Fugitives, Smugglers, and Thieves

Fugitives, Smugglers, and Thieves

Piracy and Personhood in American Literature

Sharada Balachandran Orihuela

University of North Carolina Press CHAPEL HILL

Set in Espinosa Nova by Westchester Publishing Services
Manufactured in the United States of America

The University of North Carolina Press has been a member of the
Green Press Initiative since 2003.

Library of Congress Cataloging-in-Publication Data
Names: Balachandran Orihuela, Sharada, author.
Title: Fugitives, smugglers, and thieves : piracy and personhood in American
    literature / Sharada Balachandran Orihuela.
Description: Chapel Hill : University of North Carolina Press, [2018] |
    Includes bibliographical references and index.
Identifiers: LCCN 2017044538| ISBN 9781469640914 (cloth : alk. paper) |
    ISBN 9781469640921 (pbk : alk. paper) | ISBN 9781469640938 (ebook)
Subjects: LCSH: American literature—History and criticism. |
    Pirates in literature. | Fugitives from justice in literature.
Classification: LCC PS173.P57 B35 2018 | DDC 810.9/3556—dc23
LC record available at https://lccn.loc.gov/2017044538

Cover illustration: *A smuggler chased by a brig* by Thomas Buttersworth
(Image BHC1113, National Maritime Museum Picture Library,
© National Maritime Museum, Greenwich, London).

Portions of chapter 3 were previously published in a different form as "The
Black Market: Property, Freedom, and Piracy in Martin Delany's *Blake; or, the
Huts of America*," *J19: The Journal of Nineteenth-Century Americanists* 2, no. 2
(Fall 2014): 273–300. Used here with the permission of the University of
Pennsylvania Press.

I dedicate this book to my parents, Dr. Gopalan Balachandran and Rosamaria Orihuela Basurto, who have encouraged me to follow my passions even when these pursuits take me far from home. This book is as much a product of your sacrifice and hard work as mine.

Contents

Acknowledgments

Fulfilling my dream of writing a book has required endless hours of research, writing, and revision. While I anticipated this work, I could not have predicted that a great number of people would have labored alongside me throughout this process.

For his ideas and reassurance as I pursued what seemed to be at times an overwhelming project, I thank Mark Jerng. In addition to being formative in my scholarly upbringing, Mark has been a terrific mentor throughout. His enthusiasm and belief in the project's value motivated me to become a scholar worthy of his recognition. I am also indebted to Hsuan Hsu for his contributions to this manuscript, as well as his mentorship during my time both at the University of California, Davis, and as a young academic at the University of Maryland. Riché Richardson has provided me with the personal and professional inspiration to remain true to myself even in the face of adversity.

The remarkable accomplishments of my friends and colleagues at the University of Maryland and the intellectual rigor with which they pursue their work have been a source of tremendous inspiration. I would especially like to acknowledge Robert Levine, Randy Ontiveros, Sangeeta Ray, and Edlie Wong. This book would not be what it is without their guidance, steadfast patience, support, and feedback. Despite their taxing schedules, Bob, Randy, Sangeeta, and Edlie have read my drafts, answered all my panicked emails, and been my greatest advocates. In addition to being tremendous and accomplished scholars, they are exemplary mentors, and their generosity is unparalleled. Amanda Bailey, Ralph Bauer, William Cohen, Peter Mallios, Zita Nunes, Laura Rosenthal, Martha Nell Smith, Orrin Wang, and Mary Helen Washington have at different times offered their guidance and support in the completion of this book. I am grateful for the many ways in which they have advocated on my behalf in my time at UMD. My dear friends at the University of Maryland and elsewhere deserve my appreciation for their brilliance, patience, and encouragement. These persons include Dana Carluccio, Catherine Fung, Lee Konstantinou, Julie Prieto, and Lee Walthall. They also include Kali Cyrus, John Garrison, Perla Guerrero, Nicole Johnson, Jan Padios, Riana Shaw Robinson, and Christina Walter who deserve additional recognition and my unending gratitude for their role in the completion of this book. Not only have they taught me to be courageous and fearless in every pursuit, but they have also managed to offer an excess of love and support in the most challenging of circumstances. For their friendship, I will be forever indebted, and these public acknowledgments are a small token of my immeasurable affection. My dear friend John Garrison was especially instrumental in the completion of this manuscript both morally and materially, and I am extremely fortunate to benefit from his limitless love and support, as well as his immeasurable strength as a literary scholar. Outside academia, my extraordinary family members across nations and continents deserve thanks for the selfless love they have provided for the duration of this journey. The Gopalans in India, Orihuela Basurtos in Mexico, and Harrisses, Laus, Robinsons, Walthalls, and Wests in the United States are all part of an extended family that have fed me, prayed for me, sent me loving words, and given me generous allowances for being a less-than-dutiful member of their families.

For critical monetary support as an international graduate student I wish to thank the University of California Institute for Mexico and the United States and El Consejo Nacional de Ciencia y Tecnología Doctoral Fellowship. The Marilyn Yarbrough Dissertation and Teaching Fellowship at Kenyon College provided me with a beautiful space to write in Gambier, Ohio, and the monetary support to complete the earliest iteration of this project. Several research fellowships have helped me access archives and materials that have furthered the scope of my project. For these resources, I wish to thank the Hemispheric Institute on the Americas, the Chicana/Latina Research Center, the Consortium for Women and Research, and the University of California Center for Excellence in Teaching and Learning at UC Davis. The Cuban Heritage Collection at the University of Miami was instrumental in helping me develop the initial arc of this project. A Research and Scholarship Award at the University of Maryland, along with an American Antiquarian Society Short-Term Fellowship and National Endowment for the Humanities Summer Institute Fellowship, was critical in enriching my work in property and nineteenth-century literary studies.

I very much appreciate the anonymous readers at the University of North Carolina Press. Their feedback and suggestions for revision have made this book immeasurably better. I also thank the staff at the University of North Carolina Press, my editor Lucas Church in particular, for their hard work on my behalf. Mark Simpson-Vos's initial interest in my book and Lucas's patience, encouragement, and belief in the contributions of this monograph have been buoying throughout this process. A portion of chapter 3 was published in *J19: The Journal of Nineteenth-Century Americanists*. I am appreciative of the anonymous reviewers of this article for their thoughtful comments and suggestions for revision.

Finally, I could not have embarked on this adventure without having tenacious and adoring parents. They are the loves of my life and I am lucky to be the object of their steadfast affection. I also thank my aunt, Dr. Shyamala Harris, for showing me how to pursue excellence tirelessly.

Fugitives, Smugglers, and Thieves

Introduction

Pirates, smugglers, and other outlaws have been the objects of fascination and the subjects of innumerable works of art and literature. Literary treatments of the pirate are punctuated with moments of danger and excitement so as to evoke the nonconformist and spirited life of the pirate as he pursues wealth, adventure, and independence. From Alexander O. Exquemelin's *Buccaneers of America* (1678) to Daniel Defoe's *Robinson Crusoe* (1719) to Robert Louis Stevenson's *Treasure Island* (1883), pirates have captivated the imagination. Captain Charles Johnson's *General History of the Robberies and Murders of the Most Notorious Pyrates* (1724), for example, is one of many texts that elevated the pirate to an almost mythical figure. Indeed, this widely read and reprinted text incorporated etchings of several pirates, including one of the infamous Welshman Bartholomew "Black Bart" Roberts (1682–1722).[1] The etching showcases Roberts in the foreground, standing on land while dressed in a tricorn hat and an elaborate, embroidered gown. The pirate flaunts his jewels and necklaces and proudly exhibits his rapier. In the background, numerous pirate ships rest in a cove, two of which are waving Jolly Roger flags, one portraying Roberts and Death jointly holding an hourglass, and the other picturing Roberts standing on two skulls.

The scene both captures and complicates how we have come to understand the pirate, as well as his crimes. As with many etchings of pirates in this period, Roberts is seen alone, brandishing his sword: the singular and exceptional hero of the scene. Indeed, the etching gives no indication that the pirate captain is villainous. Rather, he is represented as a proud leader and a seafarer of distinction. Given Roberts's elaborate garments and his position at the threshold between land and sea, however, he is not a common seafarer but rather clearly a person of distinction. However, Roberts exists between conflicting positions and principles: he is neither a naval officer legitimated by the state nor a lowly mariner. He is not overtly menacing, but his stance is one of a fearless commander. Finally, given the presence of the pirate ships under Roberts's command in the scene's background, he is neither altogether the embodiment of autonomy and individualism nor a communitarian everyman. This etching reflects the tensions that underwrite the pirate's unstable—and destabilizing—position within the framework of state power over its own borders, both physical and abstract. He is, in the different, shifting lights of various imaginative renderings, a nationalistic hero or an enemy of the state; an anticolonial challenger or an imperialistic expander; a model of citizenship or its troubling counterfeit. One need only examine Emanuel Leutze's *Washington Crossing the Delaware* (1851), a painting commemorating George Washington's inaugural attack on Hessian forces in 1776, to see the pervasiveness of this archetype. The spirit of piracy present in the etching of Roberts is echoed by Leutze's work, as well as by other paintings capturing the aura of rebellion, freedom, and nascent independence.

Fugitives, Smugglers, and Thieves studies piracy in American literature in light of property, citizenship, and the state. By looking closely at the primacy of property in American political and cultural life and investigating the place of piracy in expanding property rights to persons excluded from the category of the citizen, it makes a case for piracy as critical to the study of normative American citizenship. As I suggest, piracy assaults the legitimacy, integrity, and power of the state by making possession possible for those persons deliberately dispossessed by the state. Moreover, piracy is a propertied behavior that "attacks" the social, political, and economic structures of the state, as the etymological root of the word "pirate" (*peirates*), that is, one who "takes aggressive action" (*peiran*), suggests.[2] And so, this book specifically turns to the ways that late eighteenth- and nineteenth-century writers deploy the pirate as a figure who engages in aggressive actions against the state by making ownership possible for dispossessed persons. In so doing, the pirate forcibly expands the categories of personhood and citizenship in the American political imaginary. As I show, the pirate is taken up as a figure representative of egalitarianism, freedom, and resistance by authors as varied as Charles Brockden Brown and Martin Delany.

In focusing on the importance of the pirate as a figure who unmakes the unjust and dispossessive state, the writers examined in this book also expand the definitional boundaries of piracy to include aggressive actions such as counterfeiting, fugitivity, squatting, and smuggling, in which marginalized populations engage as a means of making possession possible for a range of historical actors. The pirates in the imaginative works studied in *Fugitives, Smugglers, and Thieves*, therefore, include persons living under colonial rule, Mexicans, black fugitives, and members of the Confederacy at the onset of the Civil War. This book examines the pirate in his diverse iterations as a figure that expands the notions of the American person to include subjects who engage with property illegally in order to denounce the dispossessive definitions and actions of the state.

In writers' imaginations, formerly marginalized and vulnerable subjects such as those just mentioned are transformed into the subversive and resistant figures we have come to associate with the pirate. More specifically, these figures participate in aggressive actions that undermine the state and normative conceptions of citizenship by partaking in the regime of property ownership outside the legal and territorial bounds of the state. Like the high seas, the U.S.-Mexico borderlands during the Mexican-American War, coastal Southern waters blockaded during the Civil War, and Cuba in the antebellum imaginary are sites of lawless fantasy. Therefore, while this book examines the representation of pirates in literature written primarily by U.S. authors, the works it scrutinizes necessarily reflect the transnational sensibility critical to understanding the figure of the pirate.[3]

Finally, by expanding the terrain of property ownership, these figures at the edges of the nation and at the margins of state power help to broaden the category of the citizen. Indeed, this is perhaps why the pirate is such a rich figure for so many eighteenth- and nineteenth-century American writers. However, by amplifying the figure of the pirate to include the minoritarian persons in this study, figures like the fugitive or the borderlands Mexican, all of whom trouble the naturalized relationship between property and citizenship, I help to tell a fuller story of practices of piracy both on land and at sea.

This book is indebted to an expansive archive of historical works on piracy, even as it diverges from this scholarship in its focus on imaginative writing and on forms of possession that might otherwise be overlooked as acts of piracy.[4] And so, this work interprets the seemingly inconsequential and less exciting (especially when compared to acts of piracy on the high seas) acts of theft and smuggling, those that might not be immediately recognizable as acts of piracy, as acts that assault the exclusionary nation-state, especially because these illegal propertied behaviors are largely absent from treatments on the topic, a topic that is already difficult to excavate. As Lance Grahn notes, "The history of illegal activity will always be an incomplete narrative. After all, the secrecy of an illicit act is one of its principal measures of success."[5] Indeed, this is why literature matters: while historical records might be incomplete sources for finding pirates and piracy, literature remains a rich source of both. For this reason, literary studies are a supplement to the sometimes-scant archives documenting the illegal exchanges and acts of possession.

Even so, *Fugitives, Smugglers, and Thieves* has also had to undertake a project of recovery on several different registers: not only does it recenter attention on marginalized figures in American literature, but it also recovers and rereads familiar narratives in unfamiliar ways. As I will expand on later, this happens both at the register of interpretation and in scholarship. In some instances, authors discuss piracy so obliquely that the critic is forced to read between the lines or to look to the minor and incidental moments of unlawful forms of possession as acts of piracy. In these cases, the pirate and his crimes must be carefully uncovered and situated in the broader debates about property and citizenship of the period. In so doing, this book is indebted to the important and foundational shifts that have occurred in American literary studies in the wake of those contributions made by black feminist scholars such as Saidiya V. Hartman, Katherine McKittrick, and Jenny Sharpe.[6] By recuperating and unpacking the numerous ways that black persons stage acts of resistance and self-determination, these scholars have furthered new modes of mining literature for its representations of complex negotiations of power: these are scholarly practices of discovery and recovery. And so, even as this book looks to populations that might not immediately register as abject—members of the Confederate plantocracy, for example—by recasting them as pirates, I uncover the coeval anxieties regarding property and citizenship that underwrite American life in the nineteenth century.

Manichean Pirates

The project of uncovering and recovering the pirate's formative role in expanding the category of the citizen requires an exploration of the state's rich and fascinating relationship to piracy. In an American legal tradition, piracy has been broadly defined as "a robbery committed on the high seas, although such robbery if committed on land would not by the laws of the United States be punishable with death."[7] It is a crime punishable by death in part because the crime occurs outside the territory and bounds of surveillance of any singular sovereign state: in a space considered to be "common to all men" where a nation's common law has no jurisdiction.[8] Thus piracy has been understood as a breach of *jus cogens*, or a customary norm or law to which several sovereign states have agreed. Moreover, given that captain and crew might belong to numerous states or the vessel might fly under several different national flags, William Edward Hall writes, the pirate commits an act "done under conditions which render it impossible or unfair to hold any state responsible for their commission."[9] Instead, the pirate either "belongs to no state or organized political society, or by the nature of his act he has shown his intention and his power to reject the authority of that to which he is properly subject."[10] Indeed, Hall's explanation of the position of the pirate vis-à-vis the state reflects a commonly held belief about the pirate as *hostis humani generis*, or the enemy of mankind.[11] Said differently, the pirate belongs to a class of persons that has been seen as inimical to statehood altogether.

This helps to explain why the crime of piracy is oftentimes represented as uncontrollable, hostile, and injurious to civil society: piracy is a crime so exceptional that it is only punishable by death. As William Blackstone writes, because the pirate "renounced all the benefits of society and government, and has reduced himself to the savage state of nature, by declaring war against all mankind, all mankind must declare war against him."[12] These acts of "war" against the pirate have typically included the use of military and naval power, as well as the use of extrajuridical force. In her work on the resurgence of piracy in the twenty-first century, Shannon Lee Dawdy writes that pirates can only be understood through their "extraordinary, inexplicable villainy."[13] The state thus creates an international "state of exception" used to justify a range of antipiracy tactics, such as the "extrajuridical use of force in nonsovereign spaces."[14] Dawdy's pirate is a terroristic figure whose existence justifies the expansion and deployment of the state's power.[15]

Thus, while the pirate is a figure inimical to the state, the pirate is also critical to the consolidation, strengthening, and expansion of state power.[16] In *Mercenaries, Pirates, and Sovereigns*, Janice Thomson argues that the modern state grew in part by demonstrating the need to curb piracy in order to protect the sanctity of private property.[17] More specifically, the state grew through its monopolization of violence, especially over pirates, privateers, and other outlaws, resulting in the full expression of the state's military power.[18] Using this logic, Thomson argues that the violent and violating act of the pirate requires an equally assertive response, ranging from the creation of customhouses and banks to the establishment of a navy, for example. Not only were navies created as a measure to protect the mercantilist interests of the state, but early navies were composed of privateers, themselves former pirates whose labor was redeployed in service of the state. Said differently, piracy has been formative in the expansion and strengthening of the modern nation-state through the creation of more formal models of military and economic organization. For critics including Douglas Burgess Jr.,

Mark Hanna, Jon Latimer, Julius Ruff, and others, the state and its formation must be studied alongside the practices that undermine it.

However, to view piracy in this light is to divest it of both the romantic and radical possibilities ascribed to it by Americanists in particular.[19] Peter T. Leeson and Marcus Rediker, for example, examine piracy as a practice to which those with few or no claims to protections from the state turned so as to ensure economic survival and political representation.[20] Indeed, their approach to piracy reflects recent approaches to the study of shadow economies more generally.[21] In the mid-twentieth century, amid a climate of rapid decolonization and impending neoliberalization in developing countries, Nobel Prize–winning economist W. Arthur Lewis argued that the global South had fallen behind in the race for economic progress in the postwar world.[22] Lewis conceded that informal and unlawful economic practices were the legacy of colonialism. Since then, sociologists, anthropologists, and economists have argued that participation in informal economies is the product of the historic social and economic isolation endured by poor and dispossessed persons in the United States and in developing countries. By illustrating the degree to which workers in the informal or illegal sector are by and large economically marginalized, typically rely on an unstable or low income, and often live in extreme poverty, these critics have made Eric Hobsbawm's premodern romantic social bandit relevant to the study of twentieth- and twenty-first-century life.[23]

Given their exploitability and the constraints on their economic mobility, maritime workers, including pirates of the eighteenth and nineteenth centuries, also lived life on the margins. As Dawdy writes, "The material meanings of liberty, and sometimes equality, for historical actors should be better accounted for. . . . Citizenship and membership in a new republican state may have been one means to secure economic rights, but another was to escape the territoriality of the state altogether."[24] For these historical actors escaping "the territoriality of the state," piracy was a practice of both protest and redress.[25] By choosing life on the fringe of the state and its laws, pirates revolted against it. Indeed, as Rediker writes, "illegality" was "a means of expression in a society whose institutions and customs seemed in many ways planned to worsen their very difficult lot."[26] Pirates replaced the socially, politically, and economically restrictive regimes of the state with novel forms of governance aboard the pirate ship. Dawdy and Joe Bonni write that pirate ships composed of "castaways and runaways (from slavery, military service, impressment, and/or forced immigration) living on the colonial fringe" and living outside the authority of any nation-state had no choice but to create a new organization that supplanted the preceding system.[27] Indeed, the pirate's core values of "collectivism, antiauthoritarianism, and egalitarianism" lent themselves to the creation of more populist and democratic socioeconomic relationships.[28] As Peter Linebaugh and Rediker write, "The pirate ship was egalitarian in a hierarchical age, as pirates divided their plunder equally, leveling the elaborate structure of pay ranks common to all other maritime employments. . . . Pirates were class-conscious and justice-seeking."[29]

It would seem as well from reading these scholars' works that life aboard the pirate ship gave rise to modernity and the modern man. Indeed, scholars have been attentive to the pirate's central role in the creation of the autonomous, rational, economic man, *homo economicus*.[30] Rediker has written convincingly of the maritime and piratic origins of the free-wage laborer.[31] The pirate, another critic writes, "is not chiefly a rebel against the state and its capitalist protectors, but rather represents the most advanced form of capitalism in a nascent stage of its tendential expansion and consolidation."[32] In this view, pirates help to expand the terrain of capitalist growth and private ownership, even as this expansion occurs outside the law.[33] And yet, even when piracy is an act of private gain, it also performs a public good. Hans Turley sums this up nicely in noting that the pirate is "a figure that is both *hostis humani generis* and homo economicus."[34] The pirate, therefore, has come to be the dangerous and transgressive embodiment of freedom and free will.[35]

And so, even as the pirate is a figure that recasts the regulatory and dispossessive "eye" of the state as the "I" of the pirate, and in so doing expresses his tenacious presence as the preeminent figure of modernity, by helping to create more egalitarian societies aboard the pirate ship, the pirate turns his "eye" back on the state, making visible its dispossession and exploitation of certain populations. In sum, the pirate is not simply a figure whose presence in imaginative writing makes apparent the failures of the state. Rather, the pirate's autonomy, entrepreneurship, and self-interest also mean that he is instrumental to the study of the state and membership within it, what we otherwise call citizenship. Perhaps more provocatively, read through this lens, the pirate's pursuit of freedom and property is not simply an expression of his individualism; it is also an expression of desire for citizenship. Therefore, I proceed by looking to the place of property in the creation of citizenship as both a liberal ideal and a legal mechanism that ensures protections of (and from) the state.

The Properties of the Citizen

In a tradition dating to John Locke's seminal work in *Second Treatise of Civil Government* (1690), modern citizenship as an ideal refers to the abstract rights afforded to all persons within a political community. As I show, the ideal of liberal citizenship established by Locke, specifically as it relates to the interdependence between person and property, is the foundation of American jurisprudence. Although there may be a number of traditions in the study of citizenship that *Fugitives, Smugglers, and Thieves* could draw on, I am particularly interested in the materiality of rights, otherwise referred to as the properties of citizenship, attached to lawful membership within a political community.[36]

According to Locke, the state of nature is aimed at the fulfillment of desire and the acquisition of property. For Locke, the self-possessed body is the primary property entitled to the person, and the possession of other properties stems from the primary property of the self. In his work, Locke asserts that "every man has a *property* in his own *person*. . . . The *labour* of his body, and the *work* of his hands, we may say, are properly his. . . . Whatsoever then he removes out of the state that nature hath provided, and left it in, he hath mixed his *labour* with, and joined it to something that is his own, and thereby makes it his *property*."[37] Critics have argued that this aspect of Locke's work gives rise to the free, autonomous, and self-possessed person, and this possessive individualism "borrows from property law an almost spatial sense of the bounded self—of what in the eighteenth century were called the 'fences' that constituted the liberties of free men."[38] The language used to describe the freedoms and liberties that stem from private property ownership, in other words, is critical to understanding the weight of owning the property of the self in liberal discourse. More importantly, not only is possession (of the self and of property) central to liberal philosophy, it is equally important in the creation of civil society. After all, this "property which men have in their persons as well as goods" is foundational to the fulfillment of desire and lies at the very core of civil society, since the subject will only relinquish the freedoms he experienced in the state of nature for the safety and protections attached to belonging to a civil or political society.[39] Said differently, private property serves as "the material foundation for creating and maintaining the proper social order, the private basis for the public good."[40]

The language of property and person becomes foundational to American independence and statehood. In the *Second Treatise*, Locke declares his views on the natural rights of man to be the rights to "life, liberty, and estate."[41] A slightly different iteration of this phrase makes its way into the Declaration of Independence, in which the right to property becomes the "pursuit of happiness." The phrase "life, liberty, and property," however, can be found verbatim in the Fifth and Fourteenth Amendments, both of which address the rights and privileges of national membership—the rights to due process and to citizenship and equal protection, respectively. The Fourteenth Amendment welcomed a formerly enslaved population into the fold of citizenship through the recognition and equal protection of their "life, liberty, and property."[42] These amendments both demonstrate and codify the entanglements of material properties and the properties of the citizen in American jurisprudence. Indeed, these beliefs about property demonstrate the numerous ways in which property rights are abstracted in order to generate American ideas of personhood and citizenship.

And yet, wedding property to citizenship has a much longer history in the legal imagination. In his *Commentaries* (1765–1769), Blackstone emphasizes the restrictions and limitations experienced by noncitizens, or aliens, by comparing them to propertyless bastards, writing that aliens "are on a level with bastards" because they are unable to inherit or obtain property due to their lack of "inheritable blood."[43] Blackstone dramatizes how persons without property are, in essence, perpetual outsiders. Indeed, property's attachment to rights reflects the broad shifts taking place in Europe and the Americas in the late eighteenth and early nineteenth centuries.[44] Whereas an earlier tradition of property considered property fixed both in position and in value (primarily because property was homologous to land), the development of property law in the late eighteenth and early nineteenth centuries sought to both secure property rights and bolster national economic growth by attaching to it a host of rights (what critics call the bundle of rights).[45] This bundle of rights includes positive rights and powers, such as the power of exclusion, the power of alienability, and the power of use, as well as the rights to privacy, contract, due process, and equal protection and a range of other rights recognized and protected by law.

I want to emphasize, therefore, that property is imagined to be the source *as well as* the guarantor of rights, and the distinctive features of American property rights in particular came to be attached to membership in a political and economic community. Moreover, rights themselves came to be understood as a type of property guaranteed by the state. In his work on property, Stephen Best has argued that "the claim that 'the liberty of the citizen to do as he likes so long as he does not interfere with the liberty of others to do the same' was the principle that governed an array of 'funda-mental' rights (e.g., the right of private property, the right of free con-tract)."[46] For Best, property is the marker on which American citizenship and civil society rest.[47] As Jedediah Purdy writes, the equivocation between property and propriety "was not just semantic. Rather, it expressed an idea that political membership and property rights were so integrally related that to hold property was to partake of political power, and to be without prop-erty was to fall outside the political community."[48] Moreover, the power of use one has over property, Purdy writes, "facilitated the development of free personality even as it contributed to social wealth. It made ownership a field for initiative and the affirmative expression of autonomy: not just exclusion of others from one's own space but command over the scope and character of activity there."[49] In making this claim, Purdy borrows from Blackstone, who also viewed property ownership as an ennobling action in that it cre-ates "new opportunities both to master and to contemplate the world."[50] In this sense, property is not about the thing itself. Rather, property owner-ship facilitates greater self-knowledge, as well as helping to mediate rela-tionships among people.

Best's and Purdy's analyses of the centrality of property in the creation of American personhood follow a long tradition of works detailing the exceptional nature of the nascent American state's relationship to property. For example, when visiting the embryonic United States, Alexis de Toc-queville was struck by the "equality of social conditions" in America and noted that this equality exerted an extraordinary influence on American progress and "sets up a particular direction to public attitudes, a certain style to the laws, fresh guidelines to governing authorities, and individual habits to those governed."[51] In part, Tocqueville attributes this "equality of social conditions" to property ownership. He writes, "As soon as citizens began to own land on any other than a feudal tenure and when emergence of per-sonal property could in its turn confer influence and power, all further discoveries in the arts and any improvement introduced into trade and in-dustry could not fail to instigate just as many new features of equality among men."[52] For Tocqueville, private property is at the root of American artis-tic, social, and economic growth. Thus, property promotes innovation and virtue, as well as fosters cooperation. Indeed, Alexander Hamilton trans-lates the virtues of property ownership into the need for strong property rights in the nascent U.S. nation-state. He writes, "It is a great principle of human nature that a man will be interested in whatever he possesses, in pro-portion to the firmness or precariousness of the tenure by which he holds it; will be less attached to what he holds by a momentary uncertain title, than to what he enjoys by a durable or certain title; and, of course, will be willing to risk more for the sake of the one than for the sake of the other."[53] Tocqueville's and Hamilton's views of a distinctively American relationship to property are responses to restrictive English land laws against which the U.S. state understood itself. Indeed, American principles of egalitarianism relied in part on democratizing access to real property. For this reason, the role of property in the creation of American democratic and egalitarian ideals has been taken up by contemporary critics, who have simultaneously complicated these fictions by looking to the place of race and gender alongside the development of normative American personhood.[54]

In tracing and adding to the range of meanings attached to property in this period, I mean to draw specific attention to the ways property has been embedded within a matrix of rights and claims for citizenship.[55] However, as I want to stress, national political fictions regarding property are reinforced by state policies and the American legal system. For example, alien (that is, noncitizen) property restrictions remained a common feature of colonial and postrevolutionary property laws and served to exclude noncitizens from a range of properties. For instance, although Wisconsin did not pass any provisions limiting land ownership by black persons outright, the Wisconsin Convention of 1846 "would have limited land rights to those who were eligible to becomes citizens."[56] By being excluded from naturalization, black persons were de facto excluded from the privileges of property ownership. Most significantly, however, by making state citizenship and recognition prerequisites to property ownership, states could exclude certain populations from citizenship by excluding them from property. These exclusions of black populations from landholding and from citizenship can be seen as antecedents to the *Dred Scott* decision in 1857, which formally made black people ineligible to be recognized by the nation-state as lawful citizens.[57] Indeed, for much of the eighteenth and nineteenth centuries, several states did not extend citizenship, understood as the "privileges and immunities of free citizens," to a range of different persons, including "paupers, vagabonds, and fugitives from justice," because they were considered incapable of participating in a propertied regime and the political economy of the community.[58] Although these restrictions were intended to ensure that state benefits would not be exploited, they also had the effect of restricting the right to settlement to citizens. For this reason, the state's critical role in the creation of membership or citizenship through property restrictions cannot be overstated.

In bringing to the surface what seems to be a paradox—that real property ownership is impossible without citizenship but also that property is the foundation of citizenship—I intend to underscore the mutually constitutive nature of property and citizenship in the American political and legal imagination. And although I have primarily focused on real property rights and ownership in regard to denial of citizenship, land is not the only kind of property limited and regulated for marginalized populations. The Supreme Court decision in *Heirn v. Bridault* a mere two years after *Dred Scott* perhaps best dramatized how restrictions on citizenship could severely limit not just land ownership but all kinds of property ownership for both free and enslaved black persons. This decision, which centered on the right of a free black woman to inherit property from the white man with whom she had lived, legally codified the exclusion of black people from all forms of property ownership by declaring her an "alien" and therefore unable to inherit any property.[59]

Given the importance and centrality of property in America's story, it is no surprise that scholars turn to literature to understand the collapse of property and persons under slavery.[60] As some other scholars have proposed, property comes to be restricted to white persons, so much so that whiteness itself becomes a type of property.[61] Indeed, this is Cheryl I. Harris's argument when she writes that racial identity utilizes the taxonomy of possession when it is used to parse out those "properties" afforded to the citizen and attached to citizenship.[62] When considered alongside a work such as Coviello's *Intimacy in America*, which examines how racial intimacy shaped an early U.S. national imaginary, one can easily see how property facilitates a form of racial coherence that comes to be perpetuated by access to and denials of possession.[63]

Despite these works on property and person, literary critics have rarely asked how formally dispossessed persons' property ownership can be refracted through the lens of piracy. After all, in the hands of the dispossessed, property functions as a means of disrupting the powers of the state and the state's dispensation of citizenship. Moreover, these "property outlaws" create new networks and communities of ownership that exist outside the official channels sanctioned by the state.[64] It would seem, then, that the practice of private property ownership in the hands of persons dispossessed of property and citizenship must necessarily be understood as an act of piracy.

Indeed, piracy is integral to the retelling of the American story. In addition to establishing American naval prowess, the First Barbary War (1801–1805) against Tripolitan pirates was also a significant event in consolidating American national identity.[65] The war, its heroes, and its villains also fascinated early American writers. For example, in addition to writing the renowned *History of the Navy of the United States of America*, which demonstrated his long-standing fascination with America's naval history, James Fenimore Cooper also embarked on a biography of Stephen Decatur, the first postrevolutionary hero, known for sailing the USS *United States* into victory against the pirates.[66] As Hester Blum writes, "The success of the navy in restoring autonomy to American ships in the Atlantic has often been cited as a crucial moment for the nation, when the United States could independently protect the integrity of its military and mercantile subjects."[67]

Additionally, as many scholars before me have argued, the Barbary pirates, as well as their capture of slaves and bounty, were the source for innumerable works of fiction and nonfiction, as well as the creation of a new genre—the captivity narrative.[68] Often thought of as part of the British literary tradition, the Barbary captivity narrative was especially popular in the United States. Paul Baepler writes, "The majority of written captivity accounts appear in the colonies near the end of the American War of Independence when the vulnerable new nation lost its British naval protection."[69] As Baepler acknowledges, "Scholars of American literature have often made the claim that the Indian captivity narrative represents this country's first literary genre, perhaps because the violent clash between indigenous people and colonists created the unique context for the development of what would become the prevailing culture of this nation, one predicated on liberation and freedom even as it colonized and enslaved."[70] The influence of both Barbary piracy and the captivity narrative is apparent in a range of Cooper's work, from the sea tales explored in this book to Indian captivity represented in his Leatherstocking Tales.

In order to highlight the significance of piracy in the early republic, chapter 1 looks to Cooper's sea tales more centrally, even as subsequent chapters move beyond nautical piracy. By starting with representations of nautical piracy in postrevolutionary fiction, I show how piracy is integral to the American national story, not because pirates are important historical actors, although they are, or because American maritime life is intertwined with the creation of American national identity, though it is.[71] Rather, turning to these texts for representations of how dispossessed persons trouble the foundational relationship between property, the state, and its citizen through piracy demonstrates the range of meanings attached to and associated with piracy.

By examining the numerous ways in which populations resist, oppose, and attempt to unmake a dispossessive state through unlawful property ownership, *Fugitives, Smugglers, and Thieves* helps to expand the category of piracy.[72] Given their unsettling position, fugitives, Mexicans, Confederates, and other dispossessed persons looking to escape the restrictions on property and citizenship become pirates. In focusing on the pirate figures that emerge by reading dispossessed populations as enemies of the state, I also complicate the story of both property and of piracy in the American tradition. Indeed, this book proves the richness of the figure of the pirate in understanding the mutually constitutive relationship between property and citizenship, and the place of the pirate in unsettling the naturalized relationship among the state, citizenship, and property.

Indeed, literary studies offer a unique contribution to scholarship on the relationship between national belonging and ownership by dramatizing the processes by which populations insert themselves into, or create competing national narratives and tales of citizenship. Because this work relies on imaginative literature, it supplements a sometimes-scant archive of historical records that represent the ways dispossessed populations imagine themselves within liberal narratives. This is especially significant given that the writers examined in *Fugitives, Smugglers, and Thieves* imagine their place within narratives of citizenship and liberalism in forms that unsettle, rather than strengthen, the state. And so, by reinserting, or by finding a place for, populations within narratives of the citizen and the liberal person, this project offers new ways of reading the works of both nonwhite and white writers in the story of national belonging.

Even so, I resist looking at these enactments of propertied personhood too rosily. After all, in suggesting that populations imagine ways of reinserting themselves into narratives of liberalism and citizenship through legally defiant forms of ownership, these subjects continue to be reliant on nation-statist inventions. Moreover, given that, as scholars have argued, the liberal state and its dispensation of rights and citizenship are contingent on and interdependent with colonialism, slavery, and imperialism, this study begs the question of what kind of political imaginary property offers.[73] For example, in "Dispossession and Cosmopolitan Community in Leonora Sansay's *Secret History*," Siân Silyn Roberts notes that the failures of liberal discourses of property ownership in a plantation economy make it impossible for slaves to become Locke's sovereign subjects "even once they have reclaimed their labor and the lands they cultivated."[74] In Roberts's estimation, the slave rebellion represented in Sansay's novel questions "'ownership' as the basis of humanity."[75] Given the limitations that inhere in the state, are citizenship and national membership within it inherently desirable?

To answer this question, I propose that even as the moments of piracy represented in these works of literature are expressions of redress and inclusion within a national community, they are, at least initially, challenges to the nation-state. To demonstrate the exigency and radical potential of these acts of piracy, I focus on their precariousness, their instability, and, ultimately, their unsustainability. Indeed, for this reason, I insist that this book keep its episodic structure: these minor acts of piracy must be ephemeral lest they be fully incorporated into the normative frame of liberal governance. Therefore, even as these pirates operate within the logic of the state—since they make ownership possible for dispossessed populations as an expression of their seeming desire for membership within it—their acts of piracy also threaten and upset the nation-state by imagining, to some degree, the destruction of the state. After all, what these pirates are demanding is that the state expand in unforeseen ways, beyond the scope of what has ever existed. Indeed, if the liberal state is structured on the dispossession of certain populations and their exclusion from the regime of liberal personhood, then the pirate's demand for recognition and membership threatens to destabilize the very foundations of the liberal state.

Charting New Pirates

Given the period's concerns with property, territoriality, and citizenship, it is no surprise that the pirate is taken up and expanded on by a number of eighteenth- and nineteenth-century writers. *Fugitives, Smugglers, and Thieves* examines the numerous ways in which American writers turn to or even amplify the figure of the pirate to include a number of other dispossessed persons. This approach is a departure from extant works in the study of piracy and maritime life in literary studies.[76] This book's more expansive approach to the study of possession by dispossessed persons necessarily requires that I look beyond nautical piracy in literature even as this book begins and ends in open waters: chapter 1 takes up the question of nautical piracy in early American historical fiction, while chapter 5 turns to nautical piracy in the form of blockade running in the early moments of the Civil War.

Chapter 1 closely examines how nineteenth-century American writers across the hemisphere—namely, Cooper, William Gilmore Simms, and Yucatec author Eligio Ancona—perceive piracy to be instrumental to the retelling of American national independence. For nineteenth-century writers looking back to the creation of American independent states, pirates stand in for American national heroes unsettling corrupt colonial governments and replacing them with more democratic propertied ones. More specifi-cally, these authors demonstrate the importance of property in facilitating American independence and creating the American citizen. Writers such as Simms also use the figure of the pirate to allegorize the threat of dispos-session of a Southern plantocracy in a later period. Simms in particular em-ploys nautical piracy to address the problem of slavery, which threatened the very foundations of Southern property. Piracy, once a source for the expansion of autonomous American property and the creation of the Amer-ican state, now comes to stand in for the dispossession of a certain group of Americans. As this early chapter establishes, even nautical piracy can have a range of meanings.

This chapter also establishes the importance of the romance, what Gretchen Woertendyke calls "the first fully imaginative genre to transform the ma-terials of history into national myth," in the retelling of the story of piracy.[77] By and large, the writers discussed in the book treat property, and its at-tendant privileges and freedoms, as a national ideal, even as they acknowl-edge that this ideal is limited by state law. For this reason, in this work, the romance is treated as a genre that helps to transform the unjust and dispos-sessive "materials of history" into a more capacious national story. More-over, as Woertendyke stresses, the romance's expansive temporal and spatial sensibility is well suited "to represent the mobility, volatility, and instability shaping the nineteenth-century US-Atlantic world."[78] Cooper's, Simms's, and Ancona's romances provide the foundation for the rest of the story told in the book: they establish the ways the "mobile, volatile, and unstable" figure of the pirate reflects the "mobility, volatility, and instability" of the United States in the postrevolutionary period, particularly as it relates to anxieties about territory, property, and citizenship. Thus, as chapter 1 ar-ticulates, American writers in the nineteenth century used nautical piracy to both tell the story of American independence and speak to the increas-ingly vulnerable property rights in independent America. In many ways this early treatment of piracy in the book establishes piracy as a practice that American writers acknowledge is complex. Indeed, nineteenth-century writers' treatment of nautical piracy demonstrates the range of meanings attributed to piracy in American historical romances.

Whereas chapter 1 begins with nautical piracy as an anticolonial and for-mative act in the creation of American independence and autonomy, chap-ter 2 takes up the question of property and citizenship more plainly by looking at the presence of counterfeiting in American literary life. I first examine the counterfeiter as a type of pirate before turning my attention to narratives about counterfeiting authored by Stephen Burroughs and Brown, and I argue that writers of the early republic frame counterfeiting as a damaging remnant of America's piratic past. After all, the counterfeiter produces social, political, and economic instability through his criminal enterprise. More importantly, and perhaps more damningly, the counterfeiter forges the dress, behaviors, and codes of the lawful national member, the citizen, in order to capitalize on the exchange of counterfeit currency. These writers therefore stress the importance of having both uniform paper currency and uniform definitions of citizenship lest America's piratic origins bleed into American postrevolutionary life. However, as Burroughs's memoir in particular demonstrates, counterfeiters were critical to the democratization of the property of currency in the early American period because they enabled a greater number of Americans to participate in the market and make their properties alienable. Hence these imaginative accounts dramatize the central role of counterfeit currency in the creation of new communities of exchange. As with piracy before it, chapter 2 demonstrates how the counterfeiting of both currency and person is critical to understanding American postrevolutionary life.

Following chapter 2's emphasis on citizenship, chapters 3, 4, and 5 turn their attention to figures formally excluded from the category of the citizen. Chapter 3 examines fugitive slaves as participating in an unlawful form of property ownership that resembles piracy in its capacity to upset the state management and dispensation of citizenship, as well as in its ability to foment revolutionary societies. Recognizing that the hemispheric slave trade is piracy, authors such as Delany and Frederick Douglass suggest that slaves too should engage in piracy by becoming fugitives. This resolves a tension in nineteenth-century solutions to the race problem, which wavered from emigration to economic uplift to education. I propose that these authors imagine a fourth possibility for black uplift: to remain in the shadows of U.S. regulatory bodies and to deliberately take advantage of regulatory exclusion. By enabling enslaved persons to stake claims to the primary property of the body, and, by extension, to autonomy and freedom, fugitiveness functions as a radical act of unlawful property ownership. Moreover, by analogizing black property ownership to piracy, fugitiveness emerges as a strategy that disrupts the proper operations of exchange *and* "doubly creates a 'black' market." This chapter builds powerful linkages to chapter 1 by underscoring Delany's representation of fugitives as pirates who must unyoke themselves from exploitative propertied regimes in ways that echo early national writers' representations of colonization.

Chapter 4, too, looks to a population understood as stalwarts against colonial dispossession: hidalgos living along the U.S.-Mexico borderlands in the aftermath of the Mexican-American War (1846–1848). Though the Treaty of Guadalupe Hidalgo (1848) ostensibly extended American citizenship to the Mexican landed class and ensured their property rights despite the transfer of land to the United States, they were nonetheless stripped of formal claims to their property and forced to enter into lengthy and costly legal battles to regain possession of these ranches. Hidalgos had to compete with Anglo agricultural settlers (or squatters), as well as with the railroad barons looking to expand railways in the newly annexed territories. I argue that, in the face of shifting claims to property and citizenship, María Amparo Ruiz de Burton, in her historical romances, imagines Mexican women as new and unexpected propertied subjects through inheritance and intermarriage. Read alongside the significant historical events of the period, including various land laws and preemption acts of the mid-nineteenth century, I argue that Mexican women perform forms of ownership that upend the racialized and gendered logics of citizenship and upset the intimate ties between property and rights. Thus, these are not the "foundational fictions," or national romances, that end with marriage and the birth of the mestizo child. Rather, they are foundational in their recasting of the "problem" of Mexican dispossession through squatting as the creation of Mexican American property.

Chapter 5 returns to the open water and studies the language of President Abraham Lincoln's naval blockade of Southern ports on April 19, 1861: a blockade that framed the South as a "rebellious state" and severely limited the lawful commercial activities that could take place in Southern coastal waters. Indeed, all trade taking place in Confederate waters became legally codified as piracy with the imposition of the blockade. This event catalyzed a long series of debates around diplomatic recognition, as well as revitalizing debates about property, sovereignty, and piracy. The debates taking place on an international stage, however, expressed anxieties regarding property and citizenship taking place in the South. In this final chapter, I turn my attention to two travelogues, Eliza McHatton Ripley's *From Flag to Flag: A Woman's Adventures and Experiences in the South during the War, in Mexico, and in Cuba* (1889) and Loreta Janeta Velazquez's *The Woman in Battle: A Narrative of the Exploits, Adventures, and Travels of Madame Loreta Janeta Velazquez* (1876), to unearth the piracies in which Confederate women participated due to the dispossession and economic isolation set in motion by the imposition of the blockade. These women's narratives demonstrate the need for piracy as a form of survival in such precarious times. By returning to blockade running during the Civil War, this concluding chapter reanimates piracy in a historical moment when it is thought to have perished. *Fugitives, Smugglers, and Thieves* is not, therefore, an exhaustive inventory of pirates in American literature. Rather, it invites scholars to look to more commonplace practices that might be more closely linked to the formative features of piracy than previously accounted for.

Read together, these cases tell a compelling story about a few underexamined forms of property ownership that have been left out of how we commonly understand piracy. Over the course of the book, I make a case for how these episodes, each of which recasts a dispossessed population as pirates unsettling the state through their exceptional acts of propertied villainy, tell a fuller story of what new worlds marginalized populations imagine, and mechanisms by which they envision achieving these worlds. These mechanisms include those forms of resistance and self-determination that exist not only in defiance of state law but also in defiance of the very institution of the state itself. Even as these acts of piracy, and the possession they enable, operate within the framework of liberal governance in their estimation of the power of property, these piratic forms of possession nonetheless exist in opposition to the nation-state. Indeed, it is because these populations are deliberately dispossessed by the state as a means of restricting and limiting their access to rights and citizenship that their acts of possession are subversive to the managerial powers of the state. By moving from an examination of the revolutionary potential promised by piracy as imagined by early American writers to a fuller examination of why piracy eventually comes to be synonymous with dangers posed by piracy to the integrity of the early nation-state, part II can more compellingly proceed to look at specific populations that experience crises of citizenship over the course of the nineteenth century. As I show, enslaved persons, Mexicans, and members of the Confederacy participate in piracy because they recognize the foundational importance of property in the creation of the citizen and the state. Having been deprived of the property of citizenship, these populations participate in piracy as a means of expressing protest against the state, as well as a means of accessing a form of personhood proximate to citizenship through property. These claims to personhood are tentative and precarious, but they are nonetheless worthy of scrutiny because they demonstrate the disruptive capacity and power of dispossessed persons.

Indeed, perhaps this is why the figure of the pirate, and texts and artifacts relating to piracy, continues to enthrall audiences. The pirate represents the underexamined and, sometimes, forgotten figures that threaten to irreparably harm the state. And yet, the continued representation of piracy in the culture industry demonstrates the range of meanings attached to the figure of the pirate. *Captain Phillips* (2013), based on the 2009 *Maersk Alabama* hijacking, grossed $218 million worldwide and racked up six Academy Award nominations, while the *Pirates of the Caribbean* franchise (2003–) has grossed close to $4 billion. Indeed, these along with the recently released *Pirates of the Caribbean: Dead Men Tell No Tales* constitute the global imaginary of piracy. Of course, they approach piracy very differently: whereas the *Pirates of the Caribbean* franchise consists of humorous adventure films modeled after works like *Treasure Island*, *Captain Phillips* is a work of creative nonfiction that reflects anxieties about the surge of nautical piracy off the coast of Somalia.

These generic differences reflect our continued fascination with but troubled relationship to piracy and the pirate: the pirate is either a mischievous scamp undermining British colonial governance or a terroristic figure. Indeed, to think of the pirate as the latter opens up the category of the pirate to a number of contemporary actors antithetical to civil society who exist outside the law. In writing about the secret history of torture and other forms of counterterrorism, Jane Mayer cites an interview with John C. Yoo, deputy assistant attorney general under President George W. Bush and author of internal legal memos. For Yoo, *hostis humani generis* must be expanded to include illegal combatants: "Why is it so hard for people to understand that there is a category of behavior not covered by the legal system? ... What were pirates? They weren't fighting on behalf of any nation. What were slave traders? Historically, there were people so bad that they were not given protection of the laws. There were no specific provisions for their trial, or imprisonment. If you were an illegal combatant, you didn't deserve the protection of the laws of war. ... The Lincoln assassins were treated this way, too. ... They were tried in a military court, and executed."[79]

As I have shown, Yoo's use of the term *hostis humani generis* has a long history of use in the adjudication of piracy. Citing Cicero, Daniel Heller-Roazen writes, "a pirate is not included in the number of lawful enemies, but is the common enemy of all."[80] The pirate is, in Heller-Roazen's and Jody Greene's imaginations, the first terrorist.[81] Yoo's defense of exceptional punishment for exceptional crimes, in other words, dates back to classical legal frameworks for the crime of piracy. As I address in the afterword, the terrorist, like the pirate of antiquity, is an illegal combatant, one that does not deserve the rights of the citizen. Moreover, Yoo's equivalence of a range of different exceptional crimes, from treason to piracy to terrorism, dramatizes the continued weight of these crimes in parsing the limits and powers of the state, as well as the rights and properties of the citizen. Indeed, the recent drone strikes on American citizens abroad, which violate due process clauses in the Fifth and Fourteenth Amendments, demonstrate the legal contortions undertaken by the state in order to define exceptional crimes and justify exceptional punishments. Piracy, in other words, matters now more than ever.

PART I | The Problem of Piracy
in Antebellum America

CHAPTER ONE

America's Blackbeard
Piracy and Colonial Life

Piracy is critical to understanding American property and political autonomy on both an individual and a national scale. As this chapter shows, it
matters a great deal that James Fenimore Cooper, William Gilmore Simms,
and Eligio Ancona turn to the figure of the pirate in their historical romances,
given these writers' critical positions in the development of literary nationalism in the United States and in Mexico. In their literary imaginations,
corruption, paired with property restrictions placed on Americans under
colonial rule, gave rise to piracy as the only fitting response.[1] While the pirate is instrumental in subverting the restrictions placed on property under
colonialism, he also stands in for a proto-American national hero who unsettles both British and Spanish colonial power by making possible autonomy and independence. When paired with the defeat of a colonial monopoly,
long considered an important benefit of piracy, the expansion of property
rights to colonized persons represented in these works results in what
these writers see as the distinct relationship between property and citizenship in American life. Following on the introduction's argument that property and citizenship become inextricably linked in the liberal imagination,
this chapter looks closely at how both U.S. and Mexican writers use piracy
to envision new political communities, as well as to underscore the place
of property in the nascent state.

Indeed, this is why texts from later periods turn back to the colonial period. The texts I examine in this chapter, largely published between 1829
and 1835, address the foundational questions of the nature of colonialism;
postrevolutionary citizenship, and its attendant rights and privileges; and
the creation and consolidation of the nation-state in the eighteenth century.
After all, in the United States at least, the first half of the nineteenth century
is a period of Indian removal and dispossession and the expansion of enfranchisement rights to an increasing number of white men under President Andrew Jackson, as well as a period when tensions regarding slavery
and the legal status of black persons are mounting. However, by turning to
the colonial period before the nation proper existed, the U.S. writers examined in this chapter help to stage foundational debates about the nature

of American personhood and national character in ways that will help to explain and understand these significant events of the nineteenth century.

More specifically, these texts demand uniformity regarding the place of property in American life. For example, while Ancona's, Cooper's, and Simms's romances certainly imagine private property and commercial autonomy to be critical in the creation of the U.S. nation-state and the protean American person, they are also attuned to the impact and dangers of democratizing property, especially if the privileges of property are extended to poor white (Cooper) and black (Simms) persons. For Cooper, who so valued individual rights to property as a precursor to political representation, Andrew Jackson's emphasis on enfranchisement not structured on property ownership was an affront. In Cooper's view, by untethering citizenship from property, Jackson threatened to unmoor the very privileges attached to property. Moreover, as I will discuss in greater detail in chapter 3, if the rights to property (and, thus, the rights derived from property) are extended to black persons, then Simms's anxiety about the democratization of property speaks to his anxiety about the loss of the property of whiteness in the antebellum period.

Thus, these texts also highlight increased anxieties regarding the extension of the bounds of normative American personhood and citizenship to dispossessed populations that would otherwise remain on the fringes of the rights and protections of the U.S. state. By turning back to an earlier period, these romances underline the possibilities, as well as the dangers, of extending property (and citizenship) to all persons in the period in which these writers pen their romances. Moreover, by retelling a national story that highlights the primacy of property in the creation of normative American citizenship, in their works, Ancona, Cooper, and Simms also dramatize the need for limits to property and possession lest the distinction and separation between those who possess citizenship and those who do not be negligible. Indeed, these writers imaginatively render the paradox of liberalism: that is, the noncitizen and dispossessed person underwrites the ideal, universal, liberal subject.[2]

To tell the story of America's exceptional relationship to property, I begin outside the territorial bounds of the United States with an examination of Ancona's historical romance, *El filibustero* (1864). Set in colonial Mexico, on the Yucatán Peninsula, *El filibustero*'s critical place in representing a more egalitarian and just society as a result of piracy cannot be overstated. Ancona himself was a key player in nineteenth-century cultural and political life. A teacher, lawyer, historian, journalist, and novelist, Ancona also served as governor of the state of Yucatán, where *El filibustero* is set. Indeed, Ancona was committed to locating Mexico's revolutionary zeal in a state habitually understood to be provincial and at the periphery of the Mexican nation-state. Moreover, Ancona was a fierce proponent of Mexican sovereignty, and the pirate personifies both individual and national sovereignty in his literary imagination.

After having established the utility of the fictions of nautical piracy in representing individual autonomy and national independence, this chapter turns its attention to two of Cooper's sea tales—namely, *The Red Rover* (1829) and *The Water-Witch; or, The Skimmer of the Seas* (1830). Having penned "the key forms of American fiction—the Western, the sea tale, [and] the Revolutionary romance," Cooper has long been considered the distinguished architect of distinctly American literary genres and the raconteur of American national values.[3] For Cooper as for Ancona, a colonial state exerting its power by way of dispossessing its subjects foments piracy. However, Cooper's sea tales expand on and complicate the pirate as the embodiment of American desires for autonomy. Unlike Ancona's romance, in which the pirate is both the protagonist and the subject of the romantic union, in Cooper's historical romances it is the British colonial officer, whose life is unwittingly entangled in piracy, who ascends to the position of hero. Indeed, these figures are heroic because, while they incorporate the pirate's anticolonial ideologies, they do not undo the regime of lawful property altogether. Thus, in Cooper's sea tales, the pirate always perishes, and an anticolonial, yet lawful, naval figure emerges in his place.

As I propose, the heroes in these sea tales cannot be full-blown pirates because of the sanctity of property in American life. To make this case, this study concludes with Simms's historical romance *The Yemassee: A Romance of Carolina* (1835), which dramatizes the fears nineteenth-century Americans had regarding the place of property in postrevolutionary life. Set during the Yemassee War, Simms's novel allegorizes the imminent dispossession of a Southern plantocracy at the hands of a dispossessive state.[4] However, *The Yemassee* has a much more important role in dramatizing the inextricable relationship between citizenship and property. Unlike Ancona, who represents piracy as a reparative measure against colonial exploitation and thereby redeems the figure of the pirate, for Simms, piracy stands in for problematic, damaging, and fundamentally un-American relationships to property.

While there are numerous works of criticism that look broadly to the American maritime imagination in nineteenth-century American literature, very few works look specifically to the pirate to tell a story about American property.[5] And so, I argue that the way Ancona's *El filibustero*, Cooper's sea tales, and Simms's *The Yemassee* frame the pirate's relationship to property is critical to understanding how nations across the hemisphere understood property's role in their national stories.[6] It matters greatly that these writers all employ the figure of the pirate as the embodiment of a postrevolutionary nationalism, and that these works help to establish the many meanings of piracy in a postrevolutionary transnational American imaginary.

American Piracy and Postcolonial Nationalism

Ancona's *El filibustero* is nothing if not a novel about the promises of piracy in the colonial period. The romance chronicles the evolution of its protagonist, a poor orphan named Leonel, into the notorious pirate Capitán Barbilla, a play on the name of the infamous pirate Blackbeard, who terrorized the Atlantic Ocean during the period in which the novel is set. The romance also centers on the forbidden love between Leonel and Berenguela, the daughter of the Spanish colonial officer Don Gonzalo de Villagómez. Leonel, an orphan left on the steps of Villagómez's hacienda, is very recognizably the archetypal pirate: a man who lacks lineage, family, and honor. Though he lacks these patrimonial possessions, Leonel has pride, dignity, and a keen sense of the unjust limitations imposed on him due to his lack of wealth. More importantly, Leonel's keen sense of his own dispossession gives rise to his desire for social equality. In part this is the product of his education by the Franciscan priests in Yucatán. One priest in particular, Fray Hernando de Plasencia, educates Leonel by emphasizing Jean-Jacques Rousseau's ideals of democratic citizenship and social empowerment found in *Discourse on Inequality* (1755).

However, understanding that even education will be insufficient in transgressing the social and class boundaries of colonial Mexico, Leonel resolves to leave the peninsula. While addressing Villagómez's wife, Leonel declares, "It is not the name of my parents that I will seek, since they did not believe me to be worthy of it. Instead, I will seek the name that most satisfies man's pride. I will seek a name that I create with my own merits, not the one borrowed from strangers."[7] In this sense, Leonel's desire for a "name" outside the constraints of his parentage is very identifiably the quintessentially New World, or American, break from aristocratic, European modes of social and economic hierarchization. And so, Leonel leaves in order to become an autonomous, self-made man. Barbilla soon begins patrolling the Gulf of Mexico, pillaging Spanish ships, and redistributing his amassed wealth among impoverished, indigenous Mexicans. Indeed, Barbilla's devotion to economic reorganization is so great that the historical romance ends with Barbilla's fortune being used to form a new, egalitarian community in the Yucatán.

The Yucatán serves as the ideal setting for this historical romance that recasts the pirate as the hero of Mexican independence because the concerns most prevalent in *El filibustero*—self-determination, autonomy, and the formation of a new social order—were ubiquitous in the Yucatán region. After all, the Yucatán, like the pirate colony at the end of the novel, was a rigidly anticolonial and anti-imperial state throughout the eighteenth and nineteenth centuries. Indeed, Yucatán was the site of a thriving piratic economy in the nineteenth century because of its geographic separation "from the rest of the republic by an extremely dense and barely accessible jungle."[8] Given its separation from central Mexico, the heart of Spanish colonial economic and political life in Mexico, Yucatán had "secured the rights to issue its own commercial regulations to export and import products directly to and from Europe and other American ports" starting in 1814.[9] Yucatán secured these rights in part because it had grown accustomed to trading outside the legal and permissible terms established by Spain as a way to control this rebellious and unstable region.[10] In the face of these restrictions, pirates helped to "provide the connecting tissue that articulated rural hinterlands to developing economic zones."[11] Said differently, piracy was a necessity in deliberately isolated locations barred from legal avenues for trade, and was one of many extra-legal behaviors that arose in the face of Spanish colonial restrictions. Moreover, participation in piracy served as a way for Yucatecs in particular, but also for Mexicans more generally, to demonstrate the failure of colonial Spanish legal institutions to protect the interests and the well-being of the population.

In many ways, to view the Yucatec pirate as central to the expansion, and not hindrance, of commerce and social well-being echoes Adam Smith's representation of the act of smuggling. When discussing smuggling, Smith writes that the smuggler is "a person who, though no doubt highly blameable for violating the laws of his country, is frequently incapable of violating those of natural justice, and would have been, in every respect, an excellent citizen, had not the laws of his country made that a crime which nature never meant to be so."[12] Rather than call the smuggler an individual violator of the law, Smith blames the "corrupted governments" for producing the figure of the smuggler. He asserts, "Not many people are scrupulous about smuggling, when, without perjury, they can find any easy and safe opportunity of doing so."[13] For Smith, any interruption by the state on the rights to trade is liable to produce the smuggler because the individual's natural rights to property and to trade are being infringed on. Ancona's pirate, like Smith's smuggler, is a figure who is not breaking natural law, as much as he is shedding light on the unjust economic and social communities limiting his commercial freedom.

For Ancona, piracy is not simply a means of highlighting the commercial repression engendered by colonial governments; it is also a means of representing the postrevolutionary Mexican rupture from the mores, codes, and laws of a "corrupted government" and of imagining the formation of novel political, social, and economic societies. Indeed, Barbilla's piracies off the coast of Yucatán are recast as acts of anticolonial resistance that contest and mitigate the piratic monopolization of trade by the Spanish government. The introduction to the text, for example, equivocates about the relative legitimacy of "the government agent, the friar, the governor, the bishop, [and] the pirate," because they all participate in exploiting the powerless.[14] Barbilla breaks from these antecedent figures by participating in piracy not as an act of exploitation but as an act of restitution for the powerless. Barbilla, in sum, ascends to the position of a noble figure, embarking on a quest to fight corruption in the Yucatán Peninsula while also becoming, as Nina Gerassi-Navarro has described him, "a sort of national hero who can fight for his people and culture only through piracy."[15] She writes, "Ancona's novel offers an alternative to the model of nation building . . . [and] Leonel's personal struggle for self-determination is carefully intertwined with his countrymen's fight for independence [from Spain]."[16] However, Barbilla's redistribution of property is at the heart of this independence and autonomy: he democratizes and expands access to property. In so doing, the pirate in El filibustero both unmakes the Spanish monopolistic and dispossessive state and replaces it with a more egalitarian community.

The Problem of Piracy in the Nineteenth Century

Ancona's representations of colonial governance as piracy, of the importance of breaking genealogical and patrimonial ties as a means of achieving autonomy, and of the pirate as a formative figure of national independence all find their antecedents in Cooper's sea tales. Published after the first three Leatherstocking Tales (The Pioneers, 1823; The Last of the Mohicans, 1826; and The Prairie, 1827), The Red Rover and The Water-Witch are less examined works authored by Cooper. And yet both *The Water-Witch* and *The Red Rover* must be recovered given their representation of American revolutionary zeal embodied in the figure of the pirate, "a romantic who alone in 1759 foresees the colonies' break from England and whose personal destiny is intimately related to America's."[17] After all, these historical romances begin in the prerevolutionary period and conclude in the wake of the American Revolution.

To emphasize the piratic origins of American life, Cooper highlights the omnipresence of piracy in the colonies. *The Water-Witch*, for example, follows a diverse cast of shadowy characters in early eighteenth-century New Amsterdam. They include a "flourishing" Dutch merchant, Alderman Van Beverout; Captain Cornelius Van Cuyler Ludlow, a British naval officer; the pirate Tom Tiller, known as the "Skimmer of the Seas"; Master Seadrift, Tiller's second-in-command, who we learn is Van Beverout's illegitimate daughter in disguise; Alida de Barbérie, a young woman of Norman, Huguenot, and French descent and Ludlow's love interest; and Oloff Van Staats, a young and wealthy patron in the colonies. The opening scene describes the vital Dutch colonies, which have experienced a "continued growth, that has no parallel even in the history of this extraordinary and fortunate country" and will soon rival even the "proudest capitals of Europe."[18] While the colony is described as experiencing economic growth and prosperity, we soon learn that this growth hides, or maybe even relies on, a thriving economy in the shadows. Indeed, the novel depicts a colony that is no better than the pirate ship, replete with corruption and unlawful trade taking place under Dutch colonial rule and with full support from their officials.

For this reason, Seadrift defends piracy using the language of natural law, saying, "When governments shall lay their foundations in natural justice, when their object shall be to remove the temptations to err, instead of creating them, and when bodies of men shall feel and acknowledge the responsibilities of individuals—why, then the Water-Witch, herself, might become a revenue-cutter, and her owner an officer of the customs!"[19] Seadrift blames colonial corruption for piracy on the seas. As Seadrift notes, if the colonial government unshackled its citizens from the restraints of unjust trade restrictions, the pirate might be tempted to use his vessel as a naval ship instead and, in so doing, change his profession to that of an officer. Van Beverout reaffirms this argument as he addresses Seadrift: "You bear the countenance of one who might be a useful subject, and yet are you suspected of being addicted to certain practices which—I will not say they are dishonest, or even discreditable—but which certainly have no tendency to assist her Majesty in bringing her wars to a glorious issue, by securing to her European dominions that monopoly of trade, by which it is her greatest desire to ease us of the colonies of looking any further after our particular interests, than beyond the doors of her own custom-houses."[20] Seadrift, in Van Beverout's view, may very easily pass for a proper subject of the colonials state, and yet his participation in piracy prevents him from doing so. And yet, Van Beverout cannot say that piracy is "dishonest, or even discreditable," given the monopolistic colonial state.

Indeed, Van Beverout defends his unlawful dealings on the grounds that colonial monopolies are inherently unjust and corrupt: "What are our rulers doing at home, that they need be so vociferous about a little contraband!" asks Van Beverout. "The rogues will declaim, by the hour, concerning bribery and corruption, while more than half of them get their seats as clandestinely—aye, and as illegally, as you get these rare Mechlin laces."[21] He adds, "These English are a nation of monopolists; and they make no scruple of tying us of the colonies, hand and foot, heart and soul, with their acts of Parliament, saying 'With us shalt thou trade, or not at all.'"[22] Van Beverout expresses the ways colonial governments shackle the "foot, heart and soul" of the man and, in so doing, limit the full expression of personal freedom. As Cooper underscores, both Van Beverout and Seadrift are pirates who justify their participation in the trade using the language of justice and redistribution in the face of prohibitive and dispossessive colonial monopolies.

After all, as Van Beverout also asserts in the foregoing quote, colonial monopolies are not only restrictive and dispossessive but no better than pirates, if not pirates outright, as well. Seadrift, for example, calls piracy "that system of violence and specious morality which commenced with the gifts of Ferdinand and Isabella, and the bulls of the Popes, was continued with more or less of modification, until the descendants of those single-minded and virtuous men who peopled the Union, took the powers of government into their own hands, and proclaimed political ethics that were previously as little practiced as understood."[23] He later notes,

> The gallows awaits the pickpocket; but your robber under a pennant is dubbed a knight! The man who amasses wealth by gainful industry is ashamed of his origin; while he who has stolen from churches, laid villages under contribution, and cut throats by thousands, to divide the spoils of a galleon or a military chest, has gained gold on the highway of glory! Europe has reached an exceeding pass of civiliza-

tion, it may not be denied; but before society inflicts so severe censure on the acts of individuals, notwithstanding the triteness of the opinion, I must say it is bound to look more closely to the example it sets, in its collective character.[24]

Seadrift's sharp criticism of corrupt colonial state officials serves as an attack on Van Beverout, a smuggler who benefits from his position as town alderman. Moreover, by drawing parallels between these colonial officials and early modern pirates, Seadrift's monologue highlights the close proximity between the pirate who destroys the state and the privateer instrumental in its creation. As Van Beverout and Seadrift underscore, when paired with the rampant corruption, the aforementioned exploitation necessarily requires an equally unlawful response. And so, in Cooper's *Water-Witch*, piracy has a range of different meanings. Even Ludlow, a British officer, acknowledges the unstable meaning of piracy in this text: piracy can signify the possession of "articles of commerce that are denied by the laws," and it also signifies the "deliberate and mercenary plot[s] against the revenue of the country."[25]

However, as several characters in the historical novel note, piracy is the basis of a new political community. Alida—also Van Beverout's niece—believes American colonial character to be rooted in pluralism and multinationalism, saying, "We are a people, sprung from many nations, and our effort should be to preserve the liberality and intelligence, while we forget the weaknesses, of all."[26] Seadrift's response is to say that what binds the new country together is the drive of each person to look "to his own interests."[27] Though seemingly expressing conflicting national origin stories, read through the framework of piracy, Alida's and Seadrift's beliefs appear instead to be rather similar. After all, the shared principles governing the pirate ship—namely, self-interest and autonomy outside the limiting paradigms of the state—are also the principles governing colonial New York. As Alida and Seadrift underscore, the colony, like the pirate ship, is a space where men from different nations can set aside their differences to establish a new social and political order. Indeed, the crew of Tiller's ship, like that of Heidegger's *Dolphin* in *The Red Rover*, is "composed of men of different countries," and "age and personal character seemed to have been more consulted, in their selection, than national distinctions."[28] This description of the archetypal pirate ship mirrors Alida's description of colonial New Amsterdam. And so, even though the stories depict a linguistically, socially, and nationally complex colony inhabited by British, Dutch, and French nationals, the communities share their interests in property and their participation in piracy.[29] Indeed, piracy helps to bridge ethnic and national differences that might otherwise be insurmountable in the colony. Moreover, descriptions of the pirate bridge colonial America to a postrevolutionary United States.

To this end, Cooper deliberately obfuscates the familial and national origins of the pirates, which further emphasizes the possessory self-creation so critical to representations of the early American citizen. One only needs to read descriptions of the pirates in Cooper's works for examples. In *The Water-Witch*, Tiller is described as follows:

> The dress of the stranger was quite as remarkable as his person. He wore a short pea-jacket, cut tight and tastefully; a little, low, and rakish cap, and full bell-mouthed trousers, all in a spotlessly white duck; a material well adapted to the season and the climate. The first was made without buttons, affording an apology for the use of a rich Indian-shawl, that belted his body and kept the garment tight to his frame. Faultlessly clean linen appeared through the opening above, and a collar, of the same material, fell over the gay bandanna, which was thrown, with a single careless turn, around his throat. The latter was a manufacture then little known in Europe, and its use was almost entirely confined to seamen of the long voyage. One of its ends was suffered to blow about in the wind, but the other was brought down with care over the chest, where it was confined, by springing the blade of a small knife with an ivory handle, in a manner to confine the silk to the linen; a sort of breast-pin that is even now much used by mariners. If we add that light canvas slippers, with foul anchors worked in worsted upon their insteps, covered his feet, we shall say all that is necessary of his attire.[30]

Tiller's clothing reflects the ethnic and national multiplicity of the pirate ship and the colonies. Consisting of European and Native American clothing, Tiller's attire is as inscrutable as his complexion: he is an amalgam of several different nations, ethnicities, and races. An emboldened everyman in every sense of the term, daring, cool, and obstinate, Tiller is also a stalwart against repressive British practices. In sum, Tiller stands in as the end product of Alida's vision of multinational synchronicity.

While questions of national identity and amalgamation are taken up in *The Water-Witch*, it is Cooper's *The Red Rover* that most clearly articulates the stakes of piracy in the making and unmaking of citizenship and American nationalism. In *The Red Rover*, piracy functions as an act of remediation and as an early expression of propertied autonomy in the face of the restrictions imposed by colonial states. Piracy is also foundational to the creation of the American state and its citizen. Set on and off the coast of Newport, Rhode Island, in the "early days which preceded the storm of the Revolution," *The Red Rover* follows a British naval officer named Harry Wilder as he embarks on a nautical adventure with Captain Heidegger, the "Red Rover," an infamous pirate driven to piracy due to British oppression.[31] Suspecting that the slaver stationed in Newport is Rover's cruiser, the *Dolphin*, Wilder, together with his companions Scipio Africanus and Dick Fid, joins the pirate crew so as to eventually entrap Heidegger for the British navy. However, given that the pirate captain has captured Gertrude Grayson, a colonial maiden from South Carolina, and her aunt, Miss Wyllys, the novel also charts the blossoming romance between Wilder and Gertrude. Set twenty years after the culmination of Wilder's adventure aboard the *Dolphin* and Heidegger's disappearance, the last chapter depicts Wilder, now married to Gertrude, as he reunites with a dying Captain Heidegger. In these final moments Heidegger reveals that he is Wyllys's brother and that he served as an officer in the Revolutionary War.

As with Alida and Seadrift in *The Water-Witch*, in Heidegger's view, the most critical defining feature of the pirate ship is that its multinational crew renounce their individual national affiliations. He says,

> See, here is a Dane, ponderous and steady as the gun, at which I shall shortly place him—you may cut him limb from limb, and yet he will stand like a tower until the last stone of the foundation has been sapped. And here we have his neighbors the Swede and the Russ, fit companions for managing the same piece, which I'll answer shall not be silent, while a man of them all is left to apply a match or handle a spunge. Yonder is a square built athletic mariner from one of the free towns; he prefers our liberty to that of his native city; and you shall find that the venerable Hanseatic institutions shall give way, sooner than he be known to quit the spot I give him to defend. Here you see a brace of Englishmen, and though they come from the island that I love so little, better men at need, will not be often found.[32]

On the pirate ship, national identification through *lex soli* or *lex sanguinis* falls to the wayside, and what emerges in its place is an egalitarian political system that relies on the pirate shedding his national particularities to maintain harmony. Indeed, the pirate, in Heidegger's view, is defined by this renunciation of national affiliation or citizenship, in favor of choosing life at the margins, life as *hostis humani generis*. This repudiation of national identification results in the pirate ship being described as a "sanctuary" for the multiethnic crew.[33] Even Heidegger's female prisoners feel comfortable under his care.

And yet, while the pirates in Cooper's novels are representatives of the multicultural and multinational origins of American persons, it is Wilder who most clearly embodies the spirit of the new nation. The reader learns that Wilder, like Ancona's Barbilla, is a man without a nation, having been born at sea. He declares, "I can hardly say that I am a creature of the land at all."[34] "A ship has always been my home," he proclaims.[35] Being born outside the territorial bounds of any single nation-state highlights the degree to which Wilder's decision to join the British navy functions as an act of national loyalty akin to demands for citizenship. Later, Wilder "becomes" American through his choice to participate in the Revolutionary War. And yet, as both he and the reader learn in the final pages, Wilder has perhaps always embodied the multinational American person. In the novel's denouement, we learn that he has ties to the de Lacey line of famous British naval officers while also being the nephew of the infamous pirate Heidegger. He is not a man without patrimony after all. Instead, he has always been an inchoate American, and the conclusion of the novel supports this. The final pages describe Wilder as a "middle aged, athletic man, in the naval undress of a captain of the new States. His look was calm, and his step still firm, though time and exposure were beginning to sprinkle his head with gray. He wore one arm in a sling, a proof that his service was still recent."[36] Wilder, in other words, has always been a "wilder" version of a British officer, a "wilder" British citizen who refuses to follow colonial order.[37] Indeed, he is the type of "wilder" person that is at the heart of the American citizen, and these "wild" national origins become cemented in his kinship to Heidegger, who in the final pages of the novel utters, "*We* have triumphed!"[38] In continually expressing his political fellowship with Wilder, an affinity that comes to be fortified by consanguinity, the novel assures its readers that both Heidegger and Wilder share this anticolonial sentiment, even as Wilder never overtly becomes a pirate.

Cooper's sea novels underscore that the central motivation of a pirate is not the acquisition of material properties or that he is "greedy of profiting by the services of others."[39] Rather, the pirate seeks the procurement of the ephemeral property of independence and sovereignty, as well as the property of citizenship. As Heidegger says to Wilder, "Let me tell you, it is a disheartening thing to be nothing but a dweller in a colony. It keeps down the pride and spirit of a man, and lends a hand in making him what his masters would be glad to have him. I shall say nothing of fruits and meats and other eatables that come from the land, of which both you and I have heard and know too much, unless it be to point to yonder sun and then to ask the question, whether you think King George has the power to make it shine on the bit of an island where he lives, as it shines here in his broad Provinces of America?"[40] Heidegger expresses frustration at being deprived of several properties—namely, the properties of pride and spirit—as well as of the natural resources of the land from which King George benefits. Indeed, colonialism threatens to overwhelm the independent "pride and spirit" that defines the nascent American temperament, as well as the spirit of the autonomous man expressing free will and desire for independence. And yet, through piracy, Heidegger is able to access these properties' surrogate. Through piracy, Heidegger becomes something other than a "dweller," or temporary tenant, in a foreign land. He instead becomes the permanent inhabitant or resident of a revolutionary state.

This possessory approach to independence and citizenship is perhaps most clearly demonstrated in Heidegger's use of possessive pronouns to describe the independent nation yet to come. In one of the most expressive moments articulating his frustration at being a colonial subject, Heidegger notes, "I could be a subject of a King, but to be the subject of his subjects, Wilder, exceeds the bounds of my poor patience. I was educated, I might have almost said born in one of his vessels, and how often have I been made to feel, in bitterness, that an ocean separated my birth-place from the footstool of his throne! Would you think it, Sir, one of his commanders dar'd to couple the name of *my country* with an epithet I would not wound your ear by repeating?"[41] Heidegger's anachronistic use of "my country" to describe the country yet to exist or in the process of becoming reveals his position as possessory hero indispensable to representations of the American revolutionary spirit, and to American nationalist narratives. Indeed, when placing different countries' flags on the *Dolphin*'s mast, Heidegger tells Wilder that he does not yet know the privilege of showing his country's flag in a similar way. Heidegger's underlying motivation is to not have to "succumb to the hirelings of a foreign prince" and instead to replace colonial flags with the fledgling flag of America.[42] In this way, Heidegger expresses a desire for the property of sovereignty, emblematized in the proud display of the American flag on the *Dolphin*, and even expresses ownership of national membership before the nation has formally come into existence.

In Cooper's literary imagination, Heidegger's attachment to the ephemeral property of independence is a reflection of America's long and storied attachment to property. Cooper himself sums up this position in *The American Democrat* (1838), saying, "Social station, in the main, is a consequence of property. So long as there is civilization there must be the rights of property, and so long as there are the rights of property, their obvious consequences must follow," adding, "As property is the base of all civilization, its existence and security are indispensible to social improvement."[43] Thus, Heidegger's and Tiller's desire for property through piracy stands in for a range of desirable symbolic properties, including the property of autonomy and the property of membership in a newer, more egalitarian nation. And yet, in Cooper's imagination, piracy must also be eradicated in the postrevolutionary state, which helps to explain why the enduring heroes in Cooper's sea tales are not the pirates, who eventually perish. Rather, the enduring heroes are the British deserters who become the first, pioneering Americans. In *The Red Rover*, Heidegger expires after having served in the Revolutionary War, thereby leaving Wilder to assume a resistant and revolutionary spirit. In *The Water-Witch*, it is Captain Ludlow who eventually embodies the early American hero. Indeed, Ludlow's revolutionary character comes to be accredited to his forefathers, who were agitators, "people that fled the realm for plotting against the crown, [and] are offensive to a loyal subject. . . . They are fomenters of discord, disturbers of the public mind, and captious disputants about prerogatives and vested rights."[44]

Both *The Red Rover* and *The Water-Witch* employ the pirate to exemplify the ways in which piracy tests colonial authority and is the basis for revolution. Namely, these novels' focus on freedom, democracy, and egalitarianism indicates demands for political and economic independence that cannot be achieved without a radical break with a colonial state. Given Cooper's commitment to helping form an American character distinct from its colonial predecessor, the pirate embodies the fiercest critic of colonial monopolization. The pirate also stands in as the forefather of a new postcolonial state. Retooling the storied figure of the pirate to tell a distinct national story would have been integral to the project of developing American letters as articulated in Cooper's *Letter to My Countrymen* (1834). However, Cooper's historical romances must also reconcile the desire for the ephemeral properties of autonomy and independence with a desire to protect social, political, and economic order. As Cooper sees it, harmony is both made and unmade by property. While Cooper presents Heidegger's and Tiller's piracy as a necessary form of radical insurgency, he also frames them as unsustainable or unnecessary in the postrevolutionary state. I posit that Cooper resists representing piracy in purely positive terms because piracy fundamentally threatens private property. Moreover, the pirate threatens to democratize property, which in turn threatens to devalue the real meaning of this property—namely, citizenship. Indeed, Cooper's anxieties about the unfettered expansion of the properties of citizenship expressed in *The American Democrat* betray a conservative politics one needs to look closely to find.

These novels raise a contradiction that cannot easily be reconciled by his critics: prerevolutionary, colonial America is described as a corrupt and piratic place, and yet the pirate is also a nascent American figure that, as Cooper imagines him, is the embodiment of the American revolutionary spirit. Cooper prepares his readers for this conflicted approach to piracy by allegorizing the shadowy origins of the postrevolutionary state in the shadowy familial and national origins of the pirate. Moreover, the complicated familial, racial, and national origins of the pirates evoke the confusing ethics, meanings, and outcomes of piracy, as well as the complicated position of piracy in the early republic. Unlike Ancona, who ends his novel by representing the utopian colony funded entirely by Barbilla's stolen Spanish wealth, Cooper in his endings rather clumsily promotes reconciliation between the pirate and the colonial power through the death of the pirate, and through the marriage of the nationless seaman to colonial offspring. Indeed, the forward- and backward-looking character of historical fiction, which looks to the past in order to *re*present the conditions and anxieties of the time at which the novels are written, formally mimics Cooper's Manichean approach to piracy. Piracy embodies the tension between the imagined world of America's past and its problematic present: like the historical romance, it teeters between the commonplace and the transgressive and complicates national and nationalist progressive narratives.[45] As Jason Berger argues in his analysis of Cooper's first sea novel, *The Pilot* (1824), the historical romance illustrates the internal contradictions of a young nation.[46] Read through the novels' focus on piracy and the exceptional properties of the U.S. nation-state, *The Water-Witch* and *The Red Rover* stage a complex, albeit fictional, account of the American origin story.

Together with *The Yemassee*, Cooper's novels present an intriguing case study for examining the close relationship between piracy and property in the imaginative retelling of American colonial and postrevolutionary life. Simms's pirate historical romance makes the clearest case for restricting citizenship using property. And so, Simms redeploys the pirate not as a proto-American hero but rather as a figure that endangers the nascent American state. In *The Yemassee*, the pirate threatens to expand indigenous property rights, which would thus endanger American territory. Moreover, given that claims to American territory are represented as an antecedent to national belonging, the pirate in this historical romance threatens to unmake the very foundation of American citizenship. In reconstructing an American national story around property and citizenship, Simms seems to pick up where Cooper leaves off in his imaginative representation of the promises and perils of piracy. Turning to Simms's *Yemassee* and reading it alongside Cooper's *Water-Witch* and *Red Rover* helps clarify the problem with democratizing property and citizenship as envisioned by nineteenth-century American writers.

Piracy and the Undoing of American Property

Published in 1835, years after the publication of Cooper's sea tales, *The Yemassee* represents how piracy might endanger conceptions of American nationalism should it be taken up as the foundation of American life. The novel, set during the Yemassee War in 1715, uses the event to stage a conversation about the unsettlement of populations from their lands and about how the loss of American territory threatens the property rights so foundational to the United States. In this period, the Carolinas, the setting of *The Yemassee*, were the frontier separating British from Spanish territories. *The Yemassee* dramatizes the role that piracy played in colonial struggles for power, and piracy stands in for the dangers represented by the Spanish empire to British territorial holdings in the prerevolutionary period. Indeed, "to be a pirate and a Spaniard are not such distinct matters."[47] Thus, the pirate in this romance, Captain Chorley, comes to be represented by a British naval officer who leaves his post to become a Spanish *filibustero* (privateer). The dramatic tension in *The Yemassee* centers on the conflict between the Yemassee tribe and their chief, Sanutee, and nonnative, white settlers in Yemassee territory. Chorley plays an instrumental role in these tensions when he incites Sanutee to a massacre of the white settlers, which leads to the slaughter of the Yemassee tribe instead.

Simms represents Chorley as a dangerous figure on several different registers. In becoming a Spanish privateer, Chorley represents the problematic fungibility of national identification, of citizenship, in ways that threaten the powers of the state over its territories. Unlike Wilder, who is to be admired because of his decision to become American by participat-

ing in the Revolutionary War, Chorley's choice to become a Spanish privateer threatens to cede control of these territories to the Spanish Crown. This
would of course be a problem for *The Yemassee*'s reader, who knows that
these territories must be incorporated into the postrevolutionary United
States rather than be transferred to a foreign government. Moreover, in
helping to incite the Yemassee revolt, Chorley further threatens the integrity of colonial territorial holdings. This too would have been resonant with
Simms's audience given the Indian removal under Andrew Jackson's admin-
istration taking place at the historical moment of the romance's publication. Simms stages these territorial struggles on Yemassee land as if to suggest
that Chorley's greatest piratic act is not to become a Spanish privateer but
rather to incite the Yemassee to rebel against the British colonists, which
would result in the loss of valuable territory. If, as John Mayfield has suggested, paradigms of Republican masculinity are "founded on property,
patriarchy, and citizenship," then the remainder of this chapter looks to
Simms's work to clarify how the pirate exemplifies the person whose propertied activities threaten this trinity.[48]

Simms's representation of piracy builds on Cooper's in several important ways. As a Southern writer before the Civil War, Simms uses the
Yemassee nation to trace a comparative history of colonization that anticipates the problems the South will face in the nineteenth century. Indeed,
the relationship between the Yemassee and the Confederacy is taken up
more explicitly in a later historical novel, *The Cassique of Kiawah* (1859).
Through the character of Berkeley, a privateer for the British Crown
whose expeditions begin to fall into disrepute, Simms allegorizes the
changing position of the antebellum U.S. South in relation to legal forms
of property ownership. In this novel, Simms develops the parallel conditions endured by the British privateer and the nineteenth-century slave
owner—a person whose commercial actions shift from positive to nega-
tive and from legal to illegal as the laws of the state shift around him.[49]
However, *The Yemassee* also serves as an allegory for the simmering tensions between the North and the slave-holding South.[50] To stress this
point, Simms analogizes the Yemassee tribe's loss of their land to the impending loss of a Southern plantocracy. Thus, criticism on this novel has
tended to focus on the allegorical relationship between the defeated
Yemassee in the eighteenth century and the defeated Confederacy in the
nineteenth.

However, I propose that critics have simplified Simms's historical romance by treating this novel solely as an allegory about Southern anxiety

in the years leading up to the Civil War. A closer examination of the Yemassee tribe's and Chorley's relationships to property reveals something slightly different from a mere allegorization of Southern dispossession. Rather, by tethering citizenship to territorial belonging and to real property, and using the figure of the pirate to upset this relationship, Simms deploys the pirate to tell a cautionary tale. As this novel dramatizes, if territory and property underwrite American citizenship, then Chorley's endangerment to both the regime of lawful property ownership and American territorial holdings signals his inimical relationship to citizenship.

Simms's *Yemassee* illustrates how citizenship comes to be tied to property by underscoring the problematic relationship that both the Yemassee and Chorley have to property. Indeed, both Chorley and the Yemassee are excluded from citizenship because they misunderstand the importance and place of property in the prerevolutionary state. For example, Simms suggests that both the Yemassee and their neighboring tribe, the Manneyto, have been dispossessed because they are unfamiliar with the value of their land. Chief Sanutee's distress over the loss of land is described as follows:

> He dwelt upon the limited province, even now, which had been left them for the chase; spoke of the daily incursions and injuries of the whites, and with those old forms of phrase and figure known among all primitive people, with whom metaphor and personification supply the deficiency and make up for the poverty of language, he implored them not to yield up the bones of their fathers, nor admit the stranger to contact with the sacred town, given them by the Manneyto, and solemnly dedicated to his service. But he spoke in vain; he addressed ears more impenetrable than those of the adder. They had been bought and sold, and they had no scruple to sell their country. He was supported by the few who had spoken with him against the trade, but what availed patriotism against numbers? They were unheeded, and beholding the contract effected which gave up an immense body of their best lands for a strange assortment of hatchets, knives, blankets, brads, beads, and other commodities of like character, Sanutee, followed by his three friends, rushed forth precipitately, and with a desperate purpose, from the traitorous assembly.[51]

In Sanutee's view, the Manneyto have sold their country and themselves: while the second use of "they" ("they had no scruple to sell their country") suggests that the Manneyto are guiding the terms of the exchange and sale of their lands, the first use of "they" indicates that the Manneyto are themselves the objects of purchase. This confusing language, which reveals the equivalence of Manneyto property and their bodies, matters deeply because this moment reveals the close ties between property and citizenship. Certainly the settlers swindle the Manneyto, but in giving up their territories, the Manneyto are also essentially forfeiting their claims to citizenship. Indeed, their exchange of "an immense body of their best lands for a strange assortment of hatchets, knives, [and] blankets" shows how they fail to understand the value of real property and also fail to understand the importance of preserving their lands—namely, that property underwrites claims to citizenship. After all, to have one's property protected and have property stand in for rights, one must first understand that property has a greater value than this indigenous group believes it has. In selling their lands for so little, the Manneyto dramatize why they are incapable of being incorporated into a community of propertied persons.

Simms also depicts the Yemassee as incapable of owning property properly, a problem I will discuss in greater detail in chapter 4, though in relation to Spanish and Mexican landowners during the Mexican-American War. Sanutee insists, for example, "we have no lands to sell. The lands came from our fathers—they must go to our children. They do not belong to us to sell—they belong to our children to keep. We have sold too much land, and the old turkey, before the sun sinks behind the trees, can fly over all the land that is ours. Shall the turkey have more land in a day than the Yemassee has for his children?"[52] Sanutee's declaration reveals his inability to engage in conversations about the proper operation and function of property. Property, after all, is meant to be bought and sold, to be made alienable, and this alienability underwrites the abstract equality so central to U.S. citizenship. Sanutee's failure to understand alienability signals his failure to understand the meanings attached to and importance of property. More troublingly, Sanutee's idea of property ownership more closely resembles the system of entail under English common law than the American postrevolutionary system of alienable property. In being unable to understand the ideal role of property—namely, that property must be made alienable to make material the abstract equalities tied to citizenship—Sanutee demonstrates his failure in participating in the economy of citizenship. Thus, in Simms's view indigenous populations come to be dispossessed of citizenship because they must be dispossessed of property. And yet, as Simms underscores, it is not simply the Yemassee but Chorley too who is incapable of being assimilated into the postrevolutionary American state.

Chorley is a destructive and menacing figure in the narrative because he threatens to teach the Yemassee the value and meaning of their properties by giving them the means to stage an insurrection against the colonists. Said differently, he threatens to teach the Yemassee how to reclaim their territories, and claim the protections afforded to citizens by extension, by selling them weapons and teaching them how to execute their rebellion. Paired with Chorley's lack of national affiliation, the piratical sale of weaponry to the Yemassee further illustrates how the pirate and the indigenous group threaten the integrity of the settler nation because they threaten the integrity of American territories and properties. Indeed, Chorley's participation in the Yemassee uprising marks him as a treasonous figure unfit for citizenship.

Chorley's sympathetic approach to Yemassee territorial claims, paired with his abandonment of British citizenship in favor of Spanish privateering, marks him as truly dangerous to both colonial and postrevolutionary life. Moreover, it bars him from membership in the postrevolutionary state. After all, he endangers the well-being of the population that will give rise to the first generation of postrevolutionary Americans. Said differently, Chorley can never be a citizen of the postrevolutionary state given his troubled and troubling relationship to colonial property and territory. Indeed, even before he participates in the Yemassee uprising, Chorley has already been explicitly barred from membership in the community due to his piratic dealings. The trader Granger, for example, bristles when another character compares him to the infamous pirate. He responds, "God forbid, captain. . . . I can show bills for all my goods, from worthy citizens in Charlestown and elsewhere."[53] In one interesting rhetorical maneuver, Granger reconfirms his belonging or citizenship through lawful property and marks Chorley's exclusion from Pocotaligo, the settlement first attacked by the Yemassee, on the basis of his contempt of lawful trade.

As Granger's statement underscores, the rights to membership at least in part depend on possessing the bills for goods "from worthy citizens," because the bills stand in for mutual recognition in the marketplace. Chorley's failure to either seek or value this recognition—recognition that is at the heart of egalitarian community formation—signals that he is a figure inimical to the prerevolutionary colony and postrevolutionary state. And so Chorley is marked as foreign both because of his participation in Spanish privateering and because of his injurious position to the embryonic U.S. nation-state and its territories. As if to further underscore this point, Simms highlights Chorley's foreignness by contrasting him with Craven, a "middle-class American and frontier hero."[54] While Simms presents Chorley as a national stranger, he presents Craven as an American person in the making. Thus, the final moments of the story depict Craven as the newly elected leader of Pocotaligo.

Given his exclusion from the community on account of his contempt for British property, Chorley has more in common with the indigenous population than with the British traders and settlers living in the region. After all, like Chorley, the Yemassee, too, are represented as alien. As the drama of the impending Yemassee uprising unfolds, Craven wonders "how to proceed—how to prepare on whom to rely—in what quarter to look for the attack, and what was the extent of the proposed insurrection;—was it partial, or general? Did it include the Indian nations generally—twenty-eight of which, at that time, occupied the Carolinas, or was it confined to the Yemassee and Spaniards? and if the latter were concerned, were they to be looked for in force, and whether by land or by sea?"[55] Craven frames the Yemassee attack as a fight between insiders and outsiders, and the Yemassee-Spanish alliance points to the threat faced by colonial settlers from foreign entities. In the end, both Chorley and the Yemassee are represented as foreigners and as not being capable of belonging to the fledgling nation. Indeed, the threat that they pose to its territories bars them from membership within it. In sum, Chorley's Spanish and indigenous affiliation, paired with his disregard for property and territorial integrity, marks him as a figure antithetical to the development of the postrevolutionary state. Chorley, unlike Heidegger and Tiller, is no hero, and the denouement restores order by having the colonial settlement choose Craven as its leader and hero.

American Piratic Imperialism

For American writers, the pirate helps to dramatize a range of different concerns regarding the limits of and protections attached to property. While Ancona, Cooper, and Simms all deploy the figure of the pirate to speak to the revolutionary break from British colonialism, monopoly, and property law, Simms in particular has turned to the pirate to dramatize the need for cementing and protecting property in the burgeoning nation. *Ramon, the Rover of Cuba* (1829) takes it one step further by using the figure of the pirate to make a case for the strengthening and consolidation of U.S. state power. It is the necessary endpoint to the study of piracy and property I have presented thus far.

Ramon, a fictitious first-person autobiography narrated by the titular character, tells the story of Ramon's noble birth, as well as of his dispossession at the hands of his brother and father—a formative event that catalyzes his entrée into piracy. With no legal recourse for reclaiming his property, given that he will be "outbid in bribes, or perhaps dragged to prison on a criminal charge, in consequence of my encounter in the woods," Ramon resolves to flee and become a pirate.[56] Swearing "revenge against the whole race of merchants and sailors; and resolved to lay them under contribution in a different style," Ramon describes the looting and pillaging across the Caribbean in which he participates.[57] Unlike the protagonists of the other pirate novels examined in this chapter, the titular character of this story is a violent and marauding pirate. Driven by revenge rather than by anticolonial resistance, Ramon stabs the crewmembers of seized merchant ships before tossing them overboard and inflicts bodily harm on his captives.[58] Nevertheless, halfway through the novel, Ramon expresses his desire to leave the piratic trade and eventually settles in Havana, changes his name, and reinvents himself as a wealthy bon vivant. Continuing to be tormented by his past crimes, however, and having lost the joy he experienced after leaving the trade, Ramon turns to religion in the final pages of the novel.

However, what I view as most significant about this text is how the anonymous author of *Ramon* uses the pirate and his unfettered free and unlawful trade across the hemisphere as a way to critique lax U.S. policy toward piracy. Indeed, *Ramon* seems to be more a text about the need for greater U.S. regulation and intervention in the Americas than about the political possibilities of piracy in colonial life. Ramon writes, "I have thought, after mature reflection, that the government of our eternally loyal island regards the depredations which we free rovers commit on the North American trade, with indifference, from this circumstance. It is said that great numbers of privateers are fitted out from the United States, which enter into the Colombian, Mexican, and Buenos Ayrean services, and commit immense depredations on the commerce of Spain."[59] Because of Ramon's emphasis on Cuba's wealth, as well as on the abundance of precious metals in Latin America, his commentary on the instability of the region can also be read as a demand for the United States to intervene across the hemisphere lest chaos and lawlessness overtake the continent, thereby resulting in the loss of hemispheric wealth. Ramon criticizes Cuban complicity in the trade when it turns a blind eye to piracy in Caribbean waters, as well as U.S. complicity in allowing pirate vessels to be outfitted on its territory. As Thomas Philbrick writes, "The author of *Ramon* cannot resist the temptation to use his piratical hero as the mouthpiece for propaganda in behalf of a firmer American policy in the West Indies."[60]

Although the novel describes piracy as a hemispheric problem, it envisions its regulation as the responsibility of the United States. In Ramon's view, U.S. patrolling of the hemisphere as a whole will be the natural outgrowth of increased regulation of its own territorial waters. After all, "how many South American privateers have been fitted out of one certain port in the United States within the last ten years; and how large a proportion of them have committed depredations, not only on the Spanish, but on all nations?"[61] Should the United States curb its tolerance of privateers, then piracy in Cuba and across the hemisphere would quickly end. This novel's lack of ambivalence about the need for increased state power is a natural endpoint to the debates about the need for a strong regulatory state. Indeed, these concerns about piracy are timely given the salience of piracy in the early nineteenth century. As Philbrick writes, the early nineteenth century was as much the "age of piracy" as the seventeenth, and pirate attacks on American merchant ships were widespread: the *Niles' Weekly Register* reported that "3,002 piratical assaults upon merchant shipping of all nations had taken place in the West Indies since the end of the War of 1812. At least five hundred American vessels in all, valued with their cargoes at $20,000,000, were seized by the pirates of the West Indies."[62] Writers in this period are seemingly attendant to the continuing threat of piracy to American properties. And yet, as this book proposed in the introduction, the pirate's formative role in the American literary imagination also suggests that there is something else that these writers are tapping into when redeploying this figure in their writing.

A closer look at the figure of the pirate in these nineteenth-century novels reveals the formative role of piracy in literary rehearsals about the origins and nature of American national exceptionalism. To these writers, the pirate represents a heroic, anticolonial figure from a recent colonial past, the very embodiment of American rebellion, freedom, and enterprise. And yet, as other writers acknowledge, the pirate exists at several troubling intersections. He exists between a colonial past and a protoimperial future; between a drive toward and an abhorrence of territorial expansion (and attendant state growth); between the complete disregard for and the democratization of property; between *hostis humani generis* and the citizen. The romances discussed here represent the pirate in all his complexity. More importantly, however, the pirate romances represent an intriguing case study for analyzing property and its meanings in the postrevolutionary state.

Through the figure of the pirate, the writers examined in this chapter amplify the peculiar relations to property that define the nineteenth century.

Since this book examines piracy in its diverse representations, the following chapter turns to late eighteenth-century narratives that look to the counterfeit to understand the place of property in postrevolutionary American life. As I show, the pirates in nineteenth-century historical romances present a problem very similar to that represented by counterfeiters in eighteenth-century texts. Counterfeiters, like the pirates before (and after) them, are taken up as complex figures that both expand and trouble relations to property. And yet, more than the pirate, in late eighteenth-century American literature it is the counterfeiter who seems to "forge" both currency and citizenship. More than taking up the figure of the counterfeiter, late eighteenth-century writers take up the creation of an American counterfeit, a working model for the American bill and person at a historical moment when neither has been formalized. Indeed, the writers in the following chapter seem to speak to the need for standardized currency and normative definitions of citizenship through the figure of the counterfeiter, as much as they represent the counterfeiter as helping to shape both American bills and persons. Together with this chapter, the following chapter presents a more robust view of how piracy, property, and citizenship come to be enmeshed in the American imaginary, and how the pirate can be redeployed to understand the importance of other types of propertied crimes in the American literary imagination.

CHAPTER TWO

Counterfeit States

Bootleg Currency and Postrevolutionary American Property

Whereas the previous chapter turned to nineteenth-century historical romances about pirates in American literature to tell a story about the nation's relationship to property, this chapter looks to literature written in the immediate postrevolutionary period that explores early notions of American personhood through the figure of the counterfeiter. By briefly turning to *Memoirs of the Notorious Stephen Burroughs* (1798) before embarking on a more thorough analysis of Charles Brockden Brown's serialized novel, *Arthur Mervyn; or, Memoirs of the Year 1793* (1799–1800), I argue that early American writers use the figure of the counterfeiter to present an intriguing case through which to understand postrevolutionary American property and personhood in ways that anticipate William Gilmore Simms's and James Fenimore Cooper's treatments of the figure of the pirate discussed in the previous chapter.

Burroughs's autobiography, one of the most popular texts of the antebellum period and certainly the most famous narrative authored by a counterfeiter, read alongside Brown's novel, provides a robust account of how counterfeiting captivated the postrevolutionary imaginary in ways that also reflected the anxieties about state growth and development upon the conclusion of the Revolutionary War. Therefore, this chapter does not take up the pirate per se but rather looks to piracy as an expansive term that includes acts of unlawful or unauthorized reproduction, or counterfeiting. As I show, both Burroughs and Brown represent the figure of the American counterfeiter as an incarnation of a piratic property outlaw central to the consolidation of the American bill and person. In a young republic overrun with pirated bills and persons, and where the difference between authentic and counterfeit matters little, the counterfeits in these works seemingly stand in as workable replacements for an altogether absent original, even as these texts differ in their treatment of this figure: whereas Burroughs's memoir focuses on the creation of an elusive scamp, a postrevolutionary bandit, Brown's novel, the first novel to grapple with and feature the figure of the counterfeiter in postrevolutionary American literature, dramatizes the promises and perils of counterfeiting and counterfeit items to the social and economic health of a young nation.

In many ways, the counterfeiter in these works does not differ from the pirate in that both the pirate and the counterfeiter threaten to democratize property, and they both endanger the integrity and welfare of the newly formed state. Indeed, the counterfeiter seems to be a damaging remnant of America's piratic past. The Crimes Act of 1790, which defined federal crimes (treason, piracy, and counterfeiting) and their punishment, certainly seems to locate counterfeiting as a behavior that, like piracy, is inimical to the state. Given that the counterfeiter's act—to unlawfully replicate the property of the state—threatens the very well-being of the state and its capacity to manage behaviors that imperil its power and its property, the counterfeiter (along with counterfeit properties) threatens to unmake the state.[1]

And yet, the Crimes Act's equivalence of treason, piracy, and counterfeiting is also troubling because these behaviors exist on different registers: while treason is defined as acts aiding and comforting enemies of the state, or as acts of war committed by citizens against their nation-state, counterfeiting and piracy are ostensibly propertied crimes.[2] Moreover, counterfeiting and piracy are distinct types of propertied crimes: while "counterfeiting" refers to the unlawful duplication of that property of the state we call national currency, "piracy" refers to the violent acquisition of property in those territories that lie beyond the boundaries of any single nation-state. However, the crimes of counterfeiting and piracy share the primacy of property in that category of offenses that imperil the state: while piracy is a crime that endangers the material properties of the state, counterfeiting, by threatening to undermine the value of its properties, seemingly threatens those ephemeral powers of the state to create and protect value and property. However, by looking to early discussions of counterfeits in fiction and memoirs written in the wake of the American Revolution, and to their representation of the problem of counterfeiting, this chapter posits that the greatest risk posed by counterfeiting in early American imaginative work is that the American counterfeit threatens the integrity and authenticity of the early American person.

I first turn to Burroughs's memoir, focusing specifically on how Burroughs imagines the place of the counterfeiter in postrevolutionary American society. Originally published in 1798, Burroughs's memoir describes his childhood and development into one of the most infamous counterfeiters of the eighteenth century. Burroughs, like so many pirates before him, is a man in search of a range of properties from which he has been barred. He becomes the embodiment of the "aggressive actor" against the state mentioned in the introduction. However, as with the figure of the pirate in the preceding chapter, Burroughs's representation of his sordid trade helps to give readers a more robust understanding of how propertied behaviors considered hostile to the state can instead help to expand the properties of early Americans.

In his memoirs, Burroughs takes care to describe himself as an antiauthoritarian rogue, a mischievous child and adolescent, and a trickster constantly frustrating all rule of law. Burroughs's autobiography, like so many early American memoirs, emphasizes autonomous self-invention, though in Burroughs's case this "invention" dovetails with his participation as a counterfeiter. Not only does Burroughs counterfeit currency, but he also counterfeits persons by taking on several disguises throughout the narrative. As he underscores, these disguises at once help him avoid detection and imprisonment, and also facilitate the passing of counterfeit currency since the legitimacy of currency was tethered to dress and demeanor: the rationale being that members of certain classes were more likely to pass trustworthy currency.

And yet Burroughs does not frame his engagement in counterfeiting as mere self-interest. Rather, he presents his repeated encounters with the law as central to his acquisition of the consciousness of a bandit in search of justice and the redistribution of wealth. By focusing on his dispossession and the dispossession of others as antithetical to the development of the early American person, Burroughs represents counterfeiting as a reparative measure integral to the creation and expansion of American personhood and propertied regimes. Moreover, given that in later editions Burroughs also describes setting up counterfeiting schemes along the Canadian border, his autobiography illustrates the ways in which counterfeiting helps to define the borders and edges of the American state in the wake of its independence. In other words, this autobiography speaks to the creation of the state as much as it speaks to the invention of an early American person.

However, it is Brown's *Arthur Mervyn* that most clearly illuminates the intersections of counterfeit bills and the American counterfeit person. It follows the trials of the titular hero, a man of humble origins, as he moves to Philadelphia, the largest commercial city in postrevolutionary America, to cast his lot. In Philadelphia, Mervyn encounters disease and death, the result of a yellow fever outbreak, the specter of the Haitian Revolution, and the Underground Railroad.[3] He also encounters a city overrun by counterfeit currency, and fraudulent and unscrupulous persons. In other words, counterfeiting structures the early American political economy, its social life, and, most importantly, its conception of early national persons.

Brown's titular protagonist shares some qualities with the pirate figures represented in the nineteenth-century historical romances examined in the previous chapter, as well as with Burroughs. Mervyn narrates his search for financial autonomy after having been dispossessed from the "rights of relationship," or patrimonial property upon the death of his father, who bequeaths his property to his wife rather than to Mervyn.[4] His dispossession produces what Mervyn calls a transformation from family member and property owner into "an alien and an enemy."[5] Alienated from family and nation, Mervyn seeks his fortune in Philadelphia: "Every tie which had bound me," he notes, "was dissolved or converted into something which repelled me to a distance from it."[6] Upon entering Philadelphia, he soon encounters a figure named Thomas Welbeck, the novel's primary villain and an American "counterfeit" par excellence, who takes Mervyn under his care. Soon after, Mervyn, who repeatedly insists on his own honesty and integrity, finds himself embedded in Philadelphia's shadowy economic underworld and absorbed into its counterfeit economy against his will. For example, he is able to participate in the city's exclusive social and economic networks from which he would otherwise be excluded because of his visual approximation to Welbeck as well as to other characters endowed with property and privilege, to include Clavering, the nephew of the wealthy Mrs. Wentworth, and Vincentio Lodi, the son of a wealthy planter from Guadeloupe. Thus, in addition to the counterfeit currency and properties that continuously pass hands in postrevolutionary America, the novel also presents the person as the greatest counterfeit object passing through Philadelphia.

Read together, Burroughs's and Brown's texts suggest that counterfeiting was more than just part of the eighteenth-century American literary imagination. It would seem that, in part, the authors posit that counterfeiting structures early American social and economic life, and that the counterfeit is indistinguishable from the authentic. By examining both Burroughs's autobiography and Brown's *Arthur Mervyn* through the lens of the counterfeit, I propose that these texts present a somewhat revisionary account of this illicit figure and his trade. Rather than being inimical to the postrevolutionary community, counterfeits and counterfeiters are instead integral to its formation and consolidation. After all, the counterfeiter helped to expand exchange and made property alienable in a period when currency was both unavailable and unregulated but indispensable.

In this period, currency did not simply stand in for property but also did what real property could not: it circulated and could more easily be made alienable. Along with its transferability, the ease with which currency circulated (as opposed to real property, which was cumbersome to liquidate) increased the importance of this object in the early republic. Burroughs's memoir in particular attends to the formative position of the counterfeiter in helping to expand the circulation of currency, and in broadening access to what Benjamin Franklin called "coined land."[7] Most significantly, however, Burroughs's representation of counterfeiting makes no distinction between the authentic and counterfeit bills in helping to democratize and expand ownership of this currencied property. Indeed, given the numerous banks with charters to produce bills, the rampant and insuppressible counterfeiting enterprise unintentionally resulted in a commercial backdrop where real and counterfeit bills circulated freely and interchangeably. In other words, for Burroughs as for Brown the real and counterfeit bills are indistinguishable in their function and value.

Therefore, both Burroughs and Brown use the counterfeit to explore the invention of American personhood and currency in a historical moment when there exists no normative model for either. As I show, in these novels the counterfeit bill and the counterfeit person are both pirated goods: they serve as substitutes for the original and, in so doing, render the differences between the real and its alternative negligible. By looking carefully at the ties that bind the features of counterfeit currency to the postrevolutionary person in Burroughs's and Brown's literary imaginations, we can begin to see how eighteenth-century writers conceived of the place of the counterfeit, to mean both bill and person, in the early nation-state.[8]

The resonances of viewing the early American person in particular as counterfeit are great. Rather than being defined by autonomy and originality, the early American person, like early American currency, is "shape-shifting, forging and abandoning partnerships with equanimity, constantly adapting to the needs of the moment, never remaining in one place or personality for long."[9] Moreover, given that the counterfeit bill's circulation relies at least in part on the counterfeiter's ability to pass as an honorable and respectable member of the community, a person who would not harm the community, the counterfeiter himself has to assume the guise of the citizen. Said differently, by imitating the dress, codes, and behaviors of a lawful and obedient citizen, counterfeiters demonstrate how they are themselves counterfeit. Thus, not only does counterfeiting lie at the heart of American social, political, and economic life, but the counterfeit person is foundational to understanding the postrevolutionary American person. Counterfeits and counterfeiters, in other words, are the exemplars of American self-invention and the postrevolutionary national person in that they "forge" a new propertied person in the aftermath of the American Revolution.

The Property of American Currency

Influenced by their experiences with colonial currency and the ill-fated (and widely counterfeited) Continental dollar issued by the Continental Congress during the Revolutionary War, the early architects of the nation-state struggled to determine the role of currency in the early republic.[10] Thomas Jefferson considered paper money to be nothing more than a trick "to enrich swindlers at the expense of the honest and industrious part of the nation," while John Adams believed "every dollar of a bank bill that is issued beyond the quantity of gold and silver in the vaults represents nothing and is therefore a cheat upon somebody."[11]

And yet, while Jefferson and Adams believed currency itself to be nothing more than a means of defrauding America's citizens, Alexander Hamilton writes, "Money is with propriety considered as the vital principle of the body politic; as that which sustains its life and motion, and enables it to perform its most essential functions. A complete power therefore to procure a regular and adequate supply of it, as far as the resources of the community will permit, may be regarded as an indispensable ingredient in every constitution. From a deficiency in this particular, one of two evils must ensue; either the people must be subjected to continual plunder as a substitute for a more eligible mode of supplying the public wants, or the government must sink into a fatal atrophy, and in a short course of time perish."[12] In Hamilton's view, money lies at the heart of American governance, a vital organ in the body politic, and creates egalitarianism through exchange. This egalitarianism, as noted in the previous chapter, makes possible a host of rights, privileges, and powers that aid in the formation of American citizenship even when such a national category of persons called "citizens" does not quite exist in this period.[13] Moreover, given that money sustains the life of the body politic, it is seen by Hamilton to be integral in safeguarding and fostering the growth of the embryonic nation.

While Hamilton saw currency as integral to the establishment, maintenance, and prosperity of a nascent community, James Madison saw the formative place of currency in the creation and expansion of the powers of the federal government. In Madison's view, currency's importance lies not in the relations it facilitates but rather in its capacity to assert the importance and the power of the federal government. In other words, a discussion of currency allows Madison to reflect on the powers of the state, which include its right to ensure its own growth through the establishment of mercantilist laws, as well as through the punishment of economic transactions (for example, piracy and counterfeiting) that undermine its power. Thus, in Madison's view, counterfeiting does not simply undermine the powers of the federal government, but it also undermines the integrity of the nation-state. Indeed, this position is taken up by the Continental Congress, which resolved "that if any person shall hereafter be so lost to all virtue and regard for his country, as to 'refuse to receive said bills in payment,' or obstruct or discourage the currency or circulation thereof, ... such person shall be deemed, published, and treated as an enemy of his country, and precluded from all trade or intercourse with the inhabitants of these colonies."[14] The language of counterfeiting expressed by the Continental Congress reflects the danger posed by counterfeiting to the newly independent state.[15]

However, tensions regarding whether the crime of counterfeiting was a federal or state crime presented a quagmire in nineteenth-century law. For example, the case of *State v. Antonio* (1816) centered on a counterfeiter's appeal to the courts that counterfeiting could not at once be a state *and* a federal crime lest a defendant be charged twice for the same crime. Moreover, the defendant appealed his conviction of counterfeiting on the ground that to consider counterfeiting to be a transgression of a federal statute encroached upon the jurisdiction of individual states that were charged with issuing charters for printing currency at the time. These deliberations regarding the nature of and punishment for the crime of piracy persisted until the Supreme Court case *State v. Tutt* (1831). In his majority ruling, Justice William Harper noted that counterfeiting, or "*uttering and publishing* forged coin," primarily concerned the state.[16] Notwithstanding the fascinating use of the language of literature, "uttering and publishing," which evokes the place of currency as a form of "voice" in the American political imaginary, Harper's ruling in *State v. Tutt* notes, "The offence against the Government of the United States consists in discrediting its currency. That against the State in defrauding its citizens. The offence against the State is certainly of the more palpable and dangerous character. The framers of the Constitution may have supposed that the power of punishing the actual forgery, was a sufficient security to the general Government, while to the States, it belonged to protect their citizens from the consequences of passing and circulating spurious coin."[17] The crime of counterfeiting, in Harper's view, harms the security and stability of the state and threatens to harm its citizenry. These fears are well founded. As Robert F. Batchelder writes, counterfeiting was employed as a weapon of war by England, and the Crown began to promote this practice during the Revolutionary War as a way to sabotage the rebellious state.[18]

However, as Harper sees it, counterfeit currency presents a greater threat to the state than it does to the federal government because it injures the property of the state's citizen, or resident. After all, Harper notes that counterfeiting depraves the morals of the citizen and, moreover, "embarrasses their intercourse."[19] Indeed, counterfeiting threatens to damage the very foundation of citizenship and belonging, and the meanings of property in the early state. Given the primacy of the individual state in the creation and protection of a range of properties, including the rights attached to membership in that community, Harper's condemnation of counterfeit currency as a state crime underscores the corrosive effect of counterfeiting on the health of property and the health of the citizenry. In this way, Harper's opinion seems to suggest that counterfeit currency threatens the citizen, an opinion that prevails until the ruling in *Fox v. State of Ohio* (1847), which framed counterfeiting as "an offense directly against the government, by which individuals may be affected."[20] The language adjudicating counterfeiting frames the crime as a violation against the government, *as well as* corrosive to the interactions between citizens.

Anxieties regarding the crime of counterfeiting reflect the tenuous position of currency in the antebellum period. After all, counterfeiting ran rampant throughout the country since the federal government did not have the power to print a uniform currency until the establishment of the federal "greenback" at the end of the Civil War. Instead, the rapid economic growth of the postrevolutionary period resulted in the exponential growth of charters for private banks, and "entrepreneurs . . . petitioned state legislatures for banks of their own," looking to meet the increased demand for paper currency.[21] The lack of federal oversight of these small banks peppered throughout the nation, as well as the sheer number of distinct bills circulating in the period, resulted in a nascent state overrun with counterfeit bills.[22] And yet, as Stephen Mihm has written, counterfeiting was "an integral part of the economic life in the early republic" and occasioned the rapid growth of the U.S. economy between the Revolution and the Civil War.[23] Though counterfeiting was certainly perceived to be harmful to commercial relations in this period, as demonstrated in the aforementioned Supreme Court cases, the circulation of both real and counterfeit currency indicates what early Americans saw as a distinction without a difference between real and counterfeit bills.[24] Indeed, for early Americans, counterfeiters were no different from Wildcat bankers producing bills under different charters.[25]

And yet, as I want to underscore, currency has always had a significant role in consolidating the American state. This seems especially evident in the passage of the Legal Tender Act of 1862 and the National Banking Act of 1863 during the early years of the Civil War. Faced with a financial crisis at the onset of the Civil War, Salmon P. Chase, then secretary of the treasury, proposed the creation of a national currency as a means of funding the war, as well as to assert the power and unity of the Union in a time of crisis. As Chase accurately surmised, the creation of a national currency could animate a coherent national identity. And so, this national currency, the greenback, became "a proxy for the patriotism of the people, who, under no circumstances, will depreciate them; for that would be only destroying their own public credit, and the loss would have to fall ultimately upon themselves."[26] The stability of the nation-state, in other words, came to be interdependent with the fate of its currency.

Moreover, the production and protection of currency, in turn, became the common interest of both the federal government and its citizens.[27] For this reason, the "public credit" of the nation's currency came to be protected by the Secret Service, an organization formed in 1865. Thus, the federal government eventually asserted control over all aspects of the money supply: its production and circulation, as well as its policing. More important, however, was the concurrent development of a national currency and a national citizenship in this period. Beginning with the passage of the Emancipation Proclamation of 1863 and formalized in the passage of the Fourteenth Amendment in 1868, American citizenship, like American currency, began to have a much more stable meaning. Indeed, it is because both citizenship and currency were both precarious and unstable in the antebellum period that I focus on their convergence in Burroughs's narrative and Brown's novel.

Burroughs, Currency, and the Postrevolutionary State

Memoirs of the Notorious Stephen Burroughs takes up the relationship between currency and the creation of the early American person through its treatment of currency as a type of weighted property critical to the creation and maintenance of a more egalitarian, postrevolutionary society. In his memoir, Burroughs narrates his life as an exceptional American figure: an eighteenth-century picaro, an infamous counterfeiter of currency, and an impersonator who takes on several disguises throughout the narrative. However, what stands out about Burroughs's memoir is his representation of counterfeiting as an act of propertied self-creation, as well as an act helping to democratize the enjoyments of property.[28] After all, Burroughs is a man singularly concerned with property. Like the revolutionary figure of the pirate, Burroughs represents the embodiment of an autonomous person in search of wealth and property.[29] As Barbilla does before him, Burroughs describes himself as "so far a republican, that I consider a man's merit to rest entirely with himself, without any regard to family, blood, or connexion."[30] This disregard for "family and blood" results in Burroughs casting away the laws of the father and the state in order to become a self-made man at the margins of society. However, it is Burroughs's appreciation of autonomy and of property in the early republic that makes him a remarkable figure. He notes,

> It is a truth, I believe, apparent to every one, that all cannot possess power and riches; nay, the greater part must ever remain without these acquirements; therefore, he who strives for power and riches, endeavors to take from the general good of the whole, and appropriate to his own use. He endeavors to invert the order of nature, by depriving others of equal privileges, in order to add to his own, and by inverting the order of that wisdom which has bountifully provided for all her children, misery will ensue, confusion and disorder will run through the body, and many inconveniences will be felt by every member of the community. . . . Property, even riches, acquired by industry (not by power) are of use to contribute to our happiness; by rendering us capable of lessening the necessities of our brethren and fellow members of society.[31]

As Burroughs underscores, property contributes "to our happiness" and lessens our burden on society. And yet, as Burroughs also emphasizes, the privileges of property do not come to be equally distributed.[32] For this reason, counterfeiting serves as a type of reparative measure facilitating the democratization of property and the enjoyments derived from it.

Given that not all can possess "power and riches," Burroughs notes, those who do possess them take from the "general good of the whole." Thus, in Burroughs's view, counterfeiting serves to expand property rights considered foundational to the postrevolutionary state to as many early Americans as possible. His counterfeiting is akin to banditry in which he "steal[s] from the rich and give[s] to the poor."[33] He writes, "I had formed in my own mind, schemes of conduct through life. What exquisite pleasure, said I, shall I enjoy in relieving the heart of distress? In distributing bread to the hungry, clothes to the naked, and consolation to the broken-hearted? I had already, in imagination, distributed such benefits through the land, as not to leave a poor person to inhabit his poverty. I beheld myself at the head of a people, distributing joy and gladness."[34] Most notably, Burroughs frames the democratization of property as being attached to a propertied affect: a pleasure gained from property, and a misery in being deprived of it. Early in the memoirs, Burroughs discusses the pleasure he receives from property, describing it as "enjoyment of the advantages" that property enables.[35] It would seem then that his primary interest, to democratize the "exquisite pleasure" that persons receive from property, requires counterfeiting.[36] Thus, democratizing the pleasures of currency and property lies at the heart of Burroughs's defense of counterfeiting. Indeed, Burroughs parrots the Declaration of Independence and the "pursuit of happiness" it entitles to make his case.[37]

However, I find Burroughs's appreciation of currency as a type of property critical to the creation of the postrevolutionary citizen and postrevolutionary society to be both the most interesting and most overlooked aspect of the work. After all, Burroughs views the property of currency as making possible not just the enjoyment but also the protection of certain rights and privileges that should otherwise be inalienable. In an early debate with his close associate Lysander, Burroughs invokes the representative quality of property as a surrogate for rights in order to argue for the injurious quality of counterfeiting to both person and society. In addressing Lysander, Burroughs notes, "you are sensible that counterfeiting the coin of any country is contrary, not only to the laws of that country, but likewise to the laws of our own minds, having implicitly engaged to observe and protect those laws, when we once take advantage of their efficacy to protect us in the enjoyment of our rights and privileges."[38] Burroughs argues against counterfeiting, noting that counterfeiting endangers the integrity of the properties of the state. Given that the state is the entity from which the citizen derives his "rights and privileges," as well as his protections, to imperil the state through counterfeiting is to endanger the self. Thus, in Burroughs's view, counterfeiting threatens to unsettle the state's capacity to protect its citizens.

While Burroughs emphasizes the danger posed to the citizen by counterfeiting, Lysander's response underscores the importance of counterfeiting in creating new communities of exchange. Because money itself is "of no consequence, only as we, by mutual agreement, annex to it a nominal value, as the representation of property," Lysander considers producing currency to be no different from producing diamonds.[39] Moreover, as Lysander reveals, real and counterfeit properties are indistinguishable because they both stand in for fictions of value. Real and counterfeit currency, in Lysander's view, are both endowed with representational and symbolic value: they both facilitate exchange, encourage business, and ease communication. Lysander notes, and it bears quoting at length,

> To put this art into practice, so as to enrich myself, and not destroy that due proportion between representative property and real property, is doing myself a favor, and injuring none. Gold and silver are made use of for convenience, to transact our business of barter and exchange with each other, as the representations of property, it being less cumbersome, and more easy to communicate from one to another, than real property of any kind; hence, when there is a due proportion of representative property, business can be transacted to the greatest advantage, and with the greatest ease. And when the public experience a scarcity or redundancy, they of course suffer an inconveniency; therefore, that person who contributes his mite to keep the balance between those two species of property just poised, is a blessing to himself and to the community of which he is a member.[40]

In Lysander's view, "whoever contributes to increase the quantity of cash does not only himself, but likewise the community an essential benefit."[41] The counterfeiter participates in producing a scarce and restricted product, which in turn makes possible the enrichment of community. Indeed, because of the shortage of currency in this period, Lysander ends his defense of counterfeiting by stressing that engaging in it would encourage, rather than discourage, commerce and thereby facilitate the spread of the enjoyments of property. This defense is so persuasive that at the end of this communication, Burroughs becomes convinced to participate in counterfeiting. Given that some have read Lysander as Burroughs himself—a counterfeit of sorts—the autobiography highlights the centrality of the counterfeiter in the creation and maintenance of American life.[42]

Most significantly, I see Burroughs not only as a property bandit but also as an early American testing the limits of membership within the postrevolutionary state. After all, his relationship to the nascent American state is problematic throughout the memoir.[43] For example, Burroughs repeatedly critiques what he interprets to be unjust expressions of state power. He writes, "The plain truth of the business was here: I viewed the transactions of the government towards me, to be inimical and cruel. I felt none of that confidence in her treatment which a child ought to feel towards the government of a kind parent. I considered that she had declared open war against me; and would take every opportunity to oppress me. Under this view of matters, I meant to make those arrangements in my conduct, which we see one nation making in their conduct towards another, with whom they are at open war."[44] Burroughs's use of the language of war to describe his relationship to the state underscores his deprivation of the properties of lawful inclusion within it. His participation in counterfeiting culminates in his being cast as an enemy against whom extralegal means of combat can be waged. He writes, "I had suffered many unusual, cruel and *illegal* punishments since I had been under the displeasure of the government; but whether the odium ought to be thrown on individuals or the government, I leave you to judge."[45] Burroughs repeatedly emphasizes his inimical position to the nation-state. Moreover, in calling his punishment "illegal," he questions the legitimacy of the state's use of its powers when punishing the counterfeiter. As Burroughs underscores, the postrevolutionary state's disposition of "unusual, cruel, and illegal punishments" for reparative and redistributive propertied crimes leaves him without any claims to the symbolic properties of citizenship and inclusion within it.

Thus, Burroughs's most scathing critique of imprisonment for the crime of counterfeiting invokes the language of slavery: "How is this said I to myself, that a country, that those who have tasted the bitter cup of slavery, and have known from hence the value of liberty, should so soon after obtaining that blessing themselves, deprive others of it? I know that it will be said, that for my crimes I am deprived of liberty, which is according to every dictate of justice whereas America was only struggling for her natural rights, when exercising the principles of virtue."[46] As Burroughs notes, not only does imprisonment deprive him of the symbolic attachments to the nation, critical to the foundation of republican personhood, but it also produces a condition akin to that of the "Negroes in the West-Indies": "We take away from one class of citizens a right, which we have very justly been tenacious of, and have subjected them to a state of as abject slavery."[47] Like a slave, Burroughs understands himself left without any claims to the property of personhood. Indeed, comparing himself to a slave because of his imprisonment and dispossession of currency is particularly effective in demonstrating the close attachments between property and autonomy, freedom, and personhood. After all, to be dispossessed of property is to be deprived of liberty, and thus to be deprived of those enjoyments conferred on the liberal subject and the citizen. As I will show in the following chapter, the attachments between dispossession and slavery echo beyond Burroughs's claims of being akin to a slave. In fact, Burroughs invokes slavery as a way of naming the extent of his loss of rights of political membership.

Thus, it is not surprising that upon being dispossessed of currency and liberty, Burroughs also experiences alienation from a national community. In a letter to his parents, Burroughs writes, "I view myself as an inhabitant of a vacant desolate country. There are none amongst all the world to whom I feel that glow of friendship, together with an equality of station which renders society pleasing. Long as I have remained in the converse and society of this motley collection of characters, of which the convicts are composed, yet I have no relish for their society."[48] Burroughs further laments this exile, saying he has been "shut from the enjoyment of society, from performing a part among the rest of my fellow mortals, to make some establishment for myself, in this state of dependence; and from tasting the sweets of liberty, for which we had so lately fought and bled."[49] In sum, Burroughs describes his lack of membership in the state as a deprivation of the pleasures and liberties attached to such membership. By the end of the memoirs, Burroughs is quite literally marginalized from the nascent state, and he settles in the U.S.-Canadian borderlands.

Arthur Mervyn and American Counterfeits

Both Burroughs and Brown grapple with the ways in which counterfeit currency makes possible an early American person. And yet counterfeiting is also a problem for these writers: Burroughs's narrative ends with his dispossession of all claims to personhood, while in Brown's literary imagination counterfeit currencies present a threat to the postrevolutionary state's ability to construct a narrative of its own exceptionalism. As Brown dramatizes, while America's prerevolutionary past might be piratic, its present cannot be counterfeit lest those very defining features of Americanness considered to be sui generis—autonomy, individualism, and the free expression of one's unique beliefs and opinions, for example—be undone by forgery. And so Brown takes great care to present the dangers of counterfeit properties. Given the number of frauds in *Arthur Mervyn*, no character in the novel is untouched by counterfeiting. Moreover, the novel presents all property as subject to forgery or forged outright during this period. In part, this is attributed to the historical moment in which the novel is set, in the midst of political, social, and economic upheaval in the late eighteenth century.[50]

Arthur Mervyn serves as a commentary on the precariousness of both American personhood and property in this period. The temporal setting coincides not only with the early years of the U.S. state but also with the revolutionary period in Haiti and the yellow fever epidemic in Philadelphia. In these troubling years, Brown underscores, American life and property are unstable and imperiled. Brown's treatment of the health of the American body politic and economic borrows from Mathew Carey's *A Short Account of the Malignant Fever* (1794), a text that converges the decline of Philadelphians' private property with the decline of its citizens. Along with descriptions of the death and pestilence around him, Carey's *Account* describes the "many women, then in the lap of ease and contentment," left "bereft of beloved husbands," and the destitute orphans and entire families that succumb to the terrible disease. Carey also includes accounts of the numerous "commercial houses" dissolved "by the death of the parties, and their affairs ... necessarily left in so deranged a state, that the losses and distresses which ... take place, are beyond estimation."[51] In this moment, city aldermen took possession of private homes, and persons' "effects, baggage, and merchandize" were open to seizure by the state.[52] Carey's *Account*, like *Arthur Mervyn* after it, emphasizes the defenseless and vulnerable position of a range of properties in the immediate postrevolutionary period: properties that include the health of the early American national person, as well as the integrity and health of his property in times of crisis.

This propertied upheaval results in Brown's representation of all properties as not simply imperiled but also themselves dangerous. Upon entering the city of Philadelphia, for example, Mervyn is robbed and subsequently tricked into trespassing into a private home, where he has no choice but to hide in the wardrobe until the dwellers fall asleep. Upon escaping, Mervyn notes that he has escaped the "perilous precincts of private property."[53] Similarly, Welbeck's home is a place fraught with danger. Mervyn discovers the many "secret transactions" taking place within the bounds of the home as private property.[54] Rather than being a space of safety, the private property of the home is instead a place where secrecy and danger prevail. Always the site for potential fraud, deception, and danger, Welbeck's home stands in as a location where the value and integrity of all property is at risk. For this reason, Mervyn always approaches Welbeck's home with "fear and the perturbations of wonder."[55] Likewise, upon entering the brothel in which Clemenzia Lodi (Vincentio Lodi's sister) resides so as to return her rightful fortune, Mervyn notes that he "entered these doors by fraud. I was a wretch, guilty of the last excesses of insolence and insult," and asks, "Did

I act illegally in passing from one story and one room to another?"[56] Thus, the "secret transactions" and wealth, which flow from "bad sources," as well as the "darkness" that stems from these secret transactions, structure the very operations of the novel.[57] Even the conclusion of the novel, which finds Mervyn ascending to the status of a propertied person through marriage to Ascha Fielding, a wealthy young Jewish woman, is fraught. After all, Fielding's wealth, framed as "foreign" or "alien," evokes the shadowy origins of her property.[58] In the novel all property seems to be ill begotten and dangerous, and Mervyn's anxiety regarding property persists for the duration of the text.

More importantly, in *Arthur Mervyn* property is dangerous because it is indistinguishable from the person who animates the property. Indeed, this is so because all property is animated by a person's will, and the American will in these works seems to be corrupt and counterfeit. After all, it is not simply the counterfeit bill, but the counterfeit person as well that overwhelms the postrevolutionary state. The problem of animated property is made abundantly clear in the novel's treatment of Eliza Hadwin, a young woman whom Mervyn befriends and whose inheritance is "willed" to her greedy uncle upon her father's death. Upon learning about her property being granted to her uncle, Eliza resorts to burning her father's will "because she dreaded the authority which that will gave you [her uncle], not only over her property, but person."[59] At this moment, Brown describes the importance of the will as a property in the creation of autonomy: control of Eliza's property is analogous to control over Eliza's person, in part because property and person have always been intertwined and interdependent in American social and political life. Eliza seeks to undo another's will, to undermine the posthumous resolve regarding property expressed in a legal document. To achieve autonomy, independence, and personhood, Eliza burns her father's will so as to wrest control over her body and property from the uncle, who has been given "all the power of a father."[60] Thus, upon destroying the will, Eliza exclaims, "Then I am free."[61] In this moment, Eliza's "will," which means autonomy achieved through property, supersedes her father's disinheriting and dispossessive "will," or posthumous missive. This moment helps dramatize the place of property in Brown's literary imagination: property animates a person's will, choice, and voice.

And yet, in Welbeck's imagination, counterfeit property also has a will or voice of its own. His rationale for appropriating Vincentio Lodi's assets also uses the language of "wills." Welbeck defends this unlawful appropriation, saying, "It was rather by gesture than by words that the will of Lodi was imparted. It was the topic of remote inferences and vague conjecture rather than of explicit and unerring declarations."[62] Welbeck's defense of his ownership of Lodi's property makes apparent that property conveys meaning that supersedes the individual's "explicit and unerring declarations."[63] He explains that after Lodi's death, "I forgot that this money was not mine. That it had been received under every sanction of fidelity, for another's use. To retain it was equivalent of robbery." And yet, in thinking of returning the monies, he wonders "what it was that gave man the power of ascertaining the successor to his property."[64] He continues, "During his life, he might transfer the actual possession, but if vacant at his death, he, into whose hands accident should cast it, was the genuine proprietor. It is true, that the law had sometimes otherwise decreed, but in law, there was no validity, further than it was able by investigation and punishment, to enforce its decrees; But would the law extort this money from me?"[65] Here, Welbeck points to the fascinating logic that underwrites his claim to Lodi's property. Welbeck's view mirrors the legal adage that possession is nine-tenths of the law. In physically holding the property, Welbeck designates himself as its recognized proprietor, though he acknowledges that this possession may not be lawful. Moreover, Welbeck also possesses Lodi's journals, which he intends to counterfeit using Mervyn's help. Said differently, Welbeck possesses Lodi's material properties, as well as the property of his voice, a unique and exceptional property that cannot be made transferrable unless forged and made counterfeit.

As I want to underscore, property has a voice (expressed through "wills," for example), and this voice can be corrupted and counterfeit by being copied, as Welbeck intends to do with Lodi's journals. Moreover, given that voice is foundational to understanding the person, the counterfeit voice of the person risks giving rise to a counterfeit person. Said differently, given property's foundational role in speaking for, representing, and giving rise to the early American person, persons like Welbeck threaten to unmake early American life and threaten to make the exceptional and unique figure, the American person, itself a forgery or counterfeit. *Arthur Mervyn* presents property as dangerous not only because it is constantly under siege and liable to be used to endanger otherwise innocent persons but also because property cannot be trusted to have any value, or authentic voice, in a climate where counterfeiting runs rampant. If, as Madison stated, "as a man is said to have a right to his property, he may be equally said to have a property in his rights," then it would seem that Brown's *Arthur Mervyn* seems to question what rights man can have with counterfeit property.[66]

In the section that follows, I argue that Brown's novel posits that the post-revolutionary American person is a counterfeit: a pirated, or unlawfully duplicated, working substitute for an unavailable or unattainable authentic counterpart, and this early American person speaks through a "counterfeited voice."[67] Moreover, by emphasizing the importance of counterfeit persons as effective representatives of early American personhood in the absence of a regulated alternative, Brown's novel stresses the counterfeit origins of American life. Read anew, Welbeck's theft of Lodi's properties (to include Lodi's currency and his journals) is an expression of Welbeck's forging a postrevolutionary American person in the absence of an original. And yet these counterfeits in American literature also demonstrate the need to codify both American personhood and currency lest the counterfeits come to permanently stand in as American properties.

Counterfeit Bill, Counterfeit Person

While Burroughs's memoir emphasizes the importance of the counterfeit in expanding property rights in the postrevolutionary state, *Arthur Mervyn* highlights the place of counterfeits in creating early American persons. While works of criticism have attended to the place of ventriloquism in Brown's works, for example, and have examined Welbeck's dangerous embodiment of free-market liberalism, few have looked specifically to how the numerous counterfeit voices in the text make apparent the problem of the counterfeit American person in early American life.[68] If, as Harper's ruling in *State v. Tutt* seems to suggest, currency is a type of voice, then Brown's novel seems to posit that counterfeit currencies in the early republic have the harmful effect of producing counterfeit voices or persons. More than a novel about rampant speculation, economic liberalism, and the turn away from corporatism in early America, *Arthur Mervyn* dramatizes how counterfeiting currency threatens to negatively affect the creation of early American persons.[69] For this reason, I propose that Welbeck and Mervyn are counterfeit men, and not counterfeiters.

The reader learns that Welbeck enters into counterfeiting because he has "no means of subsistence" while also being "unqualified for manual labour by all the habits of my life."[70] As he tells Mervyn, a person always needs money to "execute this scheme," and so Welbeck resorts to the production and circulation "of counterfeit bills" to attain the "pinnacle of affluence and honour."[71] However, the scheme also requires that Welbeck pass as a propertied person given that the appearance of authenticity and of being propertied enables the successful circulation of counterfeit currency.[72] As Mervyn writes soon after being outfitted in Welbeck's finery, "appearances are wonderfully influenced by dress."[73] Hence, Welbeck counterfeits Lodi as a way to access the *properties* of being a respectable and propertied person. While Welbeck counterfeits currency as a means of attaining the "pinnacle of affluence," Welbeck's greatest act of counterfeiting is to counterfeit Lodi, a deceased character whom the reader never meets. In order to complete this counterfeit, Welbeck employs Mervyn to plagiarize Lodi's journal so that Welbeck may eventually claim the narrative as his own. Said differently, Welbeck does not simply counterfeit currency and attempt to pass as Lodi, to whom Welbeck has a striking similarity. Rather, and perhaps most injuriously, Welbeck conspires to counterfeit Lodi's person.

Indeed, counterfeiting exceeds the act of impersonation. In wanting to plagiarize Lodi's journal in order to pass it off as his own, Welbeck seeks to unjustly claim the narrative or the voice of another. When describing the hidden recesses of Welbeck's home, Mervyn notes, "The business of writing was performed in the chamber of the third story. I had been hitherto denied access to this room. In it was a show of papers and books."[74] Mervyn's reference to the "business of writing" implies the presence of numerous counterfeit documents in the room, and these counterfeit documents include the inimitable properties that one associates with the person. In other words, Welbeck's "business of writing" refers as much to the production of counterfeit currency as it does to the production of Lodi's narrative with Mervyn's help. However, to assume Lodi's narrative in order to make it his own is to do more than assume the properties of another. Rather, Welbeck seeks to simulate the voice of another so as to pass as the authentic item. Said differently, Welbeck counterfeits the property of Lodi's person and, in so doing, becomes transformed into a working substitute in the absence of an original.

Welbeck's plan, it would seem, is to replace Lodi and circulate in Philadelphia in his stead, and this circulation depends on both the counterfeit bill and narrative. The equivalence of counterfeit bill and narrative in Welbeck's self-invention demonstrates the place of these texts in standing in for a person's authority, character, or even credit. Welbeck's counterfeiting of both bill and journal emphasizes the shared qualities of these "texts." When explaining to Mervyn his rationale for stealing Lodi's narrative, Welbeck notes, "My ambition has panted, with equal avidity, after the reputation of literature and opulence. To claim the authorship of this work was too harmless and specious a stratagem, not to be readily suggested.

I meant to translate it into English and to enlarge it by enterprising incidents of my own invention. My scruples to assume the merit of the original composer, might thus be removed. For this end, your assistance as an amanuensis would be necessary."[75] Welbeck's interest in Lodi's narrative is to sublimate his own narrative into that of another man so as to make the two narratives into one new whole and not simply "assume the merit of the original composer." To frame his interest in Lodi's narrative as seeking the "reputation of literature" is to dramatize the interdependence of text and currency in creating the counterfeit person.

Thus, Welbeck's "business of writing" refers to the achievement of a personal and currencied counterfeit that is so successful and effective that the difference between the authentic and the counterfeit is rendered both negligible and inconsequential. As Welbeck himself acknowledges, he descends into "dissimulation."[76] However, in "dissimulating," Welbeck threatens to undo the very system of meaning and value attributed not just to the singular and exceptional American person, but also to the singular and exceptional written narrative, as well as to the American bill. Indeed, the "show of papers and books" that Mervyn encounters in Welbeck's study suggests that all written documents emanating from Welbeck are counterfeit.

This approach to reading the novel not only helps clarify what Brown imagines as the stakes of counterfeits and counterfeiting in the early republic but also helps me reread Burroughs's memoir and its attention to the American counterfeit. After all, Burroughs repeatedly distances himself from the confidence trick and from other impostors. He writes, "The name impostor, is . . . easily fixt to my character. An impostor, we generally conceive, puts on feigned appearances, in order to enrich or aggrandize himself, to the damage of others. That I have never, in one instance, taken advantage of that confidence which the people of Pelham entertained towards me, to injure them and benefit myself, is a truth acknowledged by all. Under these circumstances, whether I ought to bear the name of impostor, according to the common acceptation, is the question?"[77] Burroughs's utterance clarifies the difference between the impostor, or the confidence man, and what this study calls the counterfeit. In Burroughs's opinion, the impostor harms his community because he "takes advantage" of the confidence of those around him, deprives his community of their enjoyments of property, and thereby injures them. Given that, as aforementioned, Burroughs sees his role as formative to democratization and not the deprivation of property, Burroughs defines himself as something other than an impostor. As with Welbeck in *Arthur Mervyn*, Burroughs assumes a position as a counterfeit man.

Indeed, the distinction between the impostor and the counterfeit underscored by Burroughs is echoed in Brown's novel. Upon meeting Mervyn, a character named Wortley notes, "Mervyn was a wily impostor; that he had been trained in the arts of fraud, under an accomplished teacher; that the tale which he had told me, was a tissue of ingenious and plausible lies; that the mere assertions, however plausible and solemn, of one like him, whose conduct had incurred such strong suspicions, were unworthy of the least credit."[78] To be a fraud and impostor, Wortley implies, means that Mervyn does not deserve public trust and credit. Wortley's skepticism of Mervyn's authenticity demonstrates the interdependence of character and financial standing in this period and also emphasizes the undesirability of being deemed an impostor. And yet, while the impostor deserves no "credit," the counterfeit operates differently. Due to the close resemblance of various characters in the novel, characters seem to be able to acquire the credit of others. Thus, the very notion of acquiring credit based on one's authenticity, reliability, and good standing is undone over the course of the novel.

Wortley is not the only character to question Mervyn's authenticity. Upon encountering the sick youth, Dr. Stevens, the first to find the severely ill Mervyn at the outset of the novel, wonders about the frauds of the young Mervyn: "Surely the youth was honest. His tale could not be the fruit of invention; and yet, what are the bounds of fraud? Nature has set no limits to the combinations of fancy. A smooth exterior, a show of virtue, and a specious tale, are, a thousand times, exhibited in human intercourse by craft and subtlety."[79] Dr. Stevens's skepticism about the truthfulness of Mervyn's story can be interpreted as Dr. Stevens's familiarity with counterfeits and frauds in the early republic. As Dr. Stevens ponders, fraud has no bounds, and fraudulent persons are as prevalent as fraudulent bills in Philadelphia. Given that he seeks to attribute authenticity and honesty to Mervyn's smooth exterior, which can be manipulated, Dr. Stevens pauses to appraise whether Mervyn's tale is real or counterfeit. Indeed, like the counterfeit bill, Dr. Stevens cannot distinguish between the counterfeit person and story, and its alternative. That the counterfeit's disguise is so convincing that even those persons closest to him cannot detect the deception is especially distressing for the integrity of American properties in the postrevolutionary period. As with the counterfeit bill, the lack of any discernible difference between the authentic and counterfeit person in *Arthur Mervyn* points to the meaninglessness of these distinctions. Unsurprisingly, then, the seemingly authentic and trustworthy titular hero, Mervyn himself, comes to be framed as untrustworthy. Thus, Brown intimates, Welbeck may not be the only counterfeit in the novel.

Indeed, Dr. Stevens's apprehension about Mervyn's authenticity echoes a pervasive anxiety about the young protagonist. As if to dissuade the reader from thinking that Mervyn might be deemed inherently authentic, Brown presents the degree to which Mervyn might himself be counterfeit. After all, both the counterfeit currency and the counterfeit narrative seduce Mervyn at different moments in the novel. Before stealing Lodi's journal from Welbeck, Mervyn notes, "In a momentary review which I took of the past, the design for which Welbeck professed to have originally detained me in his service, occurred to my mind. I knew the danger of reasoning loosely on the subject of property. To any trinket, or piece of furniture in this house, I did not allow myself to question the right of Mrs. Wentworth; a right accruing to her in consequence of Welbeck's failure in the payment of his rent; but there was one thing which I felt an irresistible desire, and no scruples which should forbid me, to possess, and that was, the manuscript to which Welbeck had alluded, as having been written by the deceased Lodi."[80] Lodi's narrative threatens to seduce even the honest Mervyn into "reasoning loosely on the subject of property." Therefore, Welbeck's "loose" reasoning regarding property, his disorienting narratives, and his presence as a counterfeit threaten to become uncontrollable and contagious, much like the yellow fever epidemic ravaging Philadelphia in this period.

Moreover, Mervyn's attachment to Lodi's narrative, as well as to the bills within it, demonstrates Brown's attention to "the subject of property" as it relates to the titular hero. Given that Welbeck claims that Lodi's bills glued between the pages of the journal are counterfeit, Mervyn's attachment to even the counterfeit bills dramatizes the decaying social and economic climate of the postrevolutionary state. Mervyn's increasingly troubling meditations on proper ownership reflect his slow descent into becoming counterfeit himself. When discussing an acquaintance's abandoned property, Mervyn states, "It now occurred to me that this youth must have left some clothes and papers, and, perhaps books. The property of these was now vested in the Hadwins. I might deem myself, without presumption, their representative or agent. Might I not take some measures for obtaining possession, or at least, for the security of these articles? The house and its furniture was tenantless and unprotected. It was liable to be ransacked and pillaged by those desperate ruffians, of whom many were said to be hunting for spoil, even at a time like this."[81] He adds, "His property might be put under the care of my new friend. But how was it to be distinguished from the property of others? It was, probably, contained in trunks, which was designated by some label or mark."[82] Mervyn describes himself as a "representative" of the property and, like Welbeck before him, increasingly considers himself to be the voice of another's property.

Moreover, while Mervyn might be giving property its voice, property increasingly also gives Mervyn a voice. The properties that Mervyn assumes and the clothing given to him by Welbeck upon Mervyn's taking the position of amanuensis allow him to become a type of counterfeit person. Finding himself outfitted in Welbeck's finery, Mervyn begins fantasizing about being adopted as his son: "Wealth has ever been capriciously distributed. The mere physical relation of birth is all that intitles us to manors and thrones. Identity itself frequently depends upon a casual likeness or an old nurse's imposture."[83] By Mervyn's own admission, his close association to Welbeck threatens to make Mervyn counterfeit as well, and it is Mervyn's appropriation of the "portable property," or Welbeck's stolen fortune, that illustrates his complete transformation into a counterfeit.

And so, the closer Mervyn comes to appropriating the properties of others, the more closely he begins to resemble the villainous Welbeck. This helps to explain why the distinctions between Mervyn and Welbeck become increasingly difficult to identify as the text progresses. Even Mervyn himself has trouble distinguishing his own behaviors from those of the crooked Welbeck. Indeed, Mervyn and Welbeck come to be indistinguishable not only because of the contagion of Welbeck's counterfeiting but rather because, as Welbeck does with Lodi, Mervyn starts fashioning himself after Welbeck. Mervyn notes, "Will it not behoove me to cultivate all my virtues and eradicate all my defects? I see that the abilities of this man are venerable. Perhaps he will not lightly or hastily decide in my favour. He will be governed by the proofs that I shall give of discernment and integrity."[84] By "eradicating" himself of all defects and being able to pass before Welbeck's "discerning" eye, Mervyn transforms himself into a convincing counterfeit, the "smooth" object feared by Dr. Stevens, rather than being transformed into a person worthy of credibility and of credit. In the novel, Welbeck's calling Mervyn a robber measures the success of Mervyn's transformation into Welbeck. Welbeck notes, "If, after this proof of the justice of my claim, you hesitate to restore the money, I shall treat you as a robber, who has plundered my cabinet and refused to refund his spoil."[85] In this final, curious inversion, Mervyn's transformation into a counterfeit reaches its fulfillment.[86]

Ultimately, I propose that the interrelation of counterfeit persons and counterfeit currency is at the heart of both Burroughs's and Brown's literary imaginations. These eighteenth-century narratives about counterfeiting dramatize the significance of this illegal behavior in the political economy of the early republic. Moreover, they also dramatize the anxiety occasioned by both the counterfeiter and the counterfeit person in the postrevolutionary state. It would seem, then, that we must read the presence of the counterfeit alongside the development of the American person and state because counterfeiting demonstrates the pervasive anxieties about American originality. Moreover, counterfeiters, as imagined by both Burroughs and Brown, help to stage how a postrevolutionary American person is animated through his engagement with property, both authentic and counterfeit.

However, the authenticity of the property matters deeply: the person animated through counterfeit currency is in danger of becoming not a counterfeiter but a counterfeit himself, thereby devaluing the authentic American person, or citizen. Given the prevalence of counterfeiters and counterfeits in the postrevolutionary period, these texts represent the danger these figures pose to the creation of a normative and legitimate U.S. citizen: they threaten to render the value of the authentic American citizen meaningless. And so, while these works dramatize how in this climate the "real self" of the American person is extremely difficult to access and assess, they also represent what is at stake in American personhood being rendered valueless.[87] As I show in the following chapter, the presence and proliferation of chattel slavery, paired with the increasing restrictions on citizenship in the nineteenth century—the *Dred Scott v. Sandford* case of 1857, for example— makes the stakes of both possession *and* American personhood much more apparent.

Thus, the counterfeit also catalyzes formative discussions about what it means to be American. The free circulation of counterfeit currency and person in the early republic suggests that the free enterprise and exchange that characterize postrevolutionary American life rest on the unlawful and extralegal reproduction of certain properties. The anxieties occasioned by the omnipresence of counterfeit bills and persons in the postrevolutionary state demand increased attention to both authenticity and authentication. As aforementioned, the concurrent rise of the Secret Service and a nationally uniform currency points to the need to homogenize currency, as well as protect it from forgery. Moreover, the increased management of currency also coincides with the emergence of nationally codified meanings of citizenship. Hence currency and citizenship come to be intertwined not only in the American imaginary but also in American political and legal life.

In the final few pages of this chapter, I would like to propose that we think of counterfeiting currency and narrative as significant in creating a more well-read public. As the popularity of both accounts of counterfeiting and counterfeit detectors increased, it would seem that Americans might have been encouraged to think of themselves as overrun with a number of different counterfeit properties—including, though not limited to, bank notes—and emboldened to become more discerning readers. Counterfeiters and their narratives, said differently, also have literary impact. As Todd Barosky writes, "The act of counterfeiting, insofar as it is successful, therefore functions as a critique of legitimized forms of monetary symbolization while also providing a model for theorizing the truth content of literary representations within a novelistic discourse characterized by the absence of durable frameworks of authority and meaning."[88] As I see it, the problem of counterfeiting in the antebellum period highlights the importance of close reading as a hermeneutic for approaching a range of texts.

Counterfeit Currency and Close Reading

In an act that closely resembles Mervyn's position as amanuensis, in his autobiography Benjamin Franklin tells us that he learns to write by *copying* script.[89] I refer to this minor biographical anecdote because of my interest in the counterfeit, the unlawfully copied material, in helping to shape early American conceptions of its citizen. Even Franklin's own autobiography, arguably charting his development into an exceptional and enterprising American hero, plays with the meanings of the counterfeit. After all, Franklin helped to design and print counterfeit-proof bills. However, his archive also demonstrates a deeper interest in paper currency as an object that sutures early American national belonging gained through economic and political autonomy to currency.[90] Given his interest in the development of financially autonomous and savvy Americans, it comes as no surprise that Franklin repeatedly describes the economic improvements derived from the circulation of currency. He writes, for example, that the first sum printed in 1723 "had done much good by increasing the trade, employment, and number of inhabitants in the province, since I now saw all the old houses inhabited, and many new ones building."[91] Franklin highlights the industry, as well as the expansion of real property, made possible by the introduction of paper currency, a point emphasized in "The Nature and Necessity of a Paper Currency" (1729). Thus, Franklin's venture into printing currency is an expression of his belief in the significance of currency (printed on the same presses as anticolonial pamphlets) in helping to undermine colonial power while simultaneously helping to create an autonomous, self-sufficient American person.

As demonstrated in Franklin's production of currency *and* revolutionary printed materials, printing texts is a deeply political act: an act with the express purpose of creating and educating an American public. Franklin's attention to the production of written materials, including currency, demonstrates the critical position of these texts in promoting economic enterprise and welfare, as well as in creating more egalitarian communities. Said differently, the text that we call the "bill" operates on a similar register as a number of other documents meant to instruct or foster new forms of social, political, and economic communities. These other instructive texts include the political pamphlets printed by Franklin, but they also include the numerous autobiographies about counterfeiters that circulated in the early national period. The counterfeiter is one of many "printers" that captivate the American literary imagination.[92]

And yet this does not fully account for the prevalence of counterfeits and counterfeiters in American print culture. Certainly, the fascination and fear of the counterfeiter, as well as counterfeit currency, can be attributed to early American concerns with the "relationship between the visibility of a person and the legibility of that person's public character," as Christopher J. Lukasik writes.[93] The counterfeiter embodies a social fluidity promised to early Americans, even when this performance is a menace. The performance is facilitated in part by literature and assisted by familiarity with books. As Lukasik writes about Franklin, "Through books, Franklin acquires not only knowledge, but access to the written performances of others in print. . . . Books furnish Franklin with behavioral models of polite performance to imitate."[94] Lukasik stresses that these performances facilitate Franklin's entrance into the business of printing, which also underscores the centrality of the printing press in the creation of national character and fostering U.S. nationalism more generally.

Indeed, it is this imitation that unsettles early Americans because it indicates malleability of character, as well as of currency. That that character can be "performed" signals the instability of the appearance of a person and his bill. Brown engages in these postrevolutionary physiognomic debates, and *Arthur Mervyn* certainly seems to center on the inability to identify authenticity and value by extension. There exists no "face value" on which postrevolutionary Americans can rely when it comes to both person and currency. As Edward Watts has written, Mervyn's inability to tell the real from the counterfeit notes he burns and to distinguish virtuous from deceitful characters at once reveals the "virtues of careful reading" and "also undermines the legitimacy of Arthur's role as a presumably reliable reader: he fails to discriminate properly. . . . His inability to distinguish undermines his claim to reliable interpretive skills, and thus casts doubt on his entire narrative."[95] Although Watts argues that this gesture serves as a critique of the role of literature inherited from the British in the prerevolutionary period, in which authors came to be trusted as "recognizable sources of instruction of information [and] stable transmitters of cultural authority inherited from British tradition," Mervyn's inability to close-read and thereby discern the authenticity of the bills and the persons around him is most demonstrably a demand for the hermeneutics of suspicious reading.

This suspicious hermeneutic would be applied not only to imaginative materials but also to bills and persons. As Mihm writes, "People receiving money looked not only for counterfeit bank notes, but also for counterfeit persons."[96] And so, as counterfeit currency increasingly floods the market, Americans come to be tasked with distinguishing the counterfeit from the real. The rise in popularity of counterfeiters' accounts, along with the popularity of counterfeit detectors in the nineteenth century, suggests that in the face of the crisis of counterfeit persons and bills, early Americans became increasingly interested in accounts of all kinds regarding counterfeiting. After all, narratives such as those by Burroughs and Brown illustrate the stakes of not reading carefully or properly and of needing to be instructed in how to read more closely so as to assess authenticity. In sum, the study of counterfeit currency in the postrevolutionary period is a rich source for information about the formation of the national person, as well as the creation of an American readerly public.

Given my interest in diverse incarnations of the American pirate, in chapter 5 I return briefly to the figure of the counterfeiter, only this time in women's autobiographies about cotton smuggling during the Civil War. While the texts examined in this chapter center on the figure of the counterfeit as a forger (or pirate) of texts and persons, chapter 5 returns again to the question of piracy outright by looking to the imposition of President Abraham Lincoln's naval blockade at the outset of the Civil War, which deprives Confederate traders of a range of properties. These properties include the material properties that ensure survival, as well as the symbolic property of citizenship. In these moments, the question of citizenship and the protections attached to citizenship become critical. Indeed, because no national definitions of citizenship exist at the onset of the war, all Confederate traders can be stripped of citizenship and of state recognition, and instead recast as pirates inimical to the state. In this climate, the Confederacy turns to counterfeiting to undermine and sabotage the Union army. Thus, postrevolutionary literature such as that examined in this chapter, as well as in chapter 5, which treats counterfeiting as central to antebellum life, is critical to understanding the concurrent rise of more stable forms of currency, as well as more reliable definitions of American citizenship.

However, to continue telling the story of piracy, in the following chapter I will turn from counterfeiting to fugitivity in order to highlight the central place of American personhood, understood not as a counterfeit production of an absent original but rather as contingent on possession of the property of the self. While this chapter has examined the replicable properties of the early American person that help to forge the American citizen, the chapter that follows looks to the self as the inalienable primary property of the American person. As the writers in the following chapter suggest, without ownership of the primary property of the self, a range of other properties, including the property of citizenship, are inaccessible. And so, the value and significance of the property of the self are made most apparent in the case of chattel slavery, where the slave is legally barred from all possessions, including the possession of the self. Indeed, by examining slave narratives that underscore the primary possession of the self in the creation of the American citizen, the following chapter looks to the unlawful or piratic ownership of the property of the self in the expansion of American personhood in the antebellum period.

The authors examined in the following chapter, all of whom excoriate the dehumanizing and dispossessive institution of slavery, look to fugitivity, or the unlawful theft of the property of the self, as an act of piracy that helps to amplify the category of the antebellum person. Given that fugitivity endangers the integrity and welfare of the properties of the Confederacy, for some of these writers fugitivity is akin to an act of piracy. This is best dramatized in Martin Delany's imaginative work *Blake; or, The Huts of America* (1859), which looks to fugitivity as a piratic act that is inimical to the Confederate state. Said differently, in Delany's imagination, the fugitive is a pirate of sorts and is the exemplar of the type of pirate whose sole crime is to possess the illegal property of the self.

CHAPTER THREE

The Black Market
Property, Freedom, and Fugitivity in Antebellum Life

Building on earlier traditions that examine the enslaved subject in terms of property, this chapter examines the presence of unlawful propertied exchanges in *Blake; or, The Huts of America* (1859) through the lens of piracy. By repositioning illegal acts of property ownership to include fugitivity at the center of enslaved subjects' demand for personhood, *Blake* uses the logic of attaching personhood to property to counter the U.S. state's exclusion of slaves from citizenship. Given that this book looks to the figure of the pirate in his diverse incarnations, this chapter proposes that the escaped slave responds to the piratic act of the slave trade through equally unlawful forms of property ownership, including fugitivity. In Martin Delany's imagination, as in the imagination of other writers taking up the question of slavery, fugitivity is an action akin to piracy because it contests the authority of the state through unlawful possessory acts, including the possession of the self. Moreover, fugitivity complicates and restructures property's foundational importance in the creation of the modern, liberal subject, and it functions as an enactment of possession powerful enough to disrupt the state that thrives on slavery.

And yet, as Delany dramatizes in *Blake*, fugitivity is not the only means of undermining state dispossessions. Rather, Delany's titular hero also participates in forms of piracy outright by taking part in a slaver's expedition, and by participating in propertied upheaval across the hemisphere. Reading *Blake* through the lens of piracy complicates portrayals of Delany as blindly adherent to free-market capitalism. Rather than having an unmediated commitment to capitalism, Delany upends commerce and exchange through piracy. Indeed, acts of piracy performed by African Americans in the antebellum period are devastating contestations of, rather than appeals to, the state for recognition.

By turning my attention more centrally to the question of self-possession in the creation of the American citizen, in this chapter I build on the previous chapters, which examined the imagined ineffable properties of the revolutionary person and the tenuous, easily reproducible properties of the postrevolutionary American person. While this chapter builds on previous

81

chapters, it very explicitly identifies the first of several instances in which populations that are intentionally dispossessed by the state stake claims to property outside the limitations of the state and its laws. Indeed, this chapter is the first that looks specifically to the property of the self as critical in the creation of the citizen. In the face of legal restrictions on a range of properties for marginalized populations, including the property of the self, possession of the self stands in as an act of piracy that expands the category of the citizen.

To demonstrate the significance of self-possession as an act of piracy, I turn to narratives about slavery authored by nineteenth-century black writers who examine the slave trade as a piratic practice. These writers also imagine resistance to the slave trade through the slave's unlawful appropriation of the property of the self. Indeed, given that the transatlantic transportation of slaves is deemed to be an act of piracy, by having *Blake*'s protagonist steal and transport the illegal property of the self across national borders, Delany suggests that any act of self-possession, too, is an act of piracy. And so, in Delany's imaginative world, fugitives are incarnations of the pirate. In *Blake*, this is dramatized not simply by the titular hero's act of fugitivity and participation in slave insurrection. Rather, the apogee of Blake's piratic ventures is to join a slaver. The only way to make Delany's imaginative intervention into questions of possession and piracy apparent, however, is to read *Blake* alongside slave narratives published in this same period. Together, these works demonstrate the significance of Blake's piratic act of self-possession to understanding the properties of citizenship.

Delany's unfinished novel is set in the shadows of the expansion of slavery and the extreme restrictions placed on black life in the United States. The novel captures a moment when the country has outlawed international slave trading yet has encouraged the growth of Southern industries that depend on slave labor. *Blake* centers on its protagonist and the novel's namesake, Henry Blake, a slave owned by Colonel Franks who escapes the institution upon witnessing the sale of his wife, Maggie. Incensed by the sale, Blake moves through plantations throughout the South, inciting slave revolt, before leaving for Cuba at the end of the first half of the novel. Part 2 opens with Blake's continued efforts to organize a black rebellion in Cuba and to locate his wife on the island. In this second part, both Blake and the reader learn that he was formerly known as Carolus Henrico Blacus, the son of a wealthy Cuban merchant mistakenly sold into slavery in his youth. Having found both his wife and his family in Cuba, Blake continues to organize a black revolution with the help of a largely wealthy, educated, and free mulatto population on the island. In the remaining issues of the serialized novel, Delany dramatizes Blake's participation in an embryonic black-led Cuban revolution.[1]

In order to highlight the incongruity and hypocrisy of a market that both relies on black labor and excludes the black body from membership in the state, Blake behaves as a pirate in three different ways. First, Blake escapes U.S. chattel slavery and, in so doing, participates in a radical act of self-ownership at the heart of liberal notions of the possession of the self. In this context, fugitivity is a form of piracy because it disregards the sanctity of private property, but also because it unsettles a state reliant on slavery and the slave trade. Second, after his escape, Blake travels around the South, inciting slave revolt and disseminating ideas about black revolution. These activities are clandestine for the additional reason that slave codes tended to prohibit not only slave escape but also "unlawful assemblies, trespasses, and seditious speeches, by a slave or slaves."[2] In this context covert speech about freedom, as well as the fugitive slave, constitute illicit "goods" being traded hemispherically along routes outside state control. Moreover, in the South, Blake encourages slaves to escape and fund their fugitivity with stolen or saved funds. By encouraging slaves to steal and engage with subversive or illegal market practices, Blake is proposing more than just an escape from slavery.[3] Rather, he encourages purchasing one's freedom and owning one's body through illegal means.

Blake's final and most radical acts of piracy are to join a slaving expedition to Africa and to manipulate the slave market in Cuba upon his return from the expedition in order to purchase the recently captured slaves at a low price and then free them with the expectation that they will join in the black revolutionary efforts on the island. In representing Blake as a pirate, Delany presents a form of black participation in the market that disrupts the proper operations of exchange and at the same time creates a black market in several different ways. Delany suggests that certain illegal economic practices allow the slave's entry into a transnational circulation of goods, not as a good him- or herself but as a subject capable of participating in trade and ownership in the shadows.

Reading this text through the lens of piracy contributes to extant criticism on *Blake*. The text has garnered a great deal of critical attention due in part to its early articulations of black transnationalism.[4] Understood from this perspective, the text advocates for political sovereignty through transnational collective black politics.[5] These critical works emphasize the transnational impulse behind Delany's articulation of rights and highlight the importance of *Blake* within larger narratives about nineteenth-century political life in the Americas.[6] A transnational reading of the text has also made possible an opening of American literature to a deliberate coverage of hemispheric social movements, as well as shifting paradigms of political and economic life in the Americas.[7] Although some criticism has examined how a transnational reading of this text might shift, given global processes of commerce and imperialism in the eighteenth and nineteenth centuries, these readings omit *Blake*'s engagement with illegal markets of exchange.[8] Moreover, although critics examine the importance and centrality of slavery in the strengthening of the U.S. nation-state and the creation of the white, male, liberal subject, few analyze how ownership of private property by enslaved black subjects can help us amplify the figure of the pirate to include dispossessed persons who participate in the subversion of these institutions.[9]

As I show, by examining property ownership among slaves using the theoretical framework of piracy, *Blake* offers a revisionary account of life under slavery: rather than a subject on the margins of the state and social and economic life, the enslaved person is at the center of novel forms of ownership. At the moment when the slave is seemingly denied all freedoms, we see that he or she is also capable of articulating a propertied autonomy outside the limitations of the state. Ultimately, Blake's piracy is a response to the systemic exclusion of black bodies from all aspects of social, political, and economic life in the United States, as well as a critical practice that undermines the state responsible for this exclusion.

Liberalism, Property, and Slavery

Because of the overwhelming quantity of Delany's writings devoted to the importance of emigration in African American emancipation and enfranchisement, he is mistakenly seen as a champion of black emigration as the sole means of black uplift.[10] In his introduction to the 1970 edition of the novel, Floyd J. Miller writes that African American intellectuals, including Delany, "flirted with the idea of a Northern American union of blacks."[11] Delany belonged to a group of abolitionists "advocating Central American emigration as well as the establishment of a Central and South American 'nation' that would contribute to the downfall of American slavery."[12] Indeed, in "The Condition, Elevation, Emigration and Destiny of the Colored People of the United States," Delany decries the failures of the U.S. nation-state and supports emigration, saying, "We love our country, dearly love her, but she don't love us—she despises us, and bids us begone, driving us from her embraces."[13] By the mid-1850s, Delany had himself settled in Canada, was privately planning a black insurrection in the United States, and was publicly advocating black emigration. In 1859, when *Blake* was serialized, Delany traveled to the Niger valley, where he purchased land that would serve as the site of black settlement, thus shifting his attention from the Americas to Africa as the location of free black communities. However, regardless of the exact site of resettlement, Delany's archives reveal his commitment to debates regarding the status of black people in the United States. For Delany, sovereignty through black emigration was the foundation for black freedom and rights, since "no people can be free who themselves do not constitute an essential part of the *ruling element* of the country in which they live," an impossibility in the United States.[14]

However, Delany's novel betrays an alternative to emigration and national sovereignty as the sole means to black freedom and independence. The propertied sovereignty and independence so crucial to Blake's escape to Cuba demonstrate Delany's acute engagement with enslaved persons' properties. Delany's political and journalistic writings reveal a shrewd and inspirational intellectual who explores the individual's relationship to property through the lens of liberal philosophy. He writes, "We must have means to be practically efficient in all the undertakings of life; and to obtain them, it is necessary that we should be engaged in lucrative pursuits, trades, and general business transactions."[15] As Delany discusses in great depth in both his fiction and nonfiction, black people are structurally excluded from participating in full expressions of social, political, and economic life and are barred from all forms of possession, including the possession of their bodies. Given that, for Delany, political personhood flows from bodily sovereignty and self-possession, without self-possession the slave cannot experience political sovereignty. When discussing the importance of self-governance, for example, Delany invokes the importance of self-possession quite literally. He writes, "For a people, to be free, [they] must necessarily be their own rulers: that is, each individual must, in himself, embody the essential ingredient—so to speak—of the sovereign principle which composes the true basis of his liberty. This principle, when not exercised by himself, may, at his pleasure, be delegated to another—his true representative."[16] For Delany, a range of political rights emanate from the primary property of the self. Indeed, this property will result in something akin to citizenship. He writes, "The thing now most required for the freedman is a home—one that he can call his own, and possess in fee simple, to insure the subsistence of himself and family," adding that in becoming possessors of land, a now-free African American population will find itself interested in, invested in, and indebted to the state.[17]

In part, Delany anticipates Booker T. Washington's belief in economic uplift expressed in *Up from Slavery* (1901), in which Washington writes, "Wherever our graduates go, the changes which soon begin to appear in the buying of land, improving homes, saving money, in education, and in high moral character are remarkable," adding that graduates are revolutionizing whole communities.[18] Education, in Washington's view, enables the black subject to "acquire property, and secure employment," allowing him to be "treated with respect in the business or commercial world," in ways that will eventually improve the destiny of the South.[19] For Washington, education is more than "the ability to read and write, the mere acquisition of a knowledge of literature and science"; rather, education "makes men producers, lovers of labour, independent, honest, unselfish, and, above all, good."[20] In making the case for an educated, and therefore economically independent, but also laboring and productive black population, Washington suggests that both the South and the nation as a whole will thrive.

In articulating the importance of transforming free black persons into propertied *homo economici* as a mode of accessing power, Washington echoes Adam Smith's foundational *Wealth of Nations*, where Smith writes that power is tied to possession: possession of one's labor and possession of the wages that one would receive in exchange for labor. For Smith as for the writers mentioned previously, slavery is an institution that limits possession and economic self-determination based on race, and therefore the institution is harmful to American political economy. Indeed, Smith makes a case against slavery on economic, not moral, grounds saying, "The experience of all ages and nations, I believe, demonstrates that the work done by slaves, though it appears to cost only their maintenance, is in the end the dearest of any. A person who can acquire no property, can have no other interest but to eat as much, and to labour as little as possible. Whatever work he does beyond what is sufficient to purchase his own maintenance can be squeezed out of him by violence only, and not by any interest of his own."[21] He adds, "Land occupied by [free] tenants is properly cultivated at the expence of the proprietor as much as that occupied by slaves. There is, however, one very essential difference between them. Such tenants, being freemen, are capable of acquiring property, and having a certain proportion of the produce of the land" gives the laborer "a plain interest that the whole produce should be as great as possible, in order that their own proportion may be so. A slave, on the contrary, who can acquire nothing but his maintenance, consults his own ease by making the land produce as little as possible over and above that maintenance."[22] In Smith's and Washington's view, power and the liberty of the individual are equated with possession of one's labor, and access to the property of the self and of one's labor is the basis of a thriving political economy.

Most importantly, for Washington, property ownership ultimately leads to the political enfranchisement of African Americans: "To permanently tax the Negro without giving him the right to vote . . . would work in the alienation of the affections of the Negro from the States in which he lives, and would be the reversal of the fundamental principles of government for which our States have stood."[23] In invoking the revolutionary slogan of "no taxation without representation," Washington deftly calls for the full enfranchisement of the African American citizens already contributing to the economic growth of the South, and his statement also reflects the extension of citizenship rights based on property rights. Washington, in other words, echoes the foundational ties between propertied personhood and political representation or enfranchisement, even as he furthers black propriety through property ownership.[24] Indeed, the numerous accounts of individual incidents of property ownership by slaves in eighteenth- and nineteenth-century texts reinforce the discourse of black respectability through property. However, given that Washington's enfranchised subject is an extension of the productive, laboring, and economically independent black body, Washington, like Delany, stresses the importance of property in the creation of "person," thereby invoking the language of liberalism alongside discourses of respectability.

Delany and Washington are not alone in this belief in the potential for black uplift through property ownership in the nineteenth century. The language of property in fact shapes African American literature both before and after the publication of *Blake*. For example, Josiah Henson's (1849), Henry Bibb's (1850), and Elizabeth Keckley's (1868) narratives all take up the formative role of property in the creation of autonomy, and they all treat black property ownership as articulations of a desire for political visibility and inclusion in the national body.[25] For example, Keckley's *Behind the Scenes; or, Thirty Years a Slave and Four Years in the White House* is a narrative about a range of properties, including the narrative itself, which she sees as a sellable product that can be used to save Mary Todd Lincoln from destitution.[26] Paired with Keckley's self-fashioning as a woman of enterprise and property, Keckley's ownership of a dressmaking shop is a demonstration of economic autonomy at the level of both the text and its circulation. And so, the text is recursive: Keckley at once presents a narrative about her assertion of economic independence while also being aware of how the text will circulate in the market and how these varied circulating properties reflect the increasing legal and economic freedoms experienced by African Americans.[27]

However, it is perhaps Henson's *Life of Josiah Henson, Formerly a Slave, Now an Inhabitant of Canada, as Narrated by Himself* that most clearly asserts the possibility for enslaved subjects to become good commercial citizens and propertied subjects. Having demonstrated his capacity for leadership on the plantation of his birth, Henson quickly becomes a farm manager there, even supplanting the overseer. A particularly significant moment in the text occurs when he is tasked with transporting his master's slaves across the Ohio River to Kentucky. During this voyage, both Henson and the slaves momentarily consider escape to the North. However, Henson thwarts these designs for escape, writing that the "idea of running away was not one that I had ever indulged. I had a sentiment of honor on the subject."[28] Henson decides to fulfill his obligation to his master by preventing the slaves from escaping: indeed, Henson believes that a demonstration of "honorable" obligation not to escape and to prevent others from escaping will culminate in being allowed to purchase his own freedom. These actions all demonstrate to some degree Henson's desire for and capacity to enter into contractual agreements and to understand the meanings of the slave body as valuable property. Unfortunately, Henson soon learns that the slave cannot enter into a contract, having been deprived of all rights and having been deprived of all legal recourse. Finding that he will never be allowed to purchase his freedom, and by extension never be allowed to own himself, at the novel's denouement Henson's only recourse is to escape to Canada, where he establishes an entrepreneurial colony of freemen.[29]

In his narrative, Bibb describes himself as a liberal subject even though this condition is denied to the slave.[30] He states that the desire to be free seemed to emanate from within, "to be a part of my nature; it was first revealed to me by the inevitable laws of nature's God. I could see that the All-wise Creator, had made man a free, moral, intelligent and accountable being; capable of knowing good and evil. And I believed then, as I believe now, that every man has a right to wages for his labor; a right to his own wife and children; a right to liberty and the pursuit of happiness; and a right to worship God according to the dictates of his own conscience. But here, in the light of these truths, I was a slave, a prisoner for life; I could possess nothing, nor acquire anything but what must belong to my keeper."[31] In describing himself as free in the state of nature and saying that this state entitles him to the privileges of laboring for a wage and to property, even the property of a wife and children, Bibb describes himself not simply as a free man but as a Lockean man in the state of nature. Bibb's expression of liberal subjectivity forcibly opens up the category of person to include himself, and, in so doing, Bibb also forces the reader to question the inherent contradiction in the logic of slavery: the reduction of a person to a thing that is impermissible in natural law.

So, too, does Frederick Douglass invoke natural rights discourse to critique the institution of slavery in *My Bondage and My Freedom* (1855). To make a case that slavery is antithetical to liberal and modern models of personhood, in *My Bondage and My Freedom*, Douglass quotes Samuel Taylor Coleridge, writing, "By a principle essential to Christianity, a PERSON is eternally differenced from a THING; so that the idea of a HUMAN BEING, necessarily excludes the idea of PROPERTY IN THAT BEING."[32] By citing Coleridge, Douglass means to emphasize the nature of property by underscoring that only things, and not persons, can be reduced to the position of a possessed object. One can find this same language in "Nature of Slavery," an extract from a longer speech delivered by Douglass five years prior to the publication of *My Bondage and My Freedom*, where Douglass notes, "to mar and deface those characteristics of its victims which distinguish *men* from *things*, and *persons* from *property*."[33] By repeatedly emphasizing the separation between person and thing using the language of property, Douglass also responds to and critiques William Brockenbrough's well-known dissent to *Commonwealth v. Turner* in 1827, which stated that a "slave was not only a *thing*, but a *person* and this well known distinction would extend its protection to the slave as person, *except so far as the application of it conflicted with the enjoyment of the slave as a thing.*"[34] While Brockenbrough's dissent separates the inalienable body of the slave from the alienable and ownable labor of the slave, in practice the person of the slave is always reduced to the thing of his labor. After all, Brockenbrough's dissent to some degree allows for ownership of the slave body through ownership of his labor, even as he echoes a foundational liberal separation between the "thing" and the "person."

Therefore, as Douglass poignantly emphasizes, it is not just that slavery counters the presumed universal rights to "justice and right and liberty" on which liberalism, as well as the U.S. state, rests, but that this rhetoric is used against the black subject to deprive him of all rights and reduce him to a thing: "the fundamental principles of the republic, to which the humblest white man, whether born here or elsewhere, may appeal with confidence, in the hope of awakening a favorable response, are held to be inapplicable to us. The glorious doctrines of your revolutionary fathers, and the more glorious teachings of the Son of God, are construed and applied against us."[35] And so, Douglass highlights the incongruity in the U.S. liberal democratic state's conception of itself, as well as the flaws inherent in the very conception of liberal individualism that allow for omissions in who is fully human. He also stresses the importance of property (of the self *together with* one's labor) in the creation and fulfillment of the abstract concept of person.

Piracy, Slavery, and Fugitivity

Given that the works mentioned previously explore how best to assert the enslaved person's humanity through his or her full expression as a laboring and economically productive person, these narratives all demonstrate a sophisticated treatment of rights' interdependence with property. However, what makes Delany's *Blake* remarkable is how it envisions a response to these injustices and dispossessions. In Delany's literary imagination, the only response to systemic exclusion is to redouble the black subject's exclusion from public life by participating in the shadows of social and economic life through fugitivity.[36] And so, *Blake* represents incidents of ownership that must be examined in the context of the overwhelming exclusion of enslaved people from the rights to property. For Delany, the Fugitive Slave Bill of 1850, passed "with the approbation of a majority of the American people," was especially unparalleled in its "tantalising insult and aggravating despotism" precisely because it both allowed the black person to lose all claims to himself and left him vulnerable to claims by any white man.[37] And so, the bill necessitated an equally unlawful response. Whereas Henson, Bibb, and Douglass all envisioned a form of inclusion in a larger political body, Delany envisions black life in the shadows of the state.

In the face of the deprivation of so many properties, Delany advances a form of illegal property ownership, including the ownership of the self through fugitivity, akin to piracy. Indeed, the property-owning slave is a figure akin to a pirate. After all, the slave cannot have lawful rights to property because, by definition, a slave cannot experience the freedoms attached to ownership of the self and, by extension, ownership of alienable property.[38] Moreover, the enslaved subject cannot own property because the slave cannot experience the recognition attached to property ownership.

Thus, incidents of illegal property ownership are demands for an unlawful possession of the self as much as they are performances of a disavowal of the state. Said differently, in claiming property, the enslaved subject demands the recognition afforded to the liberal person but does so outside the law.[39] Because state law is used to protect and enforce slavery, in breaking the law repeatedly, acts of fugitivity in *Blake* threaten to undermine the state and its markets.

And so, Delany's engagement with property must be understood as his attempt to radically restructure the relationship between the subject and the state, a notion echoed by John Locke. Since, by definition, the slave cannot be recognized as a person with rights, the slave is caught in a double bind: he is deprived of the right to property and at the same time is unable to consent to membership in civil society. Locke's response is to suggest that, because a slave has no power of consent, the slave has no obligation to be obedient. Although Locke does not directly address the question of lawful and unlawful forms of property ownership in the creation of the liberal subject, we see in Locke that the slave's relationship to state law is conflicted and that the law should not theoretically come to bear on the life of the slave. In sum, the enslaved person has no contract with the state and no obligation to follow the law. For this reason, the slave is in some ways always a pirate.

Moreover, Delany's demands for black piracy articulated in *Blake* are a response to the piracies of the slave trade. Indeed, Delany is one of many thinkers who understood slavery as an illegal economic institution akin to piracy. Douglass, for example, uses the language of illegal exchange to explain the peculiar institution.[40] He writes, "I had been cheated. . . . I treated them [slaveholders] as robbers and deceivers."[41] Upon purchasing his freedom from Hugh Auld, Douglass finds him to be "a violation of anti-slavery principles—conceding a right of property in man—and a wasteful expenditure of money."[42] Douglass views this purchase in part as "ransom, or as money extorted by a robber, and my liberty of more value than one hundred and fifty pounds sterling, I could not see either a violation of the laws of morality, or those of economy, in the transaction."[43] In a speech delivered in 1852 called "The Internal Slave Trade" and echoed in his seminal speech "What to the Slave Is the Fourth of July?," Douglass makes a case for the piratic nature of the slave trade conducted within the boundaries of the United States, saying, "That [transatlantic] trade has long since been denounced by this government as piracy. It has been denounced with burning words, from the high places of the nation, as an execrable traffic. To arrest it, to put an end to it, this nation keeps a squadron, at immense cost, on the coast of Africa. . . . It is, however, a notable fact, that, while so much execration is poured out by Americans, upon those engaged in the foreign slave trade, the men engaged in the slave trade between the states pass without condemnation, and their business is deemed honorable."[44] In his narrative, Bibb, too, minces no words and refers to the popular class of "traitors and kidnappers" of free black persons as "land pirates" who make their living through improper means.[45] Thus, in referring to slaveholders as nothing more than a "band of successful robbers" and "land pirates" Douglass and Bibb are calling slavery illegal outright: as illegal as theft or piracy.[46]

For Douglass and for Bibb, not only is the slave trade a form of piracy that threatens to reduce every slave merchant to the status of a pirate, but it also threatens to transform all economic activity into piracy. Douglass writes, "The slave is robbed, by his master, of all his earnings, above what is required for his bare physical necessities; and the white man is robbed by the slave system, of the just results of his labor, because he is flung into competition with a class of laborers who work without wages."[47] In Douglass's view, slavery is a deleterious economic system that threatens to impede economic progress in the United States. Indeed, the most virulent critiques of slavery as an economic institution come from slaves themselves, who describe slavery as a vestige of premodernity, of feudalism, and of piracy. Douglass, for example, calls Colonel Lloyd's plantation an isolated and secluded space that more closely resembles a feudal estate. After noting that the plantation's economic isolation precludes it from seeing the "glimmering and unsteady light of trade, which sometimes exerts a civilizing influence," he writes that the plantation is "grim, cold, and unapproachable by all genial influences from communities without, *there it stands*," later adding that this isolation also allows "high-handed and atrocious" crimes to be committed "with almost as much impunity as upon the deck of a pirate ship."[48] Colonel Lloyd's controlled and isolating model of conducting trade on the plantation leads to an economic stagnation that Douglass sees as antithetical to modernity. The feudal economic system on the plantation stifles competition because "there are no conflicting rights of property, for all the people are owned by one man; and they can themselves own no property."[49] The premodernity of this space, understood to originate in the lack of private property ownership, makes it opposed to the spirit of capitalism espoused by the United States. Douglass emphasizes this point by noting that in the North he encounters a more industrious race: "Everything was done here with a scrupulous regard to economy, both in regard to men and things, time and strength."[50]

Perhaps this is why the "Narrative of Albert and Mary," an abolitionist text penned by Dr. W. H. Brisbane, which allegorizes slavery in the form of a pirate captivity narrative, is so unique.[51] Even so, the story, published in Julia Griffiths's anthology of abolitionist writing, *Autographs for Freedom* (1850), is not a narrative of exploit but one of exploitation. The narrative centers on Albert and Mary, two young lovers, who discuss the ethics of slavery while traveling from their plantation homes in South Carolina to New York aboard a steamer. This debate is interrupted when an unexpected storm throws the young lovers overboard, leaving them to be rescued by a vessel commanded by the pirate captain Templeton. Though Albert and Mary resume their conversation about Christianity once aboard the pirate ship, they do so to appeal to the captain to abandon his sordid profession. And yet, from their encounter with Templeton, who confidently declares that "the argument for slavery is identically the same in principle as for piracy," it is Albert and Mary, not Templeton, who become "converts."[52] So swayed are the young lovers by Templeton's equivalence of piracy to slavery that they are transformed into abolitionists by the narrative's denouement.

Indeed, this transformation is aided by the pirate captain's insistence that neither piracy nor slavery is a sin, saying, "It is upon the ground that slavery is not under all circumstances a sin, that Christians in the Northern States hold communion with you of the South . . . and I doubt not they would as readily commune with Christian pirates, since it is evident that piracy is not, any more than slavery, *malum in se*."[53] Slowly, the pirate captain builds a case for the permissibility of the spurious trade by appealing to Albert's and Mary's ethical commitments, which make slavery permissible under the laws of Christianity.

While Templeton underscores the equivalence of piracy and slavery using the language of religion to persuade the young lovers of the acceptability of his illicit profession, he also defends his participation in piracy using the language of the law. For Templeton, piracy is like slavery not only in that they are both paternalistic and appropriative behaviors "analogous to that of parents and children" and sanctioned by religion but also because these behaviors are both legal fictions, to mean that they are legal inventions subject to revision and alteration.[54] Indeed, by framing slavery as a type of piracy, and using defenses of the peculiar institution to speak to the legitimacy of piracy in the antebellum South, Templeton's monologues in the narrative call on a legal tradition that is fungible. Manmade law, Templeton provocatively suggests, can be manipulated to such a degree so as to make the otherwise immoral and unethical ownership of human bodies lawful. Given that law is both fabricated and can be adapted so as to authorize the cruelest of practices, Templeton declares that he has a right to the properties of others because, as a pirate, he is under no social or legal obligation to follow "the laws of the society or government" whose jurisdiction he does not recognize.[55]

Finally, as the "Narrative of Albert and Mary" illustrates, it is not simply that the slave owner is a type of pirate but also that the pirate is a subject that, like the enslaved person, has a complicated relationship to property, the state, and its laws. For one, this short story highlights how the study of piracy and slavery hinges on the contingency of property. Indeed, Templeton's monologue succinctly captures a tension that is pervasive in the study of all property: property is provisional, entirely dependent on government's protection of it. And yet, should a person choose to live without any claims to rights and to the protections of properties and person, then this person has no obligations to the state and no responsibility to follow its laws. Indeed, this argument echoes Locke's above. That is, the enslaved person, legally barred from consent and from contract, lacks all properties and protections: his body is not protected by the state and he lacks even the property of his own body. For this reason, the slave, like the pirate, is illiberal and not able to participate in the economy of citizenship and has no obligations to follow the laws of a slave-holding government.

As in the "Narrative of Albert and Mary," and Bibb's and Douglass's narratives, the unlawful underpinnings of the slave trade are made apparent in the opening pages of *Blake*, which begins with a discussion of refitting the *Merchantman*, an old ship that transports slaves from Africa to Cuba and goods from Havana to Baltimore. The group discussing the retrofitting is composed of wealthy Northern, Southern, and Cuban state officials and includes the characters Colonel Stephen Franks, Major James Armsted, Captain Richard Paul, and Captain George Royer. These men, driven purely by "self-interest," are prepared to act without regard to law. The Americans, we are told, elect Baltimore as the site for the refitting, noting that the city boasts of the "greatest facilities . . . having done more for the encouragement and protection of the trade than any other known place," while the Cubans object, preferring Havana "on the ground that the continual increase of liberal principles in the various [U.S.] political parties" hinders proper economic growth.[56] The group eventually settles on Baltimore as the site of the *Merchantman* refitting.

However, given that the refitting of the *Merchantman* is in violation of several different U.S. and international laws, this opening discussion demonstrates the centrality of piracy to the plot.[57] For example, Colonel Franks, Major Armsted, Captain Paul, and Captain Royer are in violation of the Slave Trade Act of 1820 or the 1820 Piracy Law, as well as the Slave Trade Act of 1807. Delany critiques the multiple characters who continuously take part in illegal commercial activities associated with the slave trade, and the novel asserts, "It is confidently believed upon good authority that the American steamers plying between Havana and New Orleans, as a profitable part of their enterprise, are actively engaged in the slave trade between these two places. These facts, though seen and known by all employees and passengers of such vessels, are supposed to be a legal traffic of masters removing their slaves."[58] Furthermore, Delany writes that the Slave Trade Act of 1807, which outlawed the importation of slaves into the United States, "is openly and constantly trampled under foot; and those in power, the supreme Judicial and Executive authorities being generally slaveholders or their abettors, well know these facts, and by keeping silence wink at and encourage such undisguised, infamous deeds of daring."[59] The slave trade, Delany notes, is participated in with impunity by people at all social levels, perhaps most distressingly by those charged with upholding the law (for example, the various military officials mentioned earlier).

Originally an amendment to the 1819 Act to Protect the Commerce of the United States and Punish the Crime of Piracy, the Slave Trade Act of 1820 redoubled the illegality of slavery by boldly stating that any American citizen participating in the slave trade "shall be adjudged a pirate; and on conviction thereof before the circuit court of the United States for the district wherein he shall be brought or found, shall suffer death."[60] Therefore, the language of these acts categorically declares the illegality and piratic nature of participating in the slave trade. Moreover, given that the Slave Trade Act is framed as an amendment to the act protecting "commerce of the United States," the act of 1820 revealed the relationship between mercantilism, piracy, and the slave trade. In these laws, protecting and encouraging proper trade by discouraging theft and piracy (which is seen as inhibiting trade rather than promoting it) extends to the slave trade, thereby marking the slave trade as an inhibitor rather than promoter of proper trade. Thus, Delany's *Blake* brings to light a contradiction: although the slave trade is understood as necessary to the U.S. economy, in the eyes and language of the law, it is also a type of piracy on several different registers. More importantly, Blake's description of mundane and pervasive processes in the peculiar institution is in fact a portrayal of a circuit of piracy between the United States and Cuba practiced with impunity.

Recognizing that piracy contributes to the growth of the slave industry while also disrupting proper trade, Delany suggests that enslaved populations, too, should engage in piracy so as to disrupt the mechanics of slavery and test the limits of the state, which thrives on a piratic trade. He advocates illegal forms of property ownership for enslaved populations but does so using an unexpected rationale: illegal trade, in the hands of an enslaved population, is a way for enslaved bodies to stake claims to personhood and, ultimately, freedom. Unlike Colonel Franks's piracies, described at the outset of the novel, black participation in the market threatens the very state structures responsible for the subjugation they experience. The types of property ownership espoused by Delany are necessarily problematic and even unlawful, and they respond to the unlawful commerce that undergirds and perpetuates the institution of slavery. Because the law is used to protect and enforce capitalist exchange in order to contribute to national wealth, in breaking the law repeatedly, the acts of black piracy represented in *Blake* threaten to poison both the state and a healthy market. In sum, in contrast to the acts of piracy (read: the slave trade) that underpin economic growth, black acts of piracy threaten the very regulatory bodies that benefit from illegal economic activities.

Indeed, illegal exchange emerges as a necessary by-product of the legal limitations placed on the black body. For Blake, addressing a specifically black model of ownership begins with making a claim for ownership of the body through illegal means, and the logic of self-ownership extends to the slaves whom he encounters on his travels across the South. After Blake stakes a claim to his own body through escape, he proceeds to disseminate radical ideas of self-ownership across the Americas. By encouraging slaves to escape and fomenting black uprisings across the Americas, Blake encourages black persons to violate Southern slave codes and upset federal law. For example, by spreading revolutionary ideas of self-possession and aiding in the escape of slaves, Blake is violating the Fugitive Slave Act, which states that a person found to "aid, abet, or assist [an escaped slave] . . . directly or indirectly, to escape . . . or shall harbor or conceal such fugitive, so as to prevent the discovery and arrest of such person . . . shall, for either of said offences, be subject to a fine not exceeding one thousand dollars, and imprisonment not exceeding six months."[61] Given the language of the law, in advising and helping slaves to escape, Blake is breaking laws at several different levels: from the local and regional to the national.

Furthermore, the piratic act of owning one's own body, which Blake also encourages, amounts to participation in a truly black market, since a slave's ownership of his body, or self-ownership through escape, competes with the lawful claims to or ownership of the same body. In other words, fugitivity is an unlawful act of self-ownership, as well as an act of theft from Colonel Franks.[62] As Stephen Best writes in *The Fugitive's Properties: Law and the Poetics of Possession*, "The law's purpose with regards to the fugitive . . . is to manage the slave's coeval status as material property and willing self; but that purpose . . . has evolved in the direction of managing the relation between the alienable (property) and the inalienable (the self) as a simple function of the abstraction implicit in property, as a rigorous arithmetic of fungible units."[63] Blake's body is the vehicle through which piracy takes shape, while also being the principal object making self-possession possible. Blake, in other words, is the pirate, as well as the pirate ship.

Not only is black self-possession an illegal act, but Blake also proposes that enslaved subjects steal in order to make freedom possible. Delany writes, African Americans have "inherited those regions by birth, paid for the soil by toil, irrigated it with their sweat, enriched it with their blood, nothing remaining to be done but by their dependence in Divine aid, a reliance in their own ability, and strength of their own arms, but to claim and take possession."[64] The battle cry to "claim and take possession" represents a propertied call to arms that is antithetical to legal forms of ownership. Theft is framed as a necessary response to the institution of slavery, and Douglass, for example, also writes that slavery necessarily drives the slave to break the law: "In law, the slave has no wife, no children, no country, and no home. He can own nothing, possess nothing, acquire nothing, but what must belong to another. To eat the fruit of his own toil, to clothe his person with the work of his own hands, is considered stealing."[65] Therefore, Douglass steals as a means of subsistence, saying, "It was necessary that the right to steal from *others* should be established; and this could only rest upon a wider range of generalization than that which supposed the right to steal from my master."[66] He writes,

I frankly confess, that while I hated everything like stealing, *as such*, I nevertheless did not hesitate to take food, when I was hungry, wherever I could find it. Nor was this practice the mere result of an unreasoning instinct; it was, in my case, the result of a clear apprehension of the claims of morality. I weighted and considered the matter closely, before I ventured to satisfy my hunger by such means.

Considering that my labor and person were the property of Master Thomas, and that I was by him deprived of the necessaries of life—necessaries obtained by my own labor—it was easy to deduce the right to supply myself with what was my own. It was simply appropriating what was my own to the use of my master, since the health and strength derived from such food were exerted in *his* service.[67]

Douglass "steals" the food yet also considers that the food is just payment for his unpaid services. He justifies these actions using the logic of property ownership and preservation. Thus, Douglass is paradoxically stealing property in order to protect property. Indeed, he cleverly maintains that his theft of meat does not directly threaten his master's property ownership. Rather, because Douglass is merely transferring meat from one tub to another, Douglass's master continues to retain ownership of his property: "At first, he owned [the meat] in the *tub*, and last, he owned it in *me*."[68] This allows Douglass to provocatively affirm "that the slave is fully justified in helping himself to the *gold and silver, and the best apparel of his master, or that of any other slaveholder; and that such taking is not stealing in any just sense of the word*," adding that "the morality of *free* society can have no application to *slave* society."[69] He writes, "Slaveholders have made it almost impossible for the slave to commit any crime, known either to the laws of God or to the laws of man. If he steals, he takes his own; if he kills his master, he imitates only the heroes of the revolution. . . . Make a man a slave, and you rob him of moral responsibility. Freedom of choice is the essence of all accountability."[70] In being "robbed" of his "rightful liberty, and of the just reward of [his] labor," Douglass states that he is "justified in plundering in turn" in the name of "self-preservation."[71]

For Delany as for Douglass, possession of the self and of other properties through theft is critical to the creation of freedom and membership in a civic and political body. However, the acts of theft represented in *Blake* are neither minor nor inconsequential in any way: rather, they make possible new models of transnational affiliation that threaten the primary significance of the nation-state as a dispenser and guarantor of rights, personhood, and community. For this reason, Blake encourages slaves to further participate in the marketplace by persuading them to sell these claimed or stolen objects and to sell any "marketable commodities as they might chance possess."[72] These thefts and piracies have the dual purpose of funding slave escape and enabling slaves' entry into the economic sphere as propertied persons. Indeed, Blake funds his own travels around the South by taking, "by littles, some of the earnings due [him] for more than eighteen years' service to this man Franks, [which] would amount to sixteen hundred dollars more than [he] secured, exclusive of interest, which would have more than supplied [his] clothing, to say nothing of the injury done [him] by degrading [him] as a slave."[73] Indeed, before Blake steals his own body from Franks, he has already stolen a considerable sum from his owner. And yet, because the marketplace is unconcerned with the difference between legal and illegal goods (which is why piracy and black markets thrive), the marketplace is also where slaves are able to participate most freely.

Moreover, as Delany emphasizes, the theft and the sale of stolen property will result in a surrogate for political membership. For example, Blake tells a group of slaves, "With money you may effect your escape almost at any time. Your most difficult point is an elevated obstruction, a mighty hill, a mountain; but through that hill there is a gap, and money is your passport through that White gap to freedom. . . . Money alone will carry you through the White mountains or across the White river to liberty."[74] Money is described as a "passport," otherwise a marker of citizenship, that politicizes the body in economic terms.[75] As he attempts to obtain a free pass through the South, Blake notes that, for many people, the sight of the "shining gold eagle" was enough to spark their patriotism and give the escaping slaves "the right to pass as American freemen."[76] Given that this money can only be accessed through theft, the benefits of this theft are made immediately apparent: upon exchanging the shining gold eagle for the right to pass, the fugitives can then pass "as *American* freemen." This language suggests that theft gives one access to membership in the "Newnited States of America," the moniker Blake gives this country that turns a blind eye to law in favor of property and profit. In acquiring membership in the Newnited States, the escaped slaves gain not just economic personhood but a symbolic attachment to a nation-state. Money is not simply the means of securing escape; rather, the secured and saved funds enable a form of recognition that replaces national citizenship.[77] And yet, that it is "Newnited" signals that this political organization is novel and a departure from traditional models. In the face of structural exclusion from personhood and representation, *Blake* presents a model of belonging than runs counter to national inclusion. In other words, while the United States asserts white male citizenship through the illegal ownership and transportation of slave bodies, the Newnited States offers the enslaved black subject full participation in the economic sphere and enables, through piratic possession, a circuit of mutual recognition impossible in the antebellum United States.

Therefore, the reward awaiting Blake after his travels from the South to Cuba is citizenship and an opportunity to create a new society on the island. The site of Cuba coincided with economic, political, and social possibility for many Americans in the nineteenth century.[78] For Southerners, the island represented a possible future location for the expansion of U.S. chattel slavery. The port of Havana, then considered the jewel of the West Indies, presented entrepreneurs with a rich (and significantly less expensive) supply of land, coffee, sugar, and slaves.[79] Indeed, Delany's own nonfiction describes Cuba as the "great western slave mart of the world," adding, "There are at present in Cuba, probably not less than 600,000 slaves, there being in 1830 nearly twenty years ago, 450,000, with a yearly increase of trade in the slave products. These human souls, computed at the lowest estimate of $250 a-piece would amount to the sum of $150,000,000 which added to the land possessions, would bring into this country if annexed to it, no inconsiderable wealth."[80]

However, despite these popular representations of Cuba as ideologically and economically aligned with the interests of the South, for thinkers like Delany, Cuba was a site of political possibility because the island offered radical racial integration and more opportunity for mobility. Moreover, Delany writes that the annexation of Cuba to the United States "should be the signal for the simultaneous rebellion of all the slaves in the Southern States, and throughout that island."[81] In the event of Cuba's annexation, the island's large Afro-Cuban population was seen as having the potential to strengthen African American struggles for freedom. For Delany, Cuba represents a possible location for African American political, social, and economic expansion. It is therefore not surprising that Cuba is a desirable site for a variety of different subjects both black and white.

And so, at least initially, Blake finds a more racially integrated community in Cuba. For example, he learns that Cuban law "gives the slave the right, whenever desirous to leave his master, to make him a tender in Spanish coin, which if he don't accept, on proof of the tender the slave may apply to the parish priest or bishop of the district, who has the right immediately to declare such a slave free."[82] A critical difference between U.S. chattel slavery and Cuban slavery is that slaves are allowed to participate in the regime of ownership in which they can value, and ultimately purchase, their own bodies by demanding the price of freedom.[83] Framing it as an alternative to violent behavior at the hand of enslaved populations, one Cuban slave owner notes that it is "better to let the Negro have his liberty at his own expense at a price fixed by the law."[84] Seemingly, in Cuba the slave has at least the right to self-possession. Therefore, a climax occurs in the second part of the novel when Maggie, now Lotty, is able to purchase her freedom from her American owners in Cuba. Delany goes as far as to provide the text for what he calls the Magna Charta of liberty—her free papers—and these free papers frame Maggie's purchase of her own body as a material manifestation of freedom.

Blake's formal inclusion in the Cuban national body is also significant in that it represents an alternative to U.S. citizenship, which is impossible for Blake, or any black person, at the time that Delany pens the novel. Cuban citizenship stands in contradistinction to U.S. citizenship in Delany's literary imagination primarily because Cuban citizenship is not contingent on whiteness: free black persons are granted membership in the Cuban nation-state. And yet, as Blake eventually recognizes, black expressions of autonomy in Cuba are nevertheless restricted. Perhaps the greatest limitation to the full expression of black autonomy and freedom is the continued existence of chattel slavery on the island. And so, although Blake discovers he is not a Southern slave but, rather, the son of educated and well-to-do Cuban mulattos, Cuba is ultimately foreclosed as the site for black freedom. Membership in Cuba proves to be insufficient, and Blake critiques the island because it does not offer freedom and equality to all Afro-Cubans. While the island nation has a free black population recognized as citizens, this population is limited to a certain class of free black subjects that stands apart from enslaved subjects on the island. Indeed, as *Blake* suggests, free and enslaved black populations in Cuba are separated by an unbridgeable gap, as demonstrated by the fact that the group leading the revolution on the island are the free, and not enslaved, persons. Therefore, in Delany's imagination, membership within any single nation-state is seemingly always insufficient and incomplete, especially in a nation-state built on racialized slave labor.

Blake's exclusion from U.S. national membership and his unwillingness to blindly claim Cuban citizenship reflect his view of the undesirability of national membership without a radical restructuring of all aspects of social, economic, and political life in the Americas. Indeed, this is why piracy matters: while the privileges imagined by Blake through piracy are derived from those normative political properties attached to state recognition and citizenship, piracy is also a strategy that allows dispossessed persons proximity to forms of personhood that both elide and unsettle the state law. Piracy, it would seem, is the first step in forcefully expanding the bounds of citizenship by transforming the black subject into a figure who threatens to unmake the state altogether, rather than merely being subject to its repression. After all, participating in piracy enables Blake to emerge as a powerful propertied actor who also repudiates both Cuban and U.S. citizenship.

And so, for the remainder of the novel, Blake continues to engage in several other forms of piracy in violation of both U.S. property (municipal) and anti–slave trade (international) laws: first, he joins a slave expedition and participates in the piratic activity of the transatlantic slave trade. Blake's intention to seize the ship mid-ocean so as to use this vehicle in an Afro-Cuban revolution adds another dimension to his piratic actions, particularly because taking control over the ship in international waters and unlawfully appropriating the (illegal) property aboard is perhaps the most recognizable act of piracy to a modern audience. Blake's most subversive act of piracy, however, is manipulating the price of slaves upon returning to the island with the slave crew. I conclude with this particular form of piracy because it is both the most abstract and the most far reaching. Because the novel begins with a desire to participate in self-possession and the market more broadly, Blake's final act of piracy, the writing and revision of the language of value, functions as the climax, especially in the context of the missing final chapters of the novel. However, as I show, the practice of piracy, too, like membership in the U.S. and Cuban nation-states, is short-lived. Indeed, by the novel's conclusion, Blake returns to Cuba so as to lead a black rebellion on the island, the outcome of which remains unknown given the missing chapters of the text.

Blake and the Mechanics of Piracy

In many ways, Blake is emblematic of the romanticized pirate, a bandit radically testing the state's limits in regulating trade, and Blake's acts of theft and piracy exist both as the material theft of property and as a symbolic restructuring of the social and political order.[85] In his condition of statelessness and perpetual alienation from state recognition, Blake resembles the pirate who "attacks" the sanctity of private property and the inviolable state. He breaks the law and exists outside any regulation. By deliberately participating in a network of exchange that relies on his exclusion (both as a black enslaved subject and as someone who is improperly trading), Blake rewrites popular market fiction that stresses freedom of participation and equality in the marketplace. Indeed, his participation in an illegal economic sphere activates a web of social relations from which he would otherwise be excluded. Therefore, Blake's brief foray into piracy on the high seas aboard the slaving ship can be productively read alongside fugitivity, which figures prominently in the novel, since fugitivity is not an escape but, rather, a radical act of property ownership (ownership of the self) that is enabled through theft.

Blake's participation in the transatlantic slave trade as a crewmember of the slaving ship *Vulture* (formerly called the *Merchantman* at the beginning of the novel), composed of white slavers, free black crewmembers (including Blake), and a large group of slaves leased from their owners is immediately discernible as piracy. The retrofitted ship, once a legal and commercial vehicle, has now been renamed to reflect the predatory nature of its market dealings. The ship behaves like a pirate vehicle, flying different national flags in order to avoid suspicion from patrol boats while crossing the Atlantic and routinely outmaneuvering watchful British cruisers. However, in avoiding state regulatory bodies, the *Vulture*, formerly a British vessel, becomes a site of a new political economy, where the diverse crew, consisting of American and Cuban slavers, is linked by a common interest in wealth obtained by illegal means.[86] By participating in the slave trade, Blake asserts his own right to property by procuring the right to purchase slaves on the coast of Africa. This form of trade, in which Blake engages as part of the ship's crew, rather than being a commodity aboard the ship, illustrates the difference between Blake, who is able to participate in possession, and the slaves aboard the ship, who are divested of any type of recognition, thereby rendering them as property only. In this way, the *Vulture* transforms Blake into the merchant as promised by the ship's original name. However, it does so by recasting Blake as a figure operating outside the law rather than within it.

However, after the ship reaches the high seas, the condition of the enslaved subjects shifts so as to approximate Blake's privileges on board the *Vulture*, thereby dramatizing the ways in which membership on a pirate ship becomes an equalizer for all those aboard: a "hydrachy."[87] In one particularly exciting moment early in the *Vulture*'s voyage, the enslaved people sing a hymn that Delany captures, noting that it was "chanted with cheerful glee, and rather portentous mood and decisive air":

My country, the land of my birth,
Farewell to thy fetters and thee!
The by-word of tyrants—the scorn of the earth,
A mockery to all though shalt be!

Ye billows and surges, all hail!
My brothers henceforth—for ye scorn to be SLAVES,
As ye toss up your crests to the gale;
Farewell to the land of the blood-hound and chain,
My path is away o'er the fetterless main![88]

An American on board, "full of ardor and patriotism," quickly silences the chorus. This anthem, which threatens the U.S. national anthem, and, by extension, the U.S. nation-state through its mimicry of the Star-Spangled Banner calls for a rejection of the land of one's birth, the shackles of bondage, and the tyrants ruling said country. Moreover, this anthem calls for their replacement with the promises offered by the open sea. Not only does this parody of the U.S. national anthem echo the earlier discussion of monetary "passports," but also, given Blake's rejection of national affiliation, this moment aboard the ship demonstrates the multiple ways in which the enslaved characters in the novel threaten to renounce and reject U.S. citizenship and become pirates as well.

Indeed, in being aboard a pirate ship where none of the crewmembers have legal recourse, the hired slaves find themselves able to openly contest white supremacy. Eager to avoid a rebellion aboard the *Vulture*, the captain ultimately allows the hired slaves to enjoy movement aboard the ship, "enjoying all the privileges of common seamen."[89] Thus, participation in this piratic venture creates certain freedoms that even slaves are able to enjoy. These freedoms range from increased mobility to, as is the case with Blake, the privilege of owning property. Although all these articulations of freedom are technically illegal, they demonstrate that piracy alters power differentials between black and white subjects by allowing the slaves to take advantage of the slavers' lack of legal recourse. Contrary to Jeffory A. Clymer's assertion, Blake and the black crew are not *almost* pirates.[90] They *are* pirates insofar as they are participating in what, at this historical moment, would have been considered an act punishable by death. They are also pirates insofar as they are corrupting and disrupting a racial order. The slaver with the contents on board is therefore not simply a means for Blake to extend the radical framework of the possession of the self to the possession of property; it is also the means to black freedom across the Americas.

However, Blake's greatest act of piracy is to manipulate the market so as to artificially reduce the prices of the slaves in Cuba. The reader learns that Blake's participation in the transatlantic slave trade is motivated by the desire to release the slaves by encouraging his wealthy friends to purchase and then free the slaves after arriving on the island. While on board the slaving ship, Blake incites and encourages the slaves to misbehave, thereby reducing "the captives to a minimum price, which placed them in the reach of small capitalists, for whom they were purchased by agents, who pretended themselves to be spectators. These agents were among the fairest of the quadroons, high in the esteem and confidence of their people, the entire cargo of captives through them going directly into black families or their friends."[91] Upon arriving in Cuba, Blake then spreads news of the violence aboard the ship during the transatlantic voyage with the intent of lowering the price of the *Vulture*'s human cargo. His friends are thus able to procure the slaves at a cheap price in the public market, and these bodies ultimately join the revolution starting to gain momentum on the island. Thus, Blake's act of piracy is framed as the economic means for political and social upheaval on the island.

Each act of piracy in which Blake participates contributes to the creation of a new social organization based on black liberation. For Delany, freedom is both contingent on and interdependent of the very market forces that restrict black freedom, and unlawful forms of property ownership are the only means of resisting what Delany considers to be the unlawful appropriations of the black body. "The instant a person is claimed as a slave, that moment he should strike down the claimant," cries Gofer Gondolier, an Afro-Cuban revolutionary. "The natural rights of man are the faculties of option, heaven bequeathed, and endowed by God, our common Father, as essential to our being."[92] *Blake* operates within the mechanics of the market to claim rights that are associated very broadly with liberal individualism, and Delany repeatedly invokes the illegitimacy of any "claims" to black bodies, employing the very language of illegal property ownership that he later uses as a model of critique. Because slavery depends on the illegal ownership of the slave body and the divestment of the black subject's claims to property, of the self or otherwise, for Delany freedom can be achieved only through piracy.

I focus on Blake's manipulation of the market in part because it is easily overlooked. The moment passes without much fanfare. However, Blake's manipulation of the language of the market, as well as the terms of sale and ownership, is a climactic moment in the text. That his orchestration of the market is performed at the auction block at the end of the novel is especially significant, given the event that catalyzes the action in the novel: Maggie's sale. Although the novel begins with Blake's inability to own property, it concludes with a burgeoning Afro-Cuban revolution. Part of what makes this revolution possible is the now-freed slave population that Blake helped procure. This slave population, sold for an artificially low price, also means that Blake has performed one final form of theft from Colonel Franks and the delegation of Cuban and American officials initially discussing the re-fitting of the *Merchantman* (now the *Vulture*).

The climactic act of rewriting the terms, objects, and language of exchange dramatizes the economic disruptions so central to understanding *Blake* and the forms of personhood it furthers. Initially a subject incapable of participating in self-possession, let alone other forms of property ownership, Blake now demonstrates the extent of his market and economic savvy by manipulating a market designed for and thriving on his subjugation. These types of market interactions ultimately permit rights previously denied to slaves. The novel's conclusion, with numerous marriage ceremonies, for example, demonstrates the far-reaching possibilities of property ownership. In *Blake*, piracy and other unlawful activities emerge as the only possible and also the most powerful responses to what the text considers the illegal ownership of black bodies, in violation of divine and natural law. Piracy produces freedom, as well as an assortment of rights associated with freedom, including, at different times, the rights to property, protection, and representation.

Black Markets: A Coda

In a letter to Susan B. Anthony in 1857, Elizabeth Cady Stanton wrote, "When we talk of woman's rights, is not the right to her person, to her happiness, to her life, the first on the list? If you go to a southern plantation and speak to a slave of his right to property, to the elective franchise, to a thorough education, his response will be a vacant stare. . . . The great idea of his right to himself, to his personal dignity, must first take possession of his soul."[93] In analyzing this moment, the constitutional historian Hendrik Hartog suggests that "constitutional rights consciousness—at least in its typical American forms—has started from positive notions of self-ownership and of citizenship, from the ideal of an autonomous individual capable of imagining and realizing a personal future, from the Declaration of Independence's invocation of a universal right to the pursuit of happiness."[94] The American historian J. R. Pole, too, notes that equality rests on the "individual whose rights are the object of the special solicitude of the Constitution and for whose protection the Republic had originally justified its claim to independent existence."[95] For Stanton, as for the fictional Blake, abstractions of rights hinge on ownership and possession of the self. That Blake's claim to ownership begins with the right to the possession of the self is no surprise given nineteenth-century understandings of property and rights.

However, as we know, the right to ownership is foreclosed for certain populations. Certainly aware that, by and large, black people in his time have no recourse to law, Delany instead uses participation in black markets as a political and economic alternative to legal rights. What emerges as an alternative is illegal ownership. If piracy is a model of a truly "free trade" and is therefore also a threat to the state, so, too, is African Americans' participation in a market sphere in which their bodies are reclaimed illegally through escape. Furthermore, as demonstrated in *Blake*, the commodity being transmitted illegally is not limited to the slave body but includes subversive ideas about black revolt that Blake distributes across the hemisphere, from the South to Cuba. Taken together, the escaped black body and black revolutionary ideals operate as commodities that can be transmitted and exchanged freely by black subjects. Finally, Blake's participation in the manipulation of the market price of slaves demonstrates the extent of his economic autonomy and authority.

Blake's many acts of piracy dramatize the process by which certain populations are recognized only through their economic value while also demonstrating the ways in which transacting in these bodies gives both black and white subjects visibility in the market. In the text, Blake incites revolution not through violence but through economic and bodily independence. Although the slave, at the moment of escape, does not have access to any political rights, the slave can partake in a form of property ownership centered on ownership of the self and thus can be visible in the marketplace. That visibility, it would seem, can sometimes extend to other facets of slave life. In other words, participation in the market is the basis for a black revolution, and not the other way around.

The illegal economic activities in which Blake participates are compelling radical acts because they illustrate the foundational significance of black economic life in black political and social life, at the same time that they have the potential to upset white supremacist social, political, and economic order by questioning the legality of slavery. In reading Delany's approach to free "black" market capitalism, I counter a popular mythology of him that has been an impasse for critics conflicted by Delany's seemingly conservative politics. Read using the framework of black markets, Delany does not seem to espouse adherence to any particular economic, social, and legal order; instead, he advances a rejection of all managerial techniques of the state. Piracy emerges as the most harmful form of repudiation because it threatens the integrity of the social and economic fabric of the U.S. state dependent on chattel slavery.

While this chapter examines the place of America's black subjects and their possessory behaviors as acts of piracy, the next chapter takes up another case study, this time looking to Mexicans living in the U.S.-Mexico borderlands in the aftermath of the Mexican-American War. This chapter, along with the one that follows, serves as an example of how minority and marginalized populations deploy acts of piracy to critique dispossessive regimes. These acts of piracy function as acts of restitution in a state that dispossesses persons of a range of properties, including the property of citizenship. By taking up the enslaved person before turning my attention to Mexicans living in the borderlands, I show how a varied cast of persons appropriate property, even if just temporarily, in order to access those ineffable properties that are made and undone by possession and dispossession. As the chapter that follows demonstrates, the bonds between the possession of land and citizenship are as strong as the bonds between citizenship and the possession of the self. Indeed, the possession of other properties is an expression and extension of the possession of the self. And so, the following chapter expands on the property of the self to include a person's territorial holdings. In the face of U.S. territorial expansion and Mexican territorial dispossession through "squatting," Mexican American writers imagine forms of possession that unsettle the American dispossessive state. More specifically, by looking to Mexican women's central position in the creation of Mexican American property, the following chapter shows how a number of different populations claim property on the fringes of the state and its laws as a means of countering unlawful dispossessions encouraged by the state.

CHAPTER FOUR

Unsettling Subjects

Citizenship and Squatting in Historical Romances of the U.S.-Mexico Borderlands

This chapter considers the act of piratic land settlement, or squatting, as critical to understanding mid- to late nineteenth-century conceptions of U.S. citizenship. To do so, I turn to the case of Californios living in the borderlands during and in the aftermath of the Mexican-American War of 1848, as represented in the work of María Amparo Ruiz de Burton, widely considered to be the first female Mexican American novelist.[1] As I show, her most famous work, *The Squatter and the Don* (1885), makes the stakes of property in the creation of citizenship especially clear, since it depicts the state of unsettlement among the hidalgo landowners, and the concurrent acts of settlement by Anglo farmers, or squatters, in the U.S.-Mexico borderlands. In this novel, unsettlement is marked by more than a lack of fixity. Instead, "unsettlement" refers to competing claims to land that result in displacement and dispossession. More specifically, Ruiz de Burton views the Preemption Act of 1841, California Land Act of 1851, and the Homestead Act of 1861 as initiating Mexican unsettlement through Anglo squatting and settlement.

The word "unsettle," in particular, is useful in describing the political and social instability endured by this population, as well as the lack of resolution to the problem of Mexican land grants after the Treaty of Guadalupe Hidalgo. In *The Squatter and the Don*, the narrator refers to the California Land Act of 1851 as "*an Act to ascertain and settle the private land claims in the State of California*," and thus a "sad subversion of purposes [because of which] all the private land titles became *unsettled*."[2] Ruiz de Burton thus employs the language of U.S. law to criticize the complicity of the U.S. government in dispossessing Mexicans from their land, by showing that, while the act was meant to unburden Congress of adjudicating some twenty-seven thousand claims to Mexican lands after the end of the Mexican-American War and shorten the tenure of land patents, the Land Act was instead "an Act to *unsettle* land titles, and to upset the rights of the Spanish population of the State of California."[3] Indeed, this process of unsettlement of real property was pervasive in the borderlands.

While the dispensation of property rights and the dynamics of racialization both before and after the ratification of the Treaty of Guadalupe Hidalgo were different in the territories conquered by the United States (what is now Texas, California, New Mexico, and Arizona, as well as parts of Nevada, Utah, Wyoming, and Colorado), I want to underscore that these locations share their position as "borderlands" because they share a history of colonial violence and forcible incorporation into the project of American territorial expansion. Indeed, the term "borderlands," defined as "contested boundaries between colonial domains," is distinguished from the term "frontier," or a "meeting place of people in which geographic and cultural borders were not clearly defined."[4] As these areas are not so much zones of contact as territories with shifting national designations, using the term "borderlands" makes possible a reading of *The Squatter and the Don* through a lens other than one of cultural, racial, and ethnic synchronicity.[5]

Rather, borderlands allows me to tell a story of conquest that attends to this violent colonial history, a topic taken up by a number of historians and literary scholars, as well as be attentive to the ideological mechanisms through which conquered Mexicans were unsettled of those ephemeral properties attached to U.S. citizenship.[6] As I show, unsettlement allows us to understand the violence of colonialism and conquest, since it gives us insight into the importance of property and possession in the allocation of personhood in an American legal and political tradition. Indeed, as the narrator of *The Squatter and the Don* proclaims, "Our civilization is essentially one of property."[7] Thus, *The Squatter and the Don* makes a compelling case for how Mexican American unsettlement and displacement were used to cement the exclusive and exclusionary models of citizenship rooted in property that characterize the nineteenth century.

Said differently, the borderlands are where the United States practiced its exclusion of certain populations from full citizenship by dispossessing them of real property, while also conversely asserting and encouraging squatting and settlement as expressions of Anglo citizenship. Even so, this story of unsettlement is not unique to borderlands Mexicans, but rather began with the dispossession of both land and citizenship of indigenous persons in the United States. While this book does not directly address the question of Native American property and citizenship, it is indebted to the work that has been done in this area.[8] Above all, the history of Native American dispossession of property and citizenship is complex given the shifting terrain of Native American racialization; legal rights and titles to land; relations to public and private property; usufruct claims; relations to and recognition from the U.S. nation-state; dynamics of enfranchisement; subjection to U.S. state law and regulation; and relationships to tribal-national and settler-national law. This is especially true in the nineteenth century in a period of westward expansion and Indian removal. Indeed, given that these factors shift from tribe to tribe, tracking the complexities of indigenous relationships to land rights is a challenging task. And yet, while this project does not take up the question of Native American land rights, property, and citizenship, I do want to briefly gesture to a few touchstone moments in Native American legal history.[9]

More specifically, I want to highlight the ways in which the rights to and dispossession of Native American lands has underwritten Native American alienation from full U.S. citizenship. The Supreme Court cases of *Fletcher v. Peck* (1810) and *Johnson v. M'Intosh* (1823), which made Indian land title inalienable, except to the federal government, restricted the normative liberal "freedoms" tribes could experience through the occupation, ownership, and *sale* of land.[10] These restrictions reached their apogee with the ratification of the Indian Removal Act of 1830, which extinguished tribal title altogether in Southern states including Alabama, Mississippi, Georgia, North Carolina, Tennessee, and Florida, as well as in Illinois, Indiana, and Ohio. Finally, the Dawes Act of 1887, which offered U.S. citizenship to indigenous persons who accepted individual allotments of land, was passed in order to break up the communal ownership of native land, as well as encourage Native American assimilation through private property ownership. Moreover, the Dawes Act of 1887 in particular wedded private property and land rights to normative conceptions of American citizenship. These three moments in federal law not only are significant in Native American history but are also critical to understanding the mechanisms of conquest discussed in this chapter.

These three cases will demonstrate the similarities in the rationales used by the state to unsettle both indigenous persons and borderlands Mexicans. After all, both populations were considered to have anomalous or unusual relationships to property rights in land, either because these lands are owned communally, as in the case of Native Americans, or more closely resembled a feudal system of land tenure, as in the case of borderlands Mexicans. As I show, in order to justify their dispossession, borderlands Mexicans were presented as "unsettling" subjects, necessarily imperfect, but also a threat to Anglo access to property. In materials ranging from historical texts to legal statutes, Mexicans were depicted as improper property owners, incapable of being incorporated into the American nation-state, resulting in their territorial dispossession through squatting.

Unsettling Mexicans and Borderlands Dispossession

However, Ruiz de Burton's novelistic account presents a differing view of borderlands Mexicans and of the squatters encroaching on their lands. *The Squatter and the Don* follows the overlapping lives of the Alamar and Darrell families as one family attempts to preserve its land while the other struggles to build a life in new U.S. territories located in what is now Southern California.[11] The tension between the families is amplified because the patriarch of the Darrell family is a leader in the squatter movement and a defender of squatter rights in these new territories, while the Alamar family endeavors to protect its land and cattle from the recent American arrivals intent on driving the Alamars from the ranch. This tale also follows the romance between Clarence Darrell and Mercedes Alamar, children of the two competing families. As the novel progresses, Don Mariano Alamar, the Alamar patriarch, like other hidalgo ranchers, finds himself increasingly unable to defend his land and dies, leaving Clarence, who has since struck it rich in the stock market, to take care of the Alamar family. In the midst of this narrative, the reader is introduced to an additional villainous character: the railroad corporation extending the transcontinental railway to the Pacific, further dispossessing both old and recent settlers.

Arguably, Ruiz de Burton is attempting to reconstruct a history of the U.S. Southwest that incorporates the narratives of Mexican nobility and dispossession of both citizenship and land to rewrite the narrative of Latina/o subject formation in the United States. As Lázaro Lima writes regarding the Mexican-American War, "What is understood today as the 'Latino subject' surfaced along the literal and metaphorical divide between Mexico and the United States, a divide that fractured alliances, elided ethnic and racial identities, and disembodied subjects from the protocols of citizenship."[12] More specifically, the hidalgos in the borderlands, members of this nascent Latino body, illustrate the ways dispossessed persons negotiate living at the interstices of political and economic recognition. This novel is critical in representing the propertied dimension of power relations in the U.S.-Mexico borderlands in the immediate aftermath of the Mexican-American War. Said differently, in addition to reading *The Squatter and the Don* through the lens of racial and ethnic identity formation, I consider other forms of identities that might complicate these frameworks, including those identities that emerge from property.

To this end, the question of possession represented in this historical novel reflects not just an emergent Mexican American identity politics but also an emergent class of Anglo citizens who base their claims to citizenship on their claims to land.[13] Indeed, in Ruiz de Burton's literary imagination, the act of "squatting" stands in for appropriations of land that expand the category of Anglo citizenship in the Jacksonian era. For this reason, in *The Squatter and the Don* squatting is an act of colonization and territorial conquest, as well as an expression of U.S. citizenship. For example, in referring to Mr. Darrell's home, Everett, another of Mr. Darrell's sons, says that he built a "colony" to welcome the other squatters. In explaining the name, Everett elaborates, "That is the new name for the large room next to the dining room, which Clarence said he built for a '*growlery*.' Alice called it the '*squattery*' because Father always receives the settlers there; but Mother changed the name to '*colony*,' to make it less offensive, and because the talk there is always about locating, or surveying, or fencing land—always land— as it would be in a new colony."[14] In *The Squatter and the Don*, white settlement of this land is understood as an act of colonization that systemically dispossesses Mexicans of all forms of property.

However, Ruiz de Burton also represents squatting as foundational to democratic citizenship, autonomy, and freedom. Indeed, although squatting might seem to pose a great problem to the U.S. state, the intertwined histories of land ownership and U.S. citizenship reveal that squatting and other seemingly unlawful forms of land ownership and occupation on the margins of the law underwrite claims to U.S. citizenship rather than contest the state outright. Therefore, for this early Mexican American writer, the Preemption and Homestead Acts encourage squatting, or the habitation of private land without having legal ownership to it, as a means of democratizing property ownership and expanding the terrain of citizenship to Anglo-Americans. And so, in *The Squatter and the Don*, at least initially, "squatter" denotes the Anglo-American settlers in the West and Southwest, whose claims to citizenship lie in their claims to land ownership. However, given that squatting is represented as a type of piracy in *The Squatter and the Don*, piracy provides a more expansive framework for understanding the instruments of colonial invasion, occupation, and dispossession.

As I show, the mechanics of dispossession are complex. Mexicans were unsettled from their lands by having their properties designated as public lands open to possession by the U.S. state. Hidalgo dispossession was then amplified by the lengthy and costly legal battles in which hidalgos were forced to engage in order to have their titles to property recognized in U.S. courts. Given that few families held titles that were recognized and legitimated in U.S. courts, these lands were not legally "private" and thus were de facto public and subject to settlement. In *The Squatter and the Don*, George Mechlin considers this tension between private and public land, saying, "Land is not considered *private property* until the title to it is confirmed and parented. As the proceedings to obtain a patent might consume years, almost a lifetime, the result is that the native Californians (of Spanish descent), while the land-owners when we took California, are virtually despoiled of their lands and their cattle and horses. Congress virtually took away their lands by putting them in litigation."[15] The act of Mexican dispossession is structured on first designating private Mexican land as public land open to claim under the various land settlement acts of the nineteenth century, and Ruiz de Burton's italicization of "private property" in the foregoing quote visually emphasizes the lack of public recognition of Mexican possession of these lands in U.S. state law. Additionally, as Clarence later notes, his father insists on his right to locate on Alamar land or any other unconfirmed grant precisely because it is his right as an American citizen. He laments, "It is very painful to me to find my father adhering so tenaciously to his old conviction that all Mexican grants not finally confirmed to their owners are public land, and being so, they are open for settlement to all American citizens."[16] And so, this early interaction between Clarence and Don Alamar shows how Anglo land claims of "public" Mexican lands transmuted into Anglo claims to citizenship. Moreover, the designation of Mexican lands as public demonstrates that they are neither guaranteed the protections nor the rights of citizens.

It bears noting, however, that the process of transforming Mexican private lands into American public ones was also complicated. After all, like the white squatters and pioneers who occupied the borderlands after the Mexican-American War, under Spanish and Mexican rule, the hidalgos were the enterprising colonists of northern Mexican borderlands. In *The Squatter and the Don*, Don Alamar notes that the reasoning undergirding the Preemption and Homestead Acts of nineteenth-century America was no different from the rationale used by the Spanish government to settle this land. He notes,

> [The gifts made by Congress to the railroad companies provided]
> exactly the same motive which guided the Spanish and the Mexican

governments—to give large tracts of land as an inducement to those citizens who would utilize the wilderness of the government domain— utilize it by starting ranchos which afterwards would originate pueblos or villages, and so on. The fact that these landowners who established large ranchos were very efficient and faithful collaborators in the foundation of missions was also taken into consideration by the Spanish Government or the viceroys of Mexico. The landowners were useful in many ways, though to a limited extent they attracted population by employing white labor. They also employed Indians, who thus began to be less wild. Then in times of Indian outbreaks, the landowners with their servants would turn out as in feudal times in Europe, to assist in the defense of the missions and the sparsely settled country threated by the savages. Thus, you see, that it was not a foolish extravagancy, but a judicious policy which induce the viceroys and Spanish governors to begin the system of giving large land grants.[17]

By painting a rather rosy picture of the mission system in the borderlands, and comparing American forms of republican masculinity to the Mexican civilizing mission in the borderlands, this novel illustrates a logic similar to the one behind the land grant systems in both Mexico and the United States. Settlement and colonization of these lands, Ruiz de Burton stresses, is an ongoing expression of national belonging and citizenship.

Indeed, the civilizing mission of settlement in this region furthers the expansion of the physical and ideological boundaries of the nation-state. In spearheading the civilizing mission of the Spanish and Mexican governments, the hidalgos in Ruiz de Burton's literary and historical imagination are also expanding normative conceptions of Spanish personhood, or citizenship. And yet, after the war, Mexicans are recast as imperfect property owners and as unlawful occupiers of American land, rather than the pioneering figures Don Alamar imagines them to be. Indeed, given that this backwardness is in part due to the diffuse and expansive nature of Spanish (and, later, Mexican) tracts of land, as well as the feudal nature of governance on these properties, Ruiz de Burton's indictment of the U.S. government's gift of these same lands to railroad companies is meant to highlight the double binds of Mexican land ownership. Mexican ownership, suffused with representations of its backwardness due to its racialization as nonwhite (read: indigenous and mestizo), is represented as unincorporable in the rapidly advancing and technologically progressive U.S. nation-state—even as the U.S. state reproduces these same uneven propertied relations.

As Don Alamar also notes in the foregoing quote, the Spanish land grant system was depicted as an aristocratic and undemocratic system that conflicted with the American spirit of competitive capitalism. This is in part because Mexican land grants, which ranged in size from 4,000 to 133,000 acres, were inherited and not purchased in accordance with U.S. law.[18] In the Anglo-American imagination, because the size and purpose of these parcels were not restricted as they were under the Preemption and Homestead Acts, the Mexican land grant system restricted—rather than promoted—access to property and the settlement of these lands by numerous settlers.[19] Thus, Mexican occupation of land was also contested on the grounds that it was undemocratic. This undemocratic relation to property was echoed in representations of Mexicans as despotic and ungovernable, and of Mexico as a nation with values that were not compatible with those in the United States.[20] As Adrienne Caughfield has written, "Anglos questioned the viability of Mexican government. As late as 1850, the *American Whig Review* tried to fathom why Hispanic republics seemed to fail consistently. To the editors, Mexico and other Latin American states bore the oppressive burden of their Spanish legacy."[21] These representations of Mexicans and Mexico "contradicted the premise of republican virtue, which required a self-possessed, mature government of people of like mind."[22]

Mexican dispossession was also understood in terms of the greater teleology of land use, progress, and development. In these accounts, the cattle-ranching culture of the hidalgos, paired with the feudal system of the cattle ranch, stood in sharp contrast to the privately owned, capitalist farms so valued by Americans.[23] To this end, Mexicans' relationship to land, cultivation, and property contrasted Mexican stagnation and inertness with American progress, vigor, and forward momentum.[24] As Arnoldo De León writes,

> The argument that Mexican culture was firmly against innovation and deeply rooted in the past also applied to the Mexicans' farming methods. In South and West Texas, particularly, where Tejanos [Mexican Americans in southern Texas] in the last decades of the century retained some acreage, whites considered Mexican agricultural techniques as passé as other aspects of Mexican culture. They accused Tejanos of using unscientific plans, imperfect systems of cultivation, and crude implements. Mexicans were some three hundred years behind the times, it was maintained, working their land as they had in the days of Cortez, relying on a plow composed

simply of a crooked stick with an iron point. Consequently, much land still remained undeveloped, the Mexicans' backwardness having a retarding influence upon Anglo-Saxon progress.[25]

Thus, Mexican land ownership was contested on the basis of its misuse because the land was not employed for agricultural production, a tension dramatized in *The Squatter and the Don* through the conflict between the cattle-ranching hidalgos and the newly arrived farmers. Mexican claims to land "were incompatible with the family farm, with the concept of equal access to wealth, and with the Anglo-American presumption that no property rights were absolute."[26] Indeed, Americans saw the occupation of Texas and other borderlands territories as rescuing "land from tyrannical forces, making it more available to those who pursued liberty across the continent. [This population] considered land, liberty, and citizenship inseparable."[27]

Because Mexicans were seen to be misusing their land and mismanaging their territories, some historians have suggested that the hidalgo system was in a state of decline long before squatters and land speculators arrived in the newly acquired territories. Donald J. Pisani writes, "The old economic order began to crumble. Involvement in the hide and tallow trade turned the Californios into a debtor class, and they had no way to extricate themselves save by selling cattle and mortgaging their land."[28] However, these representations of Mexican hidalgos as premodern, incapable of economic and social integration, and in a state of decline are also not entirely correct. After all, upon the conclusion of the Mexican-American War, as David Montejano has written, Anglo ranchers adopted Mexican ranching culture.[29] And yet, the fiction of the "unsustainable hacienda" persists, despite the fact that "the longevity of the hacienda as a social institution was due to its resiliency: finding a market, it would respond and produce; lacking one, it would turn inward and become self-sustaining."[30]

Most significantly, the myth of Mexican misuse of land spoke more generally to the hidalgos' inability to become liberal American propertied subjects, or to become American citizens at all. In *The Squatter and the Don*, the squatters vehemently declare that "those old Spaniards never will be businessmen," and, in contrast to the Spaniard, or the Mexican incapable of economically assimilating to the United States, stands the hero of Ruiz de Burton's historical romance, Clarence Darrell, the son of the squatter rights leader.[31] Having inherited a sum of money from his aunt, Clarence invests it in the stock market. This investment conflicts with his father's ideas of proper economic livelihood in that Darrell Senior sees "stock gambling as next to robbery" because Clarence's ownership is speculative rather than material (land ownership).[32] As the narrative reads, "Clarence had been a lucky investor. With the sum of $2,000 bequeathed to him by Mrs. Darrell's aunt Newton, when he was only five years old, and which sums she ordered should be put at interest until he was twenty-one years of age, Clarence speculated, and now he was worth close to a million dollars."[33] Even as Clarence's assertion of economic selfhood through the speculative market, as opposed to merchant capitalism and land cultivation, runs counter to "traditional forms of republican virtue, masculine self-determination, and liberal subjectivity" represented in the figure of the squatter, Clarence and the Darrell family are representative of the propertied Anglo-American persons who are at the center of normative U.S. citizenship.[34] Indeed, as I will discuss later, Clarence and his father share their position as the thieves, robbers, and pirates on whom American propertied personhood rests.

Mexican Property, Mexican Liberalism

As I want to underscore, accounts of Mexican land misuse, and of Mexican land grants as aristocratic and undemocratic—all of which were used to justify assertions of Mexicans' incompatibility with American liberal governance—ignore the political and economic shifts taking place in the borderlands in this period. After all, borderlands historians and writers, including Ruiz de Burton, have proposed that the American Southwest was a site of liberal experimentation and progressivism. Américo Paredes, for example, has claimed that the Mexican borderlands are a unique site of American egalitarianism, writing, "The simple pastoral life led by most Border people fostered a natural equality among men. Much has been written about the democratizing influence of a horse culture. More important was the fact that on the Border the landowner lived and worked upon his land. There was almost no gap between the owner and his cowhand."[35]

Ruiz de Burton, too, highlights the fictions of the seemingly economically and socially disadvantageous system of Mexican enterprise, thereby countering the prevailing racialized representations of Mexican property ownership as backward. Indeed, Ruiz de Burton's novel belongs to a longer genealogy of counternarratives to fictions of Mexican cultural dissimilarity and the unassimilability of Mexicans into the American national project.[36] She repeatedly stresses the proximity of Spanish and Mexican forms of possession and ownership to a normative, Anglo tradition of property.

Moreover, through the frustrations echoed by Don Alamar earlier, Ruiz de Burton highlights a long liberal tradition that originates in Mexico. In so doing, rather than highlighting the complex and contradicting Hispanophone and Anglophone legal traditions, Ruiz de Burton instead underscores the intimacy of Hispanophone and Anglophone liberal traditions. After all, as *The Squatter and the Don* dramatizes, for these elite hidalgos, as for British and American liberal thinkers, possessions are tied to dignity. Ironically, for the dispossessed hidalgos, the foundational tenet of U.S. citizenship that was most resonant was the liberty to trade freely and to have one's own property protected by the state.

As Rosaura Sánchez writes, the Spanish Constitution of 1812, for example, "would become an important document in Latin America, particularly its policies related to Indian citizenship, secularization of Church lands, and its suppression of the Inquisition."[37] The effects of this constitution were long lasting.[38] In addition to being one of the earliest examples of constitutions expressing the foundational tenets of classical liberalism, the constitution also afforded citizenship to indigenous peoples in Spanish colonies.[39] It also reversed property restrictions, which were seen to be part of the source of restrictions on economic liberalism in Spain and its colonies. These changes reverberated across the Americas, leading eventually to the first Mexican constitution of 1824.[40] By 1830, the discourse of individual rights had reached the remote parts of Mexican territories: the borderlands. The constitutions' focus on establishing secular and private property rights resonated with a group of wealthy hidalgos tired of the Catholic mission system. Indeed, Sánchez recovered a few of the Californio *testimonios*, which show that several hidalgos, including Juan Bautista Alvarado, María no Guadalupe Vallejo, and Pío Pico, were drawn to "the constructs of free competition and the individual's right to choose, both posited within classical liberalism."[41] As Sánchez stresses, though "the missionaries tried to create a utopian land of Indian pueblos dominated by missionaries . . . liberals saw California as a place to put into effect their liberal policies and begin the process of secularization and appropriation of mission lands."[42]

However, it was the arrival of José María Echeandía, Alta California's first governor, appointed in 1825, that catalyzed changes to individual property structures in the borderlands region. Under Echeandía's guidance, the borderlands hidalgos utilized liberal-rationalist discourses of secularization and property ownership to overtake mission lands and property. Indeed, these borderlands shifts reached their apex with the failed Hijar-Páredes colonization project of 1834, an experiment that centered on reforming and modernizing all missions by introducing "a group of colonists made up of teachers, artisans, craftsworkers, and farmers" to missions in the borderlands.[43] Paired with a plan for a company aptly named the Cosmopolitan Company in California that would "develop agriculture and manufacturing . . . and promote its products on the world market," the project was aimed at the liberalization of these territories.[44] Though the plan eventually failed because of fears occasioned by the replacement of slave labor with wage labor, the project's aims lingered: the colonists stayed and brought with them a number of reforms having to do with territorial occupation and the continued secularization of land.[45] This reflects the complex location and use of the foundational principles of liberalism in the Mexican borderlands, California in particular.

And yet, even as "the discourses of liberalism in nineteenth-century Latin America were always contradictory and imprecise," the promises of liberalism "were accessible only to the criollo elite and *letrados*."[46] Moreover, liberalism was not a homogenous political and economic doctrine, nor was it unanimously appropriated in the borderlands. While "some supported liberal platforms advocating public education, popular suffrage, and the abolition of slavery . . . others supported a constitutional liberalism that guaranteed equality and freedoms for the few."[47] As Beatriz González Stephan has argued, while borderlands hidalgos were eager for reform, the desire to correct or remedy the systemic dispossession and exploitation of indigenous populations was of less interest to them. For example, Vallejo's testimonio, which Sánchez discusses in her work, reflects Californios' continued interest in controlling the "semifeudal political and economic order," as well as their continued domination of indigenous peoples in the area.[48]

Even the arrival of the colonists during the Híjar-Páredes project seemed to widen, rather than diminish, the racial and ethnic separation between various settlers in the borderlands. The colonists were, as Sánchez writes, referred to as "foreigners" in the Californio testimonios. Indeed, this reflects the complicated "nationalist discourses distinguishing between *mexicanos* and *californios* [that] serve to legitimate positions on property relations."[49] It also demonstrated how access to property in California was wedded to ideas of Mexican citizenship, itself complicated and racialized given the long history of racial taxonomy (or *castas*) in the Spanish colonial state. Said differently, the colonists, though "Mexican," were separate from the class of ethnic persons called Californios, in part because of the perceived racialized difference between the two populations. Thus, as economic liberalism was wedded to property rights, in both the Spanish and Mexican periods, and these property rights were racialized—given the exclusion of indigenous persons from the regime of property ownership extending from the Spanish to the American periods—Californios sought to defend their position as "the rightful owners" and "native sons" of this territory using the racialized language of "birthright" and "blood."[50] Indeed, Ruiz de Burton's romance is as much a story of communal resistance to legal, social, economic, and territorial dispossession and to U.S. imperialism as it is a narrative about Californio racialization, a point emphasized by her insistence on referring to the Alamar family as "Spano-Americans," rather than using the racialized term "Mexican."[51] Californios, Ruiz de Burton insists, must be racialized as white.[52]

However, as Jaime Javier Rodríguez has argued, the Mexican-American War threatened to "suspend differences between Anglo Americans and Mexicans, not only as a threat to whiteness but more critically a suspension that threatened to rewrite the narrative of the Americas."[53] Thus, Mexicans had to be constructed as "fundamentally 'non-American' in a way that transcends race and penetrates into the ideological recesses of belief— habits, language, interests," especially since Articles VIII and IX of the Treaty of Guadalupe Hidalgo promised to extend the rights to property and citizenship to Mexicans.[54] And yet, while racial difference is significant in understanding Mexican dispossession, other answers relating to property must be examined as well.[55]

Given the long history of both Californio and American attachments to property, whiteness, and liberalism, Ruiz de Burton necessarily finds other rationales for their dispossession. As she repeatedly emphasizes, Californios were dispossessed of U.S. citizenship not because they are not proximate to white—since both Californio and Anglo conceptions of whiteness are reliant on racial taxonomy, *as well as* on liberal relationships to property and freedom. Instead, this population is deemed unincorporable, and labeled as nonwhite subjects, because their properties were desirable and facilitated expansion. Using the justification of Californios' perceived premodern, or backward, relationship to land, settlers—backed by U.S. state law—systematically dispossessed them of their land, and this dispossession became the basis for dispossessing Californios of U.S. citizenship. This consideration of property relations, not racial difference, as the primary basis for the exclusion of Mexicans from U.S. citizenship complicates extant scholarship that views an Anglo-American racial order as critical to understanding Mexican exclusion from U.S. citizenship in the aftermath of the

Mexican-American War.[56] By repeatedly emphasizing that Californios are both liberal *and* white, *The Squatter and the Don* dramatizes the complicated rationale used by the U.S. state to dispossess Californios of citizenship. Indeed, it is Ruiz de Burton's attentiveness to this dynamic that most clearly demonstrates Californios' proximity and entitlement to U.S. citizenship.

Stealing, Squatting, and Propertied American Citizenship

However, what is truly fascinating about Ruiz de Burton's treatment of possession's ties to citizenship and liberalism is her treatment of Anglo squatters as property thieves, or landed pirates. After all, at the same time that the Mexican landed class was being represented as unincorporable in the American national body because of its peculiar relationship to the very property from which it was being dispossessed, the simultaneous encroachment of Americans on this land was seen as promoting a uniquely American form of property ownership and personhood through settlement and squatting. As *The Squatter and the Don* illustrates through the Darrell family, and Mr. Darrell in particular, squatting has historically been associated with liberalism, populism, and freedom, as well as with foundational American figures, including the freeholder and the pioneer.

Frederick Jackson Turner's democratic and egalitarian frontiersman, for instance, is founded on the independent farmer charged with tilling the land, and the Darrells demonstrate the importance of land ownership to the construction of a national subject. Indeed, the California historian W. W. Robinson writes that "every American is a squatter at heart—or so it seems if we think of the tide of adventurous men that began moving west at the close of the Revolutionary War, men impatient of governmental authority and as contemptuous of the rights of Indians as of wild animals, men who believed land should be as free as air."[57] He adds, "Squatterism is as old as our country. George Washington in 1784 was making entries in his diary about his experiences with squatters on lands he owned west of the Alleghenies."[58] In *Statehood and Union*, Peter Onuf explains the significance of late eighteenth-century land ordinances in the territorial growth of the United States. As agricultural historian Allan G. Bogue writes, the pioneer was at the same time "individualistic and highly competitive, qualities that were softened by the breadth of opportunity offered by the 'free lands.' . . . He was nationalistic in outlook and expansive in attitude, but at the same time cherished strong sectional loyalties [against Indians, capitalists, and foreigners]."[59] In sum, because of the close association between squatting, pioneering, and Western settlement, squatting was seen as integral to the American Manifest Destiny and national expansion.[60]

And yet, the squatter is typically a figure antithetical to the rule of law and an affront to private property ownership. In referring to the pioneers settling the West, Turner writes, "Along with individualism, self reliance, and equality, went antagonism to the restraints of government."[61] Pisani writes that "in the eyes of the first generation of California historians, society had virtually collapsed before the law-abiding rose up to restore order."[62] Not only is the frontier the "antithesis of civilization: a place beyond family, beyond church, and beyond the conventions and mores of civil society," but the "squatter is the antithesis of the rule of law."[63] These descriptions of the squatter are consistent with representations of lawless pirates or bandits living at the edge of state law. Thus, these representations of the pioneer settlement also resonate with descriptions of the democratic and egalitarian pirate ship that, like the frontier, was "marked by lack of stratification."[64] However, these descriptions also erase the differences between the unlawful squatter and the honest settler.

Indeed, though the novel, too, eventually does away with this distinction, *The Squatter and the Don* initially gives voice to Mr. Darrell's explanation of the differences between the two: "The dividing line between the squatter and the settler is very clear to anyone who honestly wants to see it," notes Willie, one of the Darrell sons. "The honest settler," he states, "only preempts government land, but the squatter goes into anybody's land before he knows who has title."[65] To help clarify her father's point, Clementine Darrell asks, "Then a squatter is a land thief?" Mrs. Darrell responds by saying, "No, because the squatter might not *intend* to steal. He might mistakenly take land which belongs to someone else. The intention is what makes the action a theft or not."[66] Clementine's confusion about the difference between squatting and legal land settlement reveals Ruiz de Burton's position on the occupation of hidalgo land. The thin line separating the squatter from the settler, both of whom are considered thieves in the novel, indicates that she views all forms of borderlands occupation as unlawful seizure of land. Indeed, this distinction without a difference is reinforced through language dramatizing the violent dispossession of Mexicans:

The squatters were in increasing majority; the Spanish natives, in diminishing minority. Then the cry was raised that our land grants were too large; that a few lazy, thriftless, ignorant natives, holding such large tracts of land would be a hindrance to the prosperity of the

State, because such lazy people would never cultivate their lands, and were even too sluggish to sell them. The cry was taken up and became popular. It was so easy to upbraid, to deride, to despise the conquered race! Then to despoil them, to make them beggars, seemed to be, if not absolutely righteous, certainly highly justifiable. Anyone not acquainted with the real facts might have supposed that there was no more land to be had in California but that which belonged to the natives. Everyone seemed to have forgotten that for each acre that was owned by them, there were thousands vacant, belonging to the Government and which anyone can have at one dollar and twenty-five cents per acre. No, they didn't want Government land. The settlers want the lands of the lazy, the thriftless Spaniards. Such good-for-nothing, helpless wretches are not fit to own such lordly tracts of land. It was wicked to tolerate the waste, the extravagance of the Mexican Government, in giving such large tracts of land to a few individuals. The American government never could have been, or ever could be, guilty of such a thing. No, never! But, behold![67]

Ruiz de Burton cleverly uses the language of conquest and the rapid prolif-eration of Anglo squatters to dramatize the unyielding nature of Mexican unsettlement. Moreover, by characterizing Anglo preemption and home-steading as "wicked" and squatters themselves as despoiling "wretches," she complicates representations of settlers and pioneers as exemplary Ameri-can subjects.

Not only is settling seen as a form of theft, indistinguishable from squat-ting, but settling and squatting are also compared to more severe illegal appropriative behaviors. In speaking of his aunt's thoughts on the suitabil-ity of Clarence and Mercedes's marriage, George Mechlin writes, "[Doña Dolores] will believe old Darrell honest in his error, and no matter whether Clarence might be the prince of good fellows, to her he will always be the son of a squatter, of one who *steals land*. No matter under whose sanction— theft is theft to her—and she would snap her fingers at the entire Senate and House of Representatives, if those honorable bodies undertook to prove to her that by getting together and saying that they can authorize Ameri-can citizens to go and take the property of other citizens (without paying for it) and keep it—and fight for it to keep it—that the proceeding is made honorable and lawful."[68] Thus, even Clarence's legal purchase of Alamar land does not prevent him from "taking" land in a dishonorable way. Fur-thermore, Victoriano, one of Don Alamar's sons, compares Mr. Darrell to a pirate.[69] This sentiment is echoed by Clarence, who, despite being an entrepreneurial character who legally purchases the Alamar land without his father's permission, reiterates the language of illegal property ownership reflected in Doña Dolores's and Victoriano's views of the squatter. Early in the novel, Clarence says that he would rather not be seen by the Alamar ladies because he "looks too rough like a smuggler or a squatter sure," thereby reflecting the ways in which squatting and settling are problematic and illegal behaviors that have more in common with the violent acts of smuggling and piracy than with the models of settling supported by the Darrell patriarch.[70]

However, the predatory nature of squatting and settling is perhaps best reflected in Ruiz de Burton's comparison of the squatter to the monstrous monopoly of the railroad corporation. Like the squatters, the railroad companies "wish to absorb all the carrying business of this coast—they want money, money, money. They want to buy steamboats, ocean steamers; street railroads and street cars; coal mines and farms; in fact, they want everything, and want it more when some poor devil loses his business thereby and goes, frozen out, into the cold world."[71] The "monstrous monopolies" are "compared to 'barnacles clinging to the body of the people,' branded as unnecessary and a 'corrupting influence' upon the state, and defined as a 'corrupt combination of individuals, formed together for the purpose of escaping individual responsibility for their acts.'"[72] The corporation, like the squatter, appropriates land using the same logic of the foundational importance of the person's rights to private property as in the Dartmouth College case (1819) and later the landmark *Santa Clara County v. Southern Pacific Railroad* (1886) decision.

Thus, what is perhaps most perverse is the ways American law legalized what it considered to be the "illegal" appropriative behaviors of frontier squatters. This is demonstrated most clearly in the language of the Preemption and Homestead Acts, which, in addition to being legislative efforts to solve the ever-increasing problem of land speculation and granting, were also the institutional mechanism designed to accommodate the evolution of nineteenth-century market capitalism, in which squatting simply made good economic sense because it could not be effectively controlled. Indeed, these acts solved the "problem" of squatting on federal lands, which was booming before passage of the Preemption Act. The Preemption Act also facilitated the settlement of new territories while limiting squatters' illegal appropriative behaviors. In passing these acts, the U.S. government tacitly acknowledged the fluid and sometimes necessary continuum from unlawful to lawful settlement of lands that aided in the reproduction of American empire through property ownership. Said differently, the legitimation of unlawful forms of property ownership through preemption and home-steading was integral to the creation and perpetuation of American liberalism, even as these acts functioned as modern letters of marque.[73]

During this period, tremendous market expansion went hand in hand with these unlawful forms of land settlement and appropriation. The Preemption and Homestead Acts "summoned the agrarian ghosts of the past and directed them in the service of the future and in doing so reinforced both the agrarian ideal as well as the forces of economic expansion and the maturation of the market economy."[74] Settlement of "public" lands was essential in the economic expansion of the United States, and the freeholder was not a vestige of an agrarian past given the changing economic climate of the mid-nineteenth century. Rather, the squatter/settler is tethered to national growth: he is a modern propertied subject at the intersection or the frontiers of legal and illegal forms of ownership. After all, these property owners were embodiments of John Locke's liberal person. The Homestead Act of 1861, for example, which gave as much as 160 acres to any male head of household twenty-one years or older, had the express purpose of creating private property owners by allowing these lands to become alienable property. Homesteaders were not the first group of settlers who believed in the foundational relationship between property and the enjoyment of American freedoms. Rooted in the seminal principles behind Locke's conception of the liberal and free subject, the Free-Soil movement and political party active from 1848 to 1852 based its occupations of land on the belief that "liberty reached its pinnacle when a free man mixed his labor with nature in pursuit of economic self-reliance and happiness."[75] The Free-Soilers also established the relationship between private property ownership and political equality and freedom. They "believed that political equality was meaningless without substantive economic equality [and] they extended the meaning of [David] Wilmot's antislavery phrase, making it also call for the federal government to guarantee the natural right of access to the earth."[76] From this perspective, rights are meaningless without access to land.

However, it was the Preemption Act in particular that reinforced the relationship between property and citizenship. Intended to create private property owners and promote settlement or colonization of new territories even if the government suffered a loss of revenue, the act allowed inhabitants of federal lands, or squatters, to purchase as much as 160 acres at a low price if the squatter qualified by being male and a citizen (or in the process of becoming naturalized). Given that only white men were able to naturalize in this period, the restrictions to property echoed in the act were ways of excluding populations from the regime of citizenship. Paired with the acts' express purpose of facilitating the settlement of hidalgo lands, the language of the acts married the dispossession of Mexicans to the acquisition of U.S. citizenship. Hubert Howe Bancroft's description of squatter populations, for example, focuses on the "strong element, mainly from the western states and Oregon, of the faith that by the 'higher law' they were entitled to the lands as free American citizens."[77] In Turner's formulation, engaging with the rugged frontier allowed "the immigrant from Europe" to be "remade in to an American citizen."[78] The term "squatter" thus legitimates illegal occupations of land that undermine claims to both property and citizenship. In sum, squatting represents not a perversion of land ownership but, rather, a foundational form of American property ownership and belonging: squatters, by extension, are foundational piratic figures staking claims to property as a means of staking claims to citizenship.

Indeed, in *The Squatter and the Don*, citizenship and enfranchisement are closely tied to questions of land ownership and occupation. Ruiz de Burton writes, "Darrell thought himself justified, and *authorized*, to 'take up lands,' as he had done before. He had more than half of California's population on his side, and though the '*Squatter's Sovereignty*' was now rather on the wane and the '*squatter vote*' was no longer the power, still the squatters would not abdicate, having yet much to say about election times."[79] The use of the language of the nation-state and citizenship (sovereignty, vote, rights) reflects the ways in which squatter claims to land are tied to the rights afforded by U.S. citizenship. In defending his claim to the contested Alamar lands, Mr. Darrell clarifies his earlier point about competing land claims by adding that they have settled on land "that other persons say belongs to them, but which land, as no one knows to whom it belongs, it is free to be occupied by any American citizen."[80] A later conversation between Clarence and Don Alamar also reveals the thin line between settler and squatter: of his father, Clarence says, "He is a settler—a '*Squatter*'—you know, and consequently very sensitive about (what they call) '*rights of settlers under the law.*' He knows my sentiments but one thing is my expressing them to him, and another is to pay money for land he thinks he has lawfully appropriated."[81] Tellingly, however, Clarence's explanation of his father's settlement/squatting of Don Alamar's land employs the language of rights: the rights of settlers, which are attached to the rights of the U.S. citizen. Thus, when Mr. Darrell firmly declares, "We aren't squatters. We are *'settlers.'* We take up land that belongs to us, American citizens, by paying the government price for it," Ruiz de Burton's deliberate use of italics emphasizes the difference between settling and squatting as hinging on the land rights associated with U.S. citizenship.[82] With these italics, Ruiz de Burton reminds us that Darrell's expression of citizenship is rooted in piracy and illegality.

Propertied Borderlands Women

Although this historical novel reveals the many ways in which Mexicans are dispossessed of both land and citizenship so that the Anglo-American squatter may rise as a propertied U.S. citizen, it also allows an important historical actor to emerge who is able to navigate the borderlands and its changing political economy: the borderlands woman. In 1834 Alfred Robinson wrote to Don José Antonio Julián de la Guerra y Noriega, a wealthy cattle rancher from San Diego, to offer a proposal of marriage to his daughter, Doña Anita. In the proposal, he expressed his wish that the marriage ensure a "mutuality in trade and a degree of continuity with familiar traditions."[83] At the time, Robinson was a young man of twenty-seven and an agent of a tallow and hide company.[84] His proposal of marriage, Albert Hurtado speculates, was to inherit through marriage the thousands of cattle raised by his prospective father-in-law. In addition to cementing a business arrangement, Robinson's establishment of kinship ties to Don José would have also ensured access to land and to social and economic networks in California. Intermarriages such as these, borderlands scholars have long argued, helped to establish long-lasting political and economic ties in the region.

Indeed, Mexican women's marriage to foreign men has been viewed by scholars of the period as facilitating the entrance of Americans into the borderlands markets, as well as aiding their access to the wealth of the region, previously held in ranchero hands. Sánchez has argued that women merely functioned "as concessions made to men, as human capital."[85] Deena González adds that to view Anglo-Mexican marriages as a choice or decision, "as self-conscious action, as mere adaptation, or . . . as an adoption of 'something new,' implies complicity or motive based on knowledge, implies—in ways consistent with liberalism—an egalitarian lineup of choices. . . . This was certainly not the case."[86] González is in favor of interpreting these mixed marriages in relation to the long, conflicted history of Mexicans in these borderlands.

However, I argue that such exchanges also granted wealthy hidalgo women access to property ownership and economic visibility, which resurrected Mexican and created Mexican American property owners at a moment of crisis. In relegating Mexican women's participation in the borderlands during this period as assimilationist, scholars have failed to perceive the politics of opposition and resistance among this population. In her analysis of women in the borderlands, Emma Peréz argues that, in the borderlands, "subjectivity is the oppositional and transformative identity that allowed [Chicanas, or Mexican American women,] to weave through the power of cultures, to infuse and be infused, to create and re-create newness."[87] Mexican women, as represented in *The Squatter and the Don*, are not simply acute observers of the dispossessions taking place around them but also the possessive figures that make possible the formation of novel propertied communities. Indeed, Ruiz de Burton's representation of the propertied lives of women in the borderlands underwrites the creation of a propertied Mexican American population. Said differently, the borderlands woman allows an emergent form of Mexican American identity to take shape through her ownership and inheritance. Moreover, because their expressions of property conflict with other demands and claims to property, Mexican women are, in effect, unsettling squatters and settlers on the borderlands. Thus, Ruiz de Burton addresses the problems of property ownership and the central role that women play in reshaping the borderlands in the emplotments of the borderlands historical romance.

In this sense, *The Squatter and the Don* presents a particularly interesting revision of the marriage plot. Rather than merely "giving new life" to the old patriarchal Mexican order through intermarriage with Anglo men who, as the historical record shows, replicated rather than contested the function and form of the Mexican hacienda, Ruiz de Burton's historical novel demonstrates models of ownership in which Mexican women dispossess Mexican men so as to facilitate the creation of Mexican American property. As George Dekker has argued, "[Ruiz de] Burton's novel signals a deviation from the traditional historical romance. *The Squatter and the Don* focuses as much on social villainies and immoral action (perforce perpetuated by men because they are as a rule the ones wielding power and agency) as on the domestic sphere wherein family relations and women are dominant."[88] In the face of American ideals of property ownership and occupation that simultaneously dispossess landed Mexicans and colonize the borderlands, Ruiz de Burton's romance demonstrates that Mexican women's property ownership and inheritance counter the law in U.S. territories, as well as existing models of property ownership.

Ruiz de Burton's interest is in dramatizing the creation of a Mexican American political body not through the birth of the Mexican American child but through the reproduction of property.[89] In sum, by being the generative creators of Mexican American property, and thus the inventors of Mexican American liberal subjectivity, as well, Californianas are instrumental in expanding the normative boundaries of U.S. citizenship. *The Squatter and the Don*, in other words, is not a historical romance about the process of nation-building that takes shape through intermarriage and the birth of the Mexican American child; rather, it shows women's intervention in the propertied regimes of the borderlands. However, it is not through intermarriage but through seemingly minor assertions of property ownership that result from inheritance and will making that borderlands women emerge as powerful political and economic actors.

In part, this relates to women's inheritance rights under Mexican law. After all, in Spanish and Mexican California, laws regarding property rights were derived from seventeenth-century civil laws called *Recopilacion de las leyes de los reynos de las indias*. Under the *leyes*, "women, like men, had the right to acquire property not only through grants but also through endowments, purchases, gifts, and inheritance. A widow would inherit half of the *bienes ganaciales* (community property) accumulated during a marriage, while her daughters and sons would share the remaining half. Women could also administer, protect, and invest their property, which they did in a variety of ways: initiating litigation; appearing in court and, if they wished, acting as their own advocate; entering into contracts; forming business partnerships; administering estates; and lending and borrowing money and other goods."[90]

Moreover, under Spanish and Mexican civil law, "married women possessed rights to property, wages, and other legal rights as an individual," unlike Anglo-American women, who, under common law, did not retain property rights after marriage.[91] Unlike English common law, marital systems in colonial Latin America recognized women's individual property rights before marriage.[92] Furthermore, unlike in English common law, "earnings from individual property (such as rent and interest), as well as assets purchased with ordinary income from 'work or industry' during the marriage, constituted the couple's community property. If the marriage was dissolved, for whatever reason, each spouse retained their individual property, as well as half of the community property."[93] Finally, under Spanish civil law, both sons and daughters had equal rights to inheritance.[94] These leyes had profound effects on women's property ownership in the borderlands.

Although women had experienced the privileges of owning property under Mexican rule, they mostly lost them after the Mexican-American War, though not in all instances. For example, the plans to establish a state government in California were formalized in its Constitutional Convention of 1849 with the ratification of the state constitution. Articulated by men "born in different climes, coming from different states, . . . [but] assembled in Convention, as Californians," the California constitution was unique in having been influenced by Mexican civil law, as well as by normative American democratic principles.[95] For example, Article I of the state constitution guaranteed that "all people are by nature free and independent and have inalienable rights. Among these are enjoying and defending life and liberty, acquiring, possessing, and protecting property, and pursuing and obtaining safety, happiness, and privacy."[96] However, these pronouncements were strategic insofar as they were meant to attract "women of fortune" to California to marry American men.[97] Indeed, Californian women were compared to and associated with California itself, "healthy, wholesome, and desirable, a fertile site for reproduction . . . eagerly awaiting the arrival of equally strong foreigners."[98] In contrast, Californio men were represented as effeminate, "weak, ineffective, indolent, and fundamentally unworthy of either their women or their land."[99]

Similarly, in *The Squatter and the Don*, Mexican masculinity is framed as being in decline, which critics have argued makes a case for foreign entitlement to the "possession of both [Californio] land and women."[100] However, works such as Deena González's and Sánchez's have overlooked how representations of a declining Mexican masculinity might change if we regard the borderlands woman, who becomes the beneficiary of family properties, as the more important propertied actor after the Mexican-American War. In *The Squatter and the Don*, land and property are foundational to the integrity and health of the body, and economic health is tied to the physical and affective health of the individual. Finding themselves dispossessed of their properties, the male heirs of Don Alamar, Victoriano and Gabriel, are crippled and injured. The disabling of the men in the novel also extends to the Anglo men. Mary Darrell's coordination of the purchase of the section of the Alamar ranch that the family inhabits "leaves Darrell, both morally and physically," injured.[101] However, although the male heirs become incapacitated (both Gabriel and Victoriano are injured and therefore unable to work), it is Doña Josefa, widow of Don Alamar, who becomes the executor of the Alamar property. She eventually sells the lands to Clarence. The final few chapters speed through the dénouement, but they nonetheless illustrate the accommodations made by Doña Josefa, who, in agreeing to sell the land to Clarence, makes a handsome profit from land that is essentially worthless because of a lack of railroad development in the region.

Thus, Ruiz de Burton's novel dramatizes how women's inheritance of borderlands properties prevents these lands from being claimed by the expanding and corrupt railroad corporation, as well as by squatters. In this view, women's maintenance of property in the face of numerous forms of dispossession stands in for a less recognizable form of piracy than those presented in preceding chapters. As I propose, the Mexican woman is a type of property outlaw who unsettles the property and integrity of a state intent on dispossession. And so, like the fugitive in the previous chapter, the Mexican woman in this chapter responds to the dispossession of property and citizenship by enacting forms of ownership that disrupt the state and its apportionment of rights and protections. Moreover, because women's ability to own and inherit property is a vestige and expression of Mexican citizenship, rather than an affirmation of U.S. personhood, women's ownership of land and property after the Mexican-American War is unsettling as well. *The Squatter and the Don* helps to clarify how the Mexican-American War occasions a crisis in private property whose aftereffects will dramatically change the shape and character of land ownership in the U.S. West and Southwest. It also presents a radical redistribution of property, a response achieved through a manipulation of Mexican and U.S. law that illustrates the solutions being imagined by borderlands women. These models of ownership between and straddling U.S. and Mexican civil law are imperfect and perhaps even unlawful insofar as they are taking advantage of the complicated legal orders in the borderlands.

Perhaps no event dramatizes how property and assertions of citizenship overlap more than Ruiz de Burton's own claim to patrimonial property, which reveals the complicated position of Mexican women in these borderlands. In their introduction to *The Squatter and the Don*, Beatrice Pita and Sánchez write that "[Ruiz de] Burton's biggest undertaking" was staking claim to a tract of land in Ensenada, originally granted to Don Jose Manuel Ruiz, Ruiz de Burton's father, "which she tried for many years to have recognized as her own."[102] Her struggle to claim this land reveals an interesting dynamic regarding Ruiz de Burton's expression of citizenship. She was considered a traitor to the Mexican community in California because of her identification as a U.S. citizen after the Mexican-American War and her marriage to Henry S. Burton, who took possession of Baja California in 1847. Paired with her assimilationist policies, Ruiz de Burton's historical novel seems to advocate Mexican incorporation into the U.S. national body.

However, the nom de plume that Ruiz de Burton used when writing this novel, C. Leal—in which the C stands for both *ciudadano* (citizen) and *sé* (to be)—reflects the tensions of national affiliation. To whom is Ruiz de Burton loyal? This question is especially difficult to answer given Ruiz de Burton struggles to claim *two* family properties: Rancho Jamul, which the Burtons purchased through homesteading, and Rancho Ensenada de Todos Santos, which belonged to Ruiz de Burton's grandfather, mentioned in the foregoing quote. It is her ownership of Rancho Jamul, settled in 1871 when Ruiz de Burton was able to confirm her homestead, that is a particularly interesting example of Ruiz de Burton's appropriation of U.S. property law.[103] After all, she staked her claim to the borderlands using the logic of homesteading, a behavior she otherwise virulently critiques in *The Squatter and the Don*. Indeed, her claims to Rancho Jamul represents how normative claims to property and citizenship in the United States are utilized by Mexican American women so as to create Mexican American property.

Indeed, Ruiz de Burton seems to do what the Alamar family does in the historical romance. Alemán writes that Don Alamar uses the "democratic government's laws . . . against itself to account for the social and economic oppression of Californios under those laws. He thus 'legalizes' his own historical critique by using the language of law to foreground what the Californios were legally promised and what was illegally taken from them."[104] Ruiz de Burton's own claim to lands reflects a clever manipulation of the various American homesteading acts. Given her belief in the injustice and illegality that inhere in these laws underpinning and encouraging Anglo claims to Mexican land, Ruiz de Burton's claim can be regarded as an expression of her rights as a naturalized U.S. citizen (to squat), as well as an act of theft.

This piratic possession at the hands of Mexican women is echoed in the conclusion of the novel, as Ruiz de Burton writes, "It seems now that unless *the people of California take the law into their own hands*, and seize the property of those men, and confiscate it, to reimburse the money *due the people*, the arrogant corporation will never pay. They are so accustomed to appropriate to themselves what rightfully belongs to others, and have so long stood before the world in defiant attitude, that they have become utterly insensible to those sentiments of fairness animating law-abiding men of probity and sense of justice. These monopolists are essentially dangerous citizens in the fullest acceptance of the word."[105] In this passage, the narrator at once claims belonging, albeit by claiming a regional identity, while couching this identity within a perverse expression of unlawful claims to property. Furthermore, through the interchangeability of "those men" with the "arrogant corporation," Ruiz de Burton does more than anticipate the corporation as interchangeable with the rights-bearing body; she also sees the only response to be one of redistribution and theft: to steal back the land from squatters and the railroad monopoly in order to redistribute it to its rightful owners. Thus, in examining the changing role of women in the U.S.-Mexico borderlands before and after the Mexican-American War, it becomes clear that Mexican women property owners became important figures in the creation of Mexican American property by behaving like squatters, or pirates, themselves.

Conclusion

The Squatter and the Don reflects the radical changes in the borderlands with regard to property and belonging in the second half of the nineteenth century. The framing of Mexicans, not American squatters, as unlawful occupiers of American land in the aftermath of the Mexican-American War caused Mexican land ownership to be perceived as a national problem. The depiction of Mexican land occupation as unlawful, unnatural, and counter to American forms of property ownership at this moment reflects U.S. anxiety over territorial expansion and ironically uses the logic of Mexican improper property ownership as a way to justify American claims to the same land. In this way, anxiety over Mexican land occupation anticipates the problems linked to Japanese American land ownership and the Alien Land Acts of 1917 and 1920, an issue explored in Colleen Lye's *America's Asia: Racial Form and American Literature, 1893–1945*.[106] The large number of European immigrants who arrived in the United States in the early twentieth century, along with a shift in the concept of U.S. citizenship from one founded on naturalization to one increasingly defined by a long family line of sanguine American whiteness, continues to make *The Squatter and the Don* relevant to the study of citizenship.

Because of the foundational ties between citizenship and property, I continue to argue that dispossessing Mexicans of their land is the foundation of their dispossession of citizenship, rather than the other way around. Said differently, perceived imperfect forms of Mexican property ownership laid the groundwork for the exclusion of Mexicans from U.S. citizenship after the end of the Mexican-American War. This framework clarifies the many ways in which Mexicans living in the borderlands were unsettled after the Mexican-American War by being deprived of rights to full civic participation and recognition, as well as to property. This relationship helps to explain why Ruiz de Burton pens her historical romance in the aftermath of the Civil War: because she shares with the Confederacy a loss of property and fortune, as well of the property of whiteness, Ruiz de Burton's historical romance is a romance of the postbellum nation that allegorizes the loss of the Confederate Southern plantocracy. The expansion and restriction of property also correlates to the expansion and consolidation of citizenship in these moments of crisis, given that the Civil War, like the Mexican-American War before it, is a war that clarifies the position of the properties of citizenship and the ways in which populations are included in and excluded from the rights granted by the state.

And so, the following chapter turns more centrally to the question of property during the Civil War. By turning to Abraham Lincoln's blockade at the onset of the Civil War, which made Confederate ownership of certain properties an unlawful act, I examine the ways that Confederate women in particular turned to smuggling as a means of asserting citizenship and ownership in a dispossessive climate. After all, the blockade's language declared that any trade taking place in Southern ports after the imposition of the blockade would be deemed unlawful. However, because the language of the blockade positioned members of the Confederacy neither as lawful belligerents or enemies nor as stateless pirates, the blockade itself helped to make contingent and perilous the citizenship of Southern property owners. Indeed, the language of the blockade dispossessed Southern property owners of claims to and protections of citizenship. In the face of these dispossessions and the creation of a Confederate pirate with the imposition of the blockade, the women's autobiographies examined in the following chapter represent smuggling both as a necessary act of survival and as an act that critiques the state. Thus, smuggling is an act of protest and redress: protest against dispossessive regimes of the state, and redress for this dispossession through participation in the regime of property ownership, even if in the shadows.

CHAPTER FIVE

Queen Cotton

Smuggling and the Exigencies of Citizenship
during the Civil War

On April 19, 1861, Abraham Lincoln issued Proclamation 81, "A Blockade of Ports in Rebellious States," which immediately affected the ports of South Carolina, Georgia, Alabama, Florida, Mississippi, Louisiana, and Texas.[1] To justify the blockade, the proclamation boldly declared it a response to "a combination of persons engaged in such insurrection [who] have threatened to grant pretended letters of marque to authorize the bearers thereof to commit assaults on the lives, vessels, and property of good citizens of the country lawfully engaged in commerce on the high seas, and in waters of the United States."[2] By declaring Confederate secession an insurrection, condemning the Confederacy's use of "pretended" or "counterfeit" letters of marque, and framing this insurrection as an affront to the "lives and property" of lawful citizens, Lincoln's blockade distinguished several different figures and behaviors: the "citizen" is distinct from the "insurrectionist," who, in the language of the blockade, is someone participating in illegitimate trade. Moreover, the use of "pretended" also distinguished the legitimate state authorized to issue lawful letters of marque from the insurrectionist region with no authority to issue such a document.

Furthermore, the language of the blockade proclaimed that "if any person, under the pretended authority of the said States, or under any other pretense, shall molest a vessel of the United States, or the persons or cargo on board of her, such person will be held amenable to the laws of the United States for the prevention and punishment of piracy."[3] In other words, not merely was Confederate trade framed as unlawful, but any persons trading in defiance of this blockade were to be recast as pirates. Said plainly, the blockade broadly marked any commercial behavior in support of the Confederacy as an act of piracy and marked all "members" belonging to this group as stateless pirates, a representation augmented by the language of the "assaults" committed by the Confederacy on the "high seas" that threaten the "good citizen" and their lawful trade. Moreover, in declaring a wide range of commercial behaviors piracy, the federal government created an "enemy," even as this enemy was unlike other belligerents in that it was not a state but rather represented the very absence of the state altogether. That is to say, the Confederates were not quite enemies, for which the Confederacy would have to be considered an autonomous state. Instead, they were closer to the category of stateless pirates, with no claims to a range of properties: the protections of a state, the material properties of goods, and the property of rights. Indeed, Lincoln's blockade delegitimized the Confederacy as an autonomous state with the authority to bestow citizenship on a subject, and thereby casting the Confederate subject as a stateless being. Additionally, the federal government suspended habeas corpus, to mean the right to "have a body" and to have the protection from unjust imprisonment, which was in direct opposition to "the maxim of the Constitution of the United States, 'that no person should be deprived of life, liberty, or property, without due process of law.'"[4] Confederates were, in sum, losing the right to their bodies, which created an uncomfortable parallel between the Confederates and their slaves.

President Lincoln's naval blockade thus catalyzed a long series of debates over diplomatic recognition and revitalized debates over citizenship, property, and piracy in the United States. In addition to surfacing anxieties regarding rights to property and trade, the blockade also made apparent the crisis faced by Confederate persons: that of being recognized by the Union as having any rights at all. Therefore, the language of the blockade helped to make apparent the stakes of Southern diplomatic recognition: Was the South merely engaging in a rebellious act, or was it an enemy state? Did Confederates lose claims to citizenship upon trading in direct violation of the blockade? More importantly, when trading in violation of the blockade, and thus being recast as pirates, did Confederates lose claims to all rights and protections altogether?

The memoirs and autobiographies of this period best capture the legally indeterminate status of Confederates and the Confederacy, and narratives describing blockade running best dramatize the high stakes of the blockade in the deprivation of citizenship and personhood for Confederates. More specifically, I examine the representational afterlife of the blockade imposed on the South at the onset of the Civil War to argue that Eliza McHatton Ripley's *From Flag to Flag: A Woman's Adventures and Experiences in the South during the War, in Mexico, and in Cuba* (1889) and Loreta Janeta Velazquez's *Woman in Battle: A Narrative of the Exploits, Adventures, and Travels of Madame Loreta Janeta Velazquez* (1876) present women's participation in blockade running as an undesirable response to the dispossession of recognition of the citizen, as well as of the self-proclaimed Confederate nation at the onset of the Civil War.[5]

As I show, in these narratives, blockade running facilitated property ownership when the declaration of war, in the Confederate view, placed a variety of properties in crisis. After all, the Civil War raises questions about who can claim property, as well as what qualities property can and cannot have.[6] As Joseph Reidy writes, "Emancipation would have direct implications for the United States, given that more than 425,000 slaves resided in the states that remained within the Union. If slave property could be confiscated, what would prevent the government from confiscating any form of private property? Even more troubling, emancipation would destroy the domestic authority of the slaveholder-citizen over his dependent family members."[7] Not only was Southern property perceived to be under siege, but the properties of citizenship were slowly being eroded for the Confederates as well. After all, in the antebellum South, property ownership ensured access to fair legal representation, with Southern courts favoring property owners' claims over propertyless employees and slaves.[8] Therefore, property came to be equated with state representation and recognition. Indeed, the suspension of habeas corpus only confirmed the extent to which the material, as well as the symbolic, properties of citizenship were under attack.

More importantly, the example of Lincoln's proclamation made apparent how the state could dispossess persons of citizenship by reframing their participation in trade in Southern coastal waters as a piratic act. What makes these narratives notable, I argue, is that they address the ways in which the shifting and highly insecure position of the blockade runner indicates the place of Southerners in the U.S. nation-state during the Civil War. As this chapter demonstrates, these texts stage how the Confederacy's lack of access to property, isolation from international markets, and deprivation of diplomatic recognition were a reflection of the experiences of dispossession and lack of recognition endured at a personal level by Southerners at this time. Given these deprivations of citizenship and of property at the hands of the federal government, memoirs penned by Confederate blockade runners tend to focus on blockade running as an expression of property ownership that extends citizenship to these newly unrecognized populations.

Therefore, blockade running, understood as part of the Confederacy's political economy, is not merely a strategy for survival but also a means of participating in state formation. In looking to the vulnerable place of the blockade runner during the Civil War, her critical position in helping to shed light on a dispossessive state, and her central place in expanding possessory rights to persons dispossessed of national recognition and of citizenship, in this chapter I demonstrate that Ripley's and Velazquez's autobiographies echo the anxieties regarding the deprivation of real property and the property of citizenship. Indeed, while the chapter prior argued that Mexicans living in the borderlands in the aftermath of the Mexican-American War were dispossessed of property so as to legitimize their dispossession of citizenship, this chapter looks to the ways that the dispossession of citizenship for Confederate persons occurred in part through the designation of their trade as piratic and the retitling of the Confederate trader as pirate. Read alongside the prior chapters, which examined the dispossession of enslaved persons and Mexicans, this chapter provides a robust story of the complex relationship between property and citizenship, and the mechanisms employed by the state to dispossess persons of both. Moreover, the works in this chapter demonstrate the extent to which blockade running becomes an expression of national belonging at a historical moment when Confederates are deprived of both property and nation. With chapter 1, which looked to the place of piracy as an expression of anticolonial resistance and nascent nationalism, this chapter examines both how Confederate traders employ blockade running as a means of claiming membership in the Confederate state, as well as resisting the dispossessive federal government. However, unlike the previous two chapters, which turn to the concept of piracy as having a liberatory potential, this chapter much like chapter 2 demonstrates how piracy can be deployed in order to shore up conservative political values, especially as those values relate to property and territory in the period of the Civil War. Indeed, that the authors examined in this chapter as well as in chapter 2 use piracy to argue against the end of slavery points to how piracy has the potential to be redeployed to engender a reactionary and conservative politics. I end with this precisely to point out the limitations of piracy, and not just piracy's liberatory possibilities.

Blockades, Property, and the Problem of Recognition

Velazquez's *Woman in Battle* follows the "adventurous career" of a young woman who in part dresses in male clothing in order to participate in Confederate war efforts.[9] Born to a Castilian family with roots in the conquest of Cuba and the discovery of Mexico, Velazquez's father loses his property to the United States after the Mexican-American War and relocates to Cuba.[10] Although she refers to Cuba as her "beautiful native island," she describes herself as "an American, heart and soul."[11] More specifically, Velazquez identifies as a Confederate woman and soldier after marrying her first husband. Thus, Velazquez's six-hundred-page narrative begins with a description of women's valor on the battlefield throughout history, comparing Velazquez favorably to Joan of Arc, then follows her through battles in the Civil War, and ends with her tour of Europe, South America, the Caribbean, and the American continent as she seeks a place for Confederates to resettle after the end of the war. More importantly, in her narrative, Velazquez overtly catalogues the various unlawful activities in which she participates, and she explicitly represents herself as a legitimate agent of the Confederacy. To this end, she takes on roles as a Confederate male soldier or combatant, as a female Union sympathizer, as a spy, as a smuggler, as a counterfeiter, and as a blockade runner to further the Confederate war effort and to assert her Confederate affiliation. Said differently, in Velazquez's view, participation in blockade running and other unlawful activities is a deeply political act.

Critical work examining *The Woman in Battle* has tended to focus on Velazquez's cross-dressing, and her sexual and national boundary crossings are interpreted as expressions of the South's rebellion.[12] Velazquez's early act of defiance of paternal authority, by refusing to marry "against my own consent," becomes representative of acts of defiance against other paternalistic structures, including that of the federal government, which she sees as unjustly impinging on the rights of an autonomous Southern region.[13] In manipulating the gendered expectations of women of the period, Velazquez's cross-dressing has also been seen by critics as an expression of a counterfeit persona.[14] Thus, critics have paid considerable attention to Velazquez's performance as Lieutenant Harry T. Buford, a Confederate soldier.[15] These scholars interpret Velazquez's cross-dressing or disguise as rooted in and a reflection of the importance of the Confederacy "as a self-determined new nation," in which both women and the Confederate states uncouple themselves from the preexisting structures of national and patriarchal power.[16]

However, few critics have examined her performance as a male soldier as a type of "contraband," as understood through the language of Lincoln's proclamation. Insofar as Velazquez assumes counterfeit identities just as she does counterfeit bills, currency plates, cotton, and other miscellaneous items, she is not simply testing the limits of federal power. Rather, her work as a Confederate spy requires that she become a type of contraband herself by assuming the disguise of a Union sympathizer (a disguise so convincing that her Confederate friends sever ties with her).[17] Said differently, Velazquez suggests that the very markers of the young Confederacy, such as stamps, insignia, and currency, are contingent on counterfeit identity, contraband bodies, and the illicit pleasures attached to the act of cross-dressing.[18] More-over, critics have missed the opportunity to examine these behaviors as part of the pursuit of international (diplomatic) recognition.[19] Therefore, while some scholars are attentive to the "contraband" of her gendered narrative of "adventure" and noticed the "illicit" pleasures experienced by Velazquez while dressed as a man, they miss an opportunity to analyze these illicit pleasures as part of the emplotment in a narrative that is essentially about avoiding personal recognition—of the many aspects of her numerous disguises—in order to gain national recognition.[20]

By breaking the blockade, Velazquez uses the ambiguities of domestic and international law regarding Confederate trade as a way to test the limits of federal control of the Confederate subject, while also helping to establish new social and political systems. Through the repeated violations of the blockade, Velazquez's memoir demonstrates the autonomy of Confederate persons, as well as the autonomy of the secessionist region. Blockade running, in her view, has a creative function: Velazquez's unlawful commercial activities help to create the nation-state whose affiliation she can ultimately claim.[21] Finally, Velazquez's prominent self-representation as an enterprising woman helps to withdraw her from participation in the conventions of genteel Southern femininity while underscoring her exceptionalism as an autonomous and self-possessed subject eager to express a form of national membership that is foreclosed at this historical moment.

In *From Flag to Flag*, Ripley, a Southern white woman and a member of the Southern plantocracy, narrates her forced exile from her Louisiana plantation at the onset of the U.S. Civil War and describes her family's difficult journey from Louisiana to Texas, Mexico, and Cuba. Ripley's travelogue dramatizes the precarious, vulnerable, and valuable position of property during the Civil War. In this way, her narrative is both similar to and different from the diaries and autobiographies written by women about commercial or economic life during the Civil War that represent women as a disabled caste, disenfranchised and excluded from all areas of public life, "denied full legal and political standing," and "permitted to exercise only a few privileges," as Nancy Isenberg describes them.[22] Ripley's travelogue is structured around her initiation into the economic sphere, albeit in a limited capacity, and is one of a number of women's diaries and memoirs of the Civil War that recount the multitude of ways in which women resisted the blockade through domestic production and industry, as well as through domestic creativity.[23]

However, Ripley's travelogue differs from other Civil War–era memoirs by taking a broader geographic perspective. In her memoir, Ripley explores questions of trade and state regulation across the Americas. Moreover, unlike other women's diaries and recollections about the onset of the Civil War, *From Flag to Flag* reveals women's networks of exchange in defiance of national laws and, in so doing, extends the parameters of Southern women's participation in war efforts in ways that reflect what Gilpin Faust has called "extreme manifestations of ambitions and strategies embraced by hundreds of Confederate females who used women's weapons but did not play by women's rules."[24]

And yet, unlike Velazquez, Ripley remains fairly secretive about her participation in blockade running and various Confederate relief efforts. Ripley's taciturn treatment of unlawful trade, paired with her general unwillingness to address the legal and ethical implications of blockade running, reflects her complicated social and political status. This combination of disclosure and secrecy, paired with the geographic range of her marginally lawful activities, allows Ripley to act as a pirate while also maintaining a position that is not completely inimical to the United States, a position that is expedient given that Ripley will eventually return to the United States at the end of the war. For example, by omitting any direct mention of her participation in cotton running when living in Texas and Cuba, locations at the margins of the nation, while repeatedly asserting her alliance to the Confederacy, Ripley represents herself as a loyal, albeit imperfect, subject capable of being reformed and reabsorbed into the reintegrated nation. Thus, by delineating and inhabiting the boundaries and margins of the American state and its laws, as well as of its citizens, Ripley represents blockade running as the undesirable outcome for subjects who have been dispossessed of citizenship.

Criticism of Ripley's *From Flag to Flag* is more limited than that of Velazquez's work: the text has been read either as a travelogue of the period and examined for its representation of Cuba and Mexico or as a text representative of the condition endured by Southerners after the war, with particular emphasis on the emigration of this population from the U.S. South.[25] Rarely have works pointed to its depiction of cotton routes along the U.S.-Mexican borderlands, which would underscore the continued significance of cotton in the U.S. economy and in the world market even after the imposition of the blockade.[26] More recently, there has been a renewed interest in the representation of Chinese indentured laborers as a reflection of the changing economies of the U.S. South and Cuba.[27] In her most recent work, Edlie Wong examines Ripley's travelogue to "explore the literary and cultural construction of the Chinese 'coolie-slave' as a circum-Atlantic racial formation," arguing that the figure of the "coolie-slave" emerges in Ripley's work as a product of "Afro-Asian" comparative racialization in the transition period from slavery to indentured servitude in Cuba.[28]

However, critics of Ripley's memoir have ignored the legal and economic dimensions of her travels to Texas, Mexico, and Cuba. More than charting new territory in the expression of women's lives in the nineteenth century, Ripley's narrative dramatizes the harmful effects of not being granted full citizenship, particularly in times of crisis. After all, the simultaneous dispossession of property and of rights catalyzes Ripley's entrance to the transnational market at the margins of the U.S. state and of law. Thus, Ripley demonstrates the reasons citizenship and recognition are critical in the maintenance of social, political, and economic order.[29]

Reading Velazquez's and Ripley's narratives for their representations of blockade running and piracy contributes to the growing critical conversation on these materials by viewing the primacy of women's engagement in new frontiers of possession, the frontiers of American space, and the frontiers of citizenship.[30] To be clear, Ripley and Velazquez are not the notorious blockade runners responsible for smuggling what some historians have conservatively estimated to be half a million bales of cotton, a thousand tons of gunpowder, half a million rifles, and hundreds of cannon during the blockade.[31] Unlike the smugglers who "provided the South with 60 percent of its weapons, one-third of the lead for its bullets and the ingredients for three-fourths of its powder, and most of the cloth for its uniforms," Ripley and Velazquez are concerned with the symbolic importance of blockade running in the creation and recognition of the property of citizenship and national belonging.[32] Therefore, their memoirs fit imperfectly in the genre of blockade-runner adventure novels.[33]

And yet, Ripley's and Velazquez's travelogues share with blockade-running adventure novels written by their male contemporaries an emphasis on the symbolic importance of unlawful trade as an act of national creation and affiliation. More interestingly, these memoirs also help to represent the creation of Confederate diplomatic recognition through acts of defiance of the blockade. For example, in the early pages of his memoir, *Running the Blockade: A Personal Narrative of Adventures, Risks, and Escapes during the American Civil War* (1896), Thomas E. Taylor addresses the peculiar position of blockade running in the legal climate of the period, noting that the inconsistency rested on the difficulty of identifying blockade running as either an expression of war or a commercial act.[34] Taylor distinguishes between the two, writing that, if blockade running were considered an act of war, then it would bestow "belligerent" status on the Confederacy and would consist "in one of them, who has obtained a working command of the sea, imprisoning the other's war fleets in their own ports."[35] However, as a commercial act, blockade running is essentially apolitical since the commercial blockade "principally concerns neutrals."[36] Therefore, as Taylor helps to illustrate, the legal designation of blockade running depends on whether the Confederacy is recognized as an enemy state, a belligerent at war with the Union, or merely a participant in trade between neutral states.

In order to clarify his own position as a blockade runner during the period, Taylor cites the norms of international law. He notes,

> One of the immediate results of this act of President Lincoln was the prompt acknowledgement of the South as belligerents by England and France. Yet the Federal States persisted in maintaining that the Confederates were rebels, and that whosoever ventured to recognise them as belligerents must be regarded as friends of rebels and no friends of the North. They ignored the fact that their interference with neutral trade, by this declaration of blockade, was a virtual concession of belligerency to the South. A declaration of blockade presupposes a state of war and not mere rebellion, and the claim by the Federals of a right to seize neutral vessels attempting to break a blockade was one which can be exercised only by a belligerent; exercised by any one else it is mere piracy.[37]

In addition to highlighting the significance of the blockade in granting the Confederacy the status of belligerent, Taylor, like other writers of the period, uses the term "blockade-running" to speak to the legitimacy of federal imposition *and* deprivation of Confederate recognition. As Taylor claims, the difference between military and commercial blockades is that the first concerns ships of war or the military warships of the state, while the second concerns "neutrals," or simple trading vehicles. And yet, a trading vehicle may be designated as an enemy ship if it has been identified as such by belligerents; and in protecting itself, a neutral ship might very quickly be designated as a pirate vehicle.

As a response to what Taylor sees as a problematic overreach of the federal government, he writes, "It must always be remembered that for a belligerent to be entitled to exercise these high prerogatives he must first have constituted a real and effective blockade."[38] In this ambiguous statement, Taylor questions the legitimacy of Lincoln's blockade using the international norms of war. However, paired with his assessment of the federal government as interfering with neutral trade by not declaring the Confederacy to be a belligerent, and unlawfully appropriating their goods in defiance of international law, Taylor recasts the Union and not the Confederacy as the law-breaking entity. Thus, Taylor appropriates the language of the blockade in order to designate the appropriative/dispossessive acts of the Union as piracy.

Published in 1892, William Watson's *The Adventures of a Blockade Runner; or, Trade in Time of War* takes a different approach from Taylor's memoir by interpreting blockade running during the Civil War as a just act of war.[39] Like Velazquez before him, Watson elevates the blockade runner to the status of a lawful enemy, as opposed to an unlawful pirate. Most notably, Watson highlights the uneasy position blockade runners occupy between hostile combatants and private traders. Watson notes that cotton was "considered as contraband, and by some an unholy trade, and those engaged in it regarded as reckless, lawless fellows, subject to be shot or drowned for their tricks."[40] However, blockade running was an assertion and expression of property ownership, not necessarily simply a breach of law. He continues,

> Blockade-running was not regarded as either unlawful or dishonourable, but rather as a bold and daring enterprise. It was no surreptitious breach of any law, but merely defiance of a barrier placed and maintained by no other right than by the force of arms; and those who attempted to brave it did so at their own risk, subject by the laws of war to be fired upon, their vessel sunk or captured, themselves drowned, killed, or wounded in the course of the capture, but that was the extent of the liability. They had broken no law, and no charge for such could be brought against them, and no punishment beyond confiscation of the vessel and cargo. It was simply an act of war, subject to the laws of war, and to me who had little or no knowledge or experience in the mercantile line it was much more congenial than the extortions and deceitful wheedling and trickeries of the *legitimate* trade.[41]

Blockade running, in Watson's estimation, is an act that defies colonization or invasion: it is not inherently an unlawful act. He writes,

Over the whole length and breadth of the land all commercial industries, business pursuits, and even pleasures and enjoyments, were suppressed by the authority and din of war. Shut off from communication with the outer world, and surrounded by a hostile force, the whole country might be compared to one vast besieged garrison, where but one object was paramount, that of resistance to the enemy, and the will of the commander the only law, and the only liberty such as he chose to grant. The Northern States, with a view of crushing the South into obedience, had, with a powerful fleet, blockaded every Southern port, and completely shut off the Southern States from all communication with other nations.[42]

In this view, all blockade runners are engaging in acts of war, and in so doing, they represent the Confederacy as a sovereign state capable of entering into war (a position of belligerency denied to the Confederate states at the onset of the war). In labeling the trade "*legitimate*," Watson calls into question the arbitrariness and the power of law in legitimating trade, while also characterizing blockade running as an act of resistance to unjust and unlawful domestic and international laws. Watson's characterization of the Confederacy as a sovereign state also has the additional effect of legitimating the citizenship of the Confederate person. They are not stateless pirates at all, but rather Confederate citizens.

Property and Citizenship in the State at War

Indeed, the question of the legal position of Confederates is only settled with the Prize Cases of 1863, which were debated in the Supreme Court more than two years after the imposition of the blockade and the Confederate declaration of an insurrection. In addition to rehearsing the close attachments between property and national recognition on the judicial stage, the cases helped to settle the position of Confederates not as stateless subjects hostile to the very idea of the state (or pirates) but rather as foreign enemies.[43] The Prize Cases were particularly important given that the Confiscation Act passed by Congress in 1862, which allowed the federal government to seize Confederate property by invoking Congress's power to punish treason, had the secondary effect of casting Confederates as domestic enemies as well. These competing rationales used to seize Confederate property reveal the federal government's problematic classification of Confederates as both treasonous subjects (that is, bad citizens) and foreign enemies (that is, noncitizens). Moreover, this confusing and competing taxonomy of Confederates as recognized, albeit imperfect, American subjects *and as* subjects with no claims to American citizenship at all was echoed in the federal government's treatment of Confederate property. The cases, which ostensibly only debated the status of Confederate properties seized during the blockade, settled the question of what type of subjects Confederates were vis-à-vis domestic and international law.

The Prize Cases centered on claims to property made by the owners of a number of seized vessels bound for Confederate ports before the official declaration of a state of insurrection on July 13, 1861, but after the declaration of the blockade in April: a three-month period when the subject position of Confederates was most critical. In court, the appellants argued that the seizure of their property was unlawful because the president's blockade was unconstitutional. The majority opinion, written by Justice Robert Grier, stated, "The proclamation of blockade by the President is, of itself, conclusive evidence that a state of war existed which demanded and authorized recourse to such a measure."[44] This tautology (that a state of war exists because of the proclamation of a blockade, and that a blockade is the product of a state of war) exposed the complicated position of Southerners at the onset of the war, as well as the category of person whose property could be confiscated with impunity in a nation whose bedrock principles included the protection of property. In the view of the federal government, it was engaged in a state of war with the South—a war that demonstrated executive overreach, at best, and that legitimated a range of unjust federal appropriative behavior, at worst. As Grier states in the court's opinion, while the question of the constitutionality of the blockade is resolved in the tautology of the president's authority, the question of whether Confederate property was subject to proper seizure is more complex.[45]

The appellants contested the seizure of their property, stating, "The term 'enemy' is properly applicable to those only who are subjects or citizens of a foreign State at war with our own" and not to members of their own state.[46] By highlighting that U.S. citizens may be deemed "rebels and traitors" but not "enemies," the appellants argued that their property could not legally be seized.[47] Furthermore, the appellants contended that since "insurrection is the act of individuals, and not of a government or sovereignty," the "confiscation of their property can be effected only under a municipal law [and not international law]."[48] Because under federal law the confiscation of property could not take place without the commission of a crime, the appellants were, de jure, entitled to the protection of property promised to all U.S. citizens. Finally, and perhaps most importantly, the appellants claimed that the "secession ordinances are nullities" and were "ineffectual to release any citizen from his allegiance to the national Government."[49] The appellants claimed they were therefore entitled to the protections afforded to citizens, which includes the protection of property. Moreover, they asserted that their citizenship could not be revoked: their property, in other words, was unjustly seized. In sum, the appellants used the lack of Confederate diplomatic recognition to claim that blockade running was not an act of war (as Velazquez and Watson argue) but, rather, an act of theft or rebellion subject to federal law.

The Prize Cases raised the problem of the legal position of Confederates: Were Southerners treasonous enemies, pirates, or foreigners? In fact, Grier's second question articulated earlier hinged on the question of the condition of Confederate subjectivity: Were these properties the properties of enemies, the properties of pirates, or the lawful properties of citizens? Grier acknowledges that the difference in the Confederates' subject position (which has material consequences for the legal standing of Southern property) rests on recognition. He asks, "Is the property of all persons residing within the territory of the States now in rebellion, captured on the high seas, to be treated as 'enemies' property,' whether the owner be in arms against the Government or not?"[50] Grier determines that in declaring "their independence" and casting "off their allegiance," the Confederacy affirmed its intention of establishing a sovereign state, thereby making this property vulnerable to seizure under international laws of war.[51] In other words, by declaring their independence, members of the Confederacy became "enemies" whose properties were subject to confiscation.[52]

However, the courts had to reckon with the fact that Confederates did not belong to a foreign nation-state. Rather, they belonged to a domestic state, thereby giving rise to the question of whether members of a domestic state could be deprived of property simply by "casting off their allegiance." Moreover, if the reason the courts had to settle this question was that, in the past, the category of "enemy" or "belligerent" had been synonymous with the category of "foreigner," then the courts had to settle on whether they could relabel a citizen as a "foreigner." In other words, the courts had to grapple with the difference between "enemies" and "foreigners." To settle the issue, the courts concluded that subjects who inhabited the "revolted province or State" de facto showed allegiance to that state rather than the federal government: after all, "under the very peculiar Constitution of this Government, although the citizens owe supreme allegiance to the Federal Government, they owe also a qualified allegiance to the State in which they are domiciled. Their persons and property are subject to its laws. Hence, in organizing this rebellion, they have acted as States claiming to be sovereign over all persons and property within their respective limits, and asserting a right to absolve their citizens from their allegiance to the Federal Government."[53] In the opinion of the court, there was no discernible difference between belonging to an insurrectionist region and belonging to a belligerent nation-state, especially because in the antebellum United States, persons received their rights and property protections from individual states rather than from the federal government. The courts, in other words, saw no difference between the domestic state and the international nation-state.

Moreover, given their allegiance, Grier notes, the members of an insurrectionist region could be used to "increase the revenues of the hostile power" and thus "are, in this contest, liable to be treated as enemies though not foreigners."[54] Therefore, in Grier's opinion, a state could be regarded as an "enemy" without necessarily being "foreign." In declaring that all persons who belonged to hostile powers and territories were to be treated as enemies and traitors (not foreigners), Grier expressed the complicated position of Southerners during the Civil War, a condition that is reasserted in Ripley's and Velazquez's narratives. The Confederates were enemies, and their status as enemies suspended all legally bound contracts: it made any intercourse, "commercial or otherwise," unlawful.[55] And so, while Ripley and Velazquez were not "foreigners," narratives like theirs point to the alienation that Confederates experience not simply through their dispossession of property and citizenship but also through being labeled national enemies.

I want to underscore the importance of the legal position of Confederate property in the adjudication of their citizenship. Even in his dissenting opinion, Justice Samuel Nelson echoed Grier's argument regarding the status of Confederate property given the belligerency of the Confederacy. He writes,

The insurance of enemies' property, the drawing of bills of exchange or purchase on the enemies' country, the remission of bills or money to it, are illegal and void. Existing partnerships between citizens or subjects of the two countries are dissolved, and, in fine, interdiction of trade and intercourse direct or indirect is absolute and complete by the mere force and effect of war itself. All the property of the people of the two countries on land or sea are subject to capture and confiscation by the adverse party as enemies' property, with certain qualifications as it respects property on land, ... all treaties between the belligerent parties are annulled, the ports of the respective countries may be blockaded, and letters of marque and reprisal granted as rights of war, and the law of prizes as defined by the law of nations comes into full and complete operation, resulting from maritime captures, *jure belli*.[56]

The Prize Cases thus helped to settle the question of the relationship between property and citizenship: in belonging to an enemy, Confederate property was subject to seizure and confiscation. The Confederates, in other words, lost their right to the protection of property. The debates over the equivalence of property and citizenship persisted after the war, when the Southern Claims Commission began to award compensation for lost property should the claimants demonstrate that they had been loyal citizens during the war.[57] Through the process of depositions and of compiling the testimonies of the claimants, people were marked with "recognition as ... loyal citizen[s]," and the "right to claim the Union as [their] own."[58] During the proceedings of the commission, the interrogatories replicated language underscoring the interdependence of property and the "person," understood as a subject recognized as a member of a national community: a citizen. For example, during these proceedings, the interrogator's questions included, "Were you in any service, business, or employment for the confederacy? ... Did you ever have any charge of any stores, or other property, for the confederacy? ... Did you ever subscribe to any loan of the so-called Confederate States? ... Were you at any time a member of any society or organization for equipping volunteers or conscripts?"[59] These questions, intended to weed out Confederate sympathizers and members of the Confederacy, focused on and affected claims to property. However, as these questions make apparent, to be granted claims to property and thereby to the protection of property (and nation) also meant that one had demonstrated an affiliation with and attachment to the federal government. Through these proceedings, the commission legitimated claims to property but, more importantly, legitimated inclusion in the national body.

As these legal cases demonstrate, the question of property's interrelation with a person was debated continuously throughout the Civil War, as well as after the end of the conflict. These incidents are echoed in Velazquez's and Ripley's narratives: subjects vulnerable to the total loss of personhood and recognition are also subject to the total loss of property. Having been designated as enemies belonging to a belligerent state, Confederates like Velazquez and Ripley are left without any capacity to defend or own property. Moreover, defending or owning property conversely leaves Velazquez and Ripley without any claims to federal recognition as citizens. Thus, both Ripley and Velazquez spend a considerable portion of their memoirs describing their dispossession and the ways in which it translates into their dispossession of autonomy and recognition. However, they also describe their attempts to reclaim property through behaviors that range from participating in blockade running and counterfeiting (as Velazquez does) to functioning as a bank while temporarily guarding the money of Confederate traders in Mexico (as Ripley does).

Cotton, Currency, and Commerce in the Shadows of War

In order to dramatize the importance of their work in the shadows of the Confederacy, Ripley and Velazquez begin their narratives by describing their dispossession at the onset of the war, even when, as mentioned earlier, the confiscation of property by the Union serves to acknowledge the belligerency of (and thus bestow recognition on) the Confederacy. Ripley's travelogue reflects the subject position experienced by a dispossessed Southern plantocracy, and the effects of this dispossession on personhood. Property takes center stage in Ripley's travelogue. It is clear that, for Ripley, the protection of personal property is indicative not only of just governance but also of what just governance affords: representation, protection from unlawful seizure, and legal recognition. And so, the text posits that the dispossession of property and recognition drives the Ripley family to transgress both domestic and international law by participating in the underground economy of cotton running.

At the onset of the war, Ripley finds that the only way to escape systematic brutalization by the "arbitrary rule of the army of occupation" is to hastily leave Louisiana, what she calls her "exile."[60] Ripley packs a carriage with the equipment necessary for the hasty "midnight flight."[61] In this particularly poignant scene early in her memoir, Ripley recalls the utter devastation of property endured at the hands of the federal army:

> No words can tell the scene that those deserted rooms presented. The grand portraits, heirlooms of that aristocratic family, men of the

Revolutionary period, high-bred dames of a long-past generation in short bodices, puffed sleeves, towering headdresses, and quaint golden chains—ancestors long since dead, not only valuable as likenesses that could not be duplicated, but acknowledged works of art—these portraits hung upon the walls, slashed by swords clear across from side to side, stabbed and mutilated in every way! The contents of store-closets had been poured over the floors; molasses and vinegar, and everything that defaces and stains, had been smeared over walls and furniture. Up-stairs, the *armoires* with mirror-doors had been smashed in with heavy axes or hammers, and the dainty dresses of the young ladies torn and crushed with studied, painstaking malignity, while china, toilet articles, and bits of glass that ornamented the rooms were thrown upon the beds and broken and ground into a mass of fragments; desks were wrenched open, and the contents scattered not only through the house, but out upon the streets, to be wafted in all directions; parts of their private letters as well as letters from the desks of other violated homes, and family records torn from numberless bibles, were found on the sidewalks of the town, and even on the public roads beyond town limits![62]

This early moment serves to inventory her loss for the reader, particularly the loss of her private properties. The destruction of the items in her home also reflects the permeability of her personal space. Most importantly, however, is that this trespass on her property drives Ripley's sense of her dispossession of any rights after the declaration of war. To underscore the extent of her dispossession, she describes how armoires and desks are destroyed alongside portraits and heirlooms, which, as she points out, can be traced to the Revolutionary War and the origins of the American nation-state.

Therefore, Ripley's destroyed and "slashed" heirlooms and paintings of her forefathers make the reader aware of the effects of the war's deprivation of all possessions and claims to the nation. Ripley continues,

Of the china, pictures, books, etc., sent to various supposed places of safety when our Louisiana home was threatened, nothing could be found, when we had once more an abiding-place, but a box of books. The house where the pictures were stored was robbed in the absence of its owner, and years after I heard that some of our family portraits had been seen in the cabins of neighboring negroes. The china—a wedding anniversary gift, and therefore doubly prized—had never been wholly unpacked; the few sample pieces that were taken out at Arlington were carefully replaced, and the cask sent to my widowed sister's plantation on Bayou Fordoche. While General Lawlor was in command in the vicinity, the enterprising colonel of a New York regiment "captured" it while passing through the plantation. Some efforts were made for the recovery of the china, but they were unsuccessful, and later my sister was informed that it had been shipped North. . . . In the general and indiscriminate custom of "appropriating" that prevailed during that exciting period we were thankful that nobody took the books.[63]

Throughout this passage, Ripley uses the language of theft, putting "captured" and "appropriating" in quotation marks to illustrate the dispossession that she experiences at the hands of the federal army but also to underscore the injustice and illegality of this dispossession. Moreover, in describing property as both a material object and person, Ripley underscores the intertwined and mutually constitutive relationship between material properties and the properties belonging to the person. To "capture" an object, for example, seems grammatically imprecise, yet Ripley highlights the ways in which she sees these behaviors as part of a larger context about the intersections of property and person. These goods, like her American citizenship at the onset of the war, are stolen, appropriated, robbed, and captured without any legal recourse.

Like Ripley, Velazquez bemoans the loss of Confederate property, especially the property of those she calls noncombatants. She writes, for example, "No matter how peaceably disposed [Confederates] might be, they could satisfy neither party, and were made [to] suffer by both. The proprietor of the Bowman House was forced to witness a fine property destroyed before his eyes through the reckless and unthinking anger of men who never stopped to inquire whether he was guilty or not of any offence against them or their cause before taking vengeance upon him. He was reduced to poverty by the burning of his hotel."[64] She also describes the historically significant fall of New Orleans, writing, "Late in the morning of the 25th of April, 1862, the Federal fleet could be seen coming up the river, but it must have dampened the enthusiasm of the Yankee sailors somewhat to find steamboats, cotton, and all kinds of combustible property blazing for miles along the levee. It was a terribly magnificent spectacle, but one the like of which I earnestly hoped I might never witness again, for it fairly made me shudder to see millions of dollars worth of property being utterly destroyed in this reckless manner, and it impressed me more strongly with an idea of the horrors of warfare than all the fighting and slaughter I had ever seen done."[65] The desolation of New Orleans, she notes, is not the "legitimate" result of war but, rather, the product of "ambitious and unscrupulous politicians" taking advantage of the "forlorn condition of the South."[66] What Velazquez witnesses is the destruction of Confederate property—ranging from the devastation of New Orleans to the destruction of the Bowman House in Jackson, Mississippi—as the first step in the loss of Confederate citizenship. The property destruction witnessed by Velazquez is alarming because, unlike Ripley's personal property, the property that Velazquez saw destroyed was of a public nature and therefore symbolic of the destruction of the Confederacy.

Velazquez also witnesses a range of unlawful acts committed by the federal government, including bounty jumping, the flooding of the South with counterfeit currency, and forced conscription.[67] Velazquez describes the thriving market in enlistment papers, or the practice of purchasing a military substitute for federal conscription, taking place in the North, which she describes as "traffic in human flesh and blood."[68] She writes that agents in interior counties "came for the purpose of filling their quotas, and they always found a horde of brokers ready to accommodate them with real and bogus enlistment papers, each of which was supposed to represent an able-bodied man. . . . Whether the papers were bogus or genuine mattered very little to those who purchased, so long as they could obtain credit on them from the authorities at Washington."[69] Velazquez describes one such application for a substitute made at an office with which she was connected: the applicant was "a very prominent and very wealthy gentleman of New York, who was willing to pay as high as twenty-one hundred dollars for some one to take the place of his son, who had been drafted . . . [and the man] was willing to send any number of substitutes if necessary, but not his son."[70] Because this is what Velazquez calls "all in the way of business," she persuades a "hearty young colored fellow" to enlist "as a substitute for the old man's son."[71]

Velazquez also describes the enlistment of poor Irish and German immigrants, who were "surrounded by crowds of shouting and yelling brokers until they were fairly bewildered, and found themselves enlisted before they well knew what was the matter with them."[72] She describes these men as being "marched off to act as substitutes for able-bodied American citizens."[73] With no recourse to the privileges of language, this group of immigrants is left vulnerable to exploitation. Indeed, this population has no recourse to rights; she describes its members as "human cargo," and she says they are "shipped for this side of the ocean just like so many cattle. Captain P [captain of these vessels carrying immigrants] considered himself as their owner, and he sold them to the government exactly as he would have sold cattle, if that sort of traffic had been as profitable as dealing in white, human beings."[74] By using the language of "cattle," Velazquez indicates that this human cargo being traded by Northerners is left entirely devoid of claims to personhood, much like enslaved persons. The exploitation of this vulnerable immigrant population without access to language or to knowledge of the American legal system points to their alienation from a system of representation and recognition. Her condemnation of the trade also functions not as an indictment of slavery in the Americas but as Velazquez's proof of the existence of slavery in the North, as well as the South. In the North, she sees a form of bodily trade and exchange made manifest in times of crisis that is concurrent with the thwarting of chattel slavery in the South. Although there seems to be no awareness in the narrative that what she is describing parallels closely the experience of transporting other forms of human cargo, Velazquez has two objectives: to highlight the many unlawful activities taking place in the North and to underscore her own engagement in unlawful forms of exchange as a necessary response in the face of Northern piracy.

Indeed, much like Martin Delany, Velazquez, too, describes the acts of piracy that are taking place with impunity on American land at the hands of Northerners and Southerners. Although many Southerners suffered due to the war and the blockade, "in all of the large cities were men and women, many of them in government employ, who were in constant communication with the Confederate agents, and in all of them were merchants who were rapidly growing wealthy by sending goods of all kinds, including arms and ammunition, to the South, either by having them smuggled through the lines, or by shipping them to some neutral port for the purpose of having them transferred to blockade runners."[75] The result is that "millions of dollars' worth of goods . . . were sold for the Southern market by men who were loud in their protestations of loyalty to the Federal government, who bitterly denounced the South, in public and in private, who contributed largely to aid in carrying on the war, and who enjoyed, in the fullest manner, the confidence of the government, and of those of their fellow-citizens who honestly believed that the war was a just one."[76] These men "were more than anxious to sell to any one who would buy, but in case the buyer was known to be, or was suspected of being, a Confederate agent, the question of the moment was, to sell without being found out."[77] What Velazquez describes, to echo the foregoing discussions, is not a traitorous act but, rather, an act of piracy in the sense that it is driven by the search for pure profit. Thus, what Velazquez observes is a system of possession and dispossession that benefits those who claim loyalty to the Union (and who were therefore also bestowed with federal recognition) at the expense of those who have been actively deprived of recognition and the right to their property. In this climate, Velazquez posits that some forms of property deprivation and depredation can only be countered with similar acts of theft, and *The Woman in Battle* makes a case for blockade running and other unlawful commercial activities as the only response to the extreme restrictions placed on Southerners.

Velazquez sees the vast and transnational network of blockade running as giving her a means of expressing political and economic sovereignty, and she views blockade running as acting "under orders from the only government the authority of which [she] acknowledged, and animated only by an ardent desire to advance the interests of the cause which [she] had espoused."[78] In framing her work as a blockade runner as a justifiable act of war, Velazquez separates herself from both the federal soldiers participating in acts of theft and destruction of property and Confederate-identified traders looking to make a profit through blockade running. Rather, Velazquez is both a politicized and politicizing figure for a Confederate cause, and participation in shadow economies comes to define Velazquez as a Confederate citizen. These acts are ultimately "of a character that, under ordinary circumstances, would admit of no extenuation," but because they are an assertion of her allegiance to the "only government" that she acknowledges, she is "justified in aiding that government by every means in her power, as well by fighting its enemies in the field."[79] Rather than an act of private gain, for Velazquez, blockade running is an act of war that is instrumental in the creation of an autonomous Confederate state.

Velazquez understands her participation in blockade running as a fulfillment of her Confederate duty, confirmed by the editor's note to the memoir, which encourages that the Confederacy be understood by the reader as a "belligerent."[80] This helps the reader consider Velazquez's behaviors within a range of those that approximate acts of war even though, as aforementioned, the "belligerency" of the Confederacy is denied on the international stage. Recognizing the Confederacy as a belligerent, the editor notes, helps the reader understand the acts described in the memoir as "patriotic" because Confederate subjects had to do "all in their power to defeat their enemies, not only by opposing them with armies in the field, but by demoralizing them by insidious attacks in the rear. . . . From a military point of view, therefore, what was proper and justifiable for one side, was proper and justifiable for the other, and will so be considered by impartial critics."[81] Velazquez writes, "I was acting as best I knew how to promote the success of a cause which I felt to be a just one, and that I considered myself as justified in doing the Federals all injury I could, and in promoting the interest of the Confederacy by every means in my power."[82]

Moreover, blockade running provides Velazquez with the opportunity to emerge as a shrewd businesswoman. In a chapter titled "Blockade Running," Velazquez describes herself as so "efficient in managing matters that required to be managed with skill, boldness, and discretion" that she soon enters the business of blockade running with relative ease and with the trust of her Confederate associates. For the first time in the narrative, Velazquez benefits from dressing in women's clothing, since "it was thought that, as in the cases of the proposed raid, a woman would be able to do a great many things without exciting suspicion."[83] Thus, it is important that Velazquez enter the economic sphere in women's clothing because it allows her more mobility. In this role as blockade runner, she is entrusted with purchasing goods in Philadelphia and New York and transporting them to the West Indies and then arranging shipment to blockaded Southern ports. Purchasing goods in the North, while sometimes difficult because of "fastidious" loyalty to the federal government, was for the most part easy, and Velazquez writes that "the majority of business houses" welcomed all customers without any regard for the customers' state affiliation.[84] Velazquez thus uses her economic position in conjunction with what she considers just acts of war to claim the rights attached to legally recognized populations, or those persons who can legally claim inclusion in the Confederacy. Blockade running, Velazquez suggests, is an act of war that legitimates Confederate recognition in the absence of the state, and participation in this form of exchange extends recognition to the individual that is akin to citizenship; and yet, for this recognition to take place, these activities in part must also remain hidden. Said differently, blockade running is critical in creating a new state, as well as membership within it.

After all, the diplomatic and personal recognition made possible through blockade running helps to make possible a fuller expression of a national community or family that exists in response to unjust and repressive political systems. For example, Velazquez is struck by the designation of Confederate spies as "outlaws" who are "liable to be hung if detected—the death of a soldier even being denied him," even though they are "nothing more nor less than a detective officer, and there cannot be any good and sufficient reason assigned for the discredit which attaches to his occupation."[85] She continues, "The agent of a secret service bureau ought to have the same immunity that any other combatant has. We shoot guerrillas, or unauthorized combatants, and so, perhaps we might continue to hang unauthorized spies; but a regular attaché of a secret service bureau should have some recognized rights, which even the enemy would be bound to respect."[86] Velazquez uses the language of law and of rights to understand her own subject position, as well as those "outlaws" that she recasts as citizen-soldiers in wartime. Moreover, in Velazquez's view these Confederate citizens, like those Cubans liberating themselves from "the Spanish yoke," express a collective national affiliation that is a response to and a struggle against an unwelcome colonial force.[87] By highlighting the many ways in which her participation in the shadows of trade is a defense of the autonomous statehood of the Confederacy, Velazquez discursively *creates* the nation that she can lawfully defend.

However, it is not only through blockade running but also through counterfeiting and bond speculation that Velazquez expresses an understanding of the importance of circulation, both financial and physical, of unlawful materials as an expression of Confederate belonging. Along with a number of Confederate agents, Velazquez breaks into the Treasury and makes away with an electrotype to print a hundred dollars' worth of compound interest notes and another for printing fractional currency. She prints "eighty-five thousand dollars' worth of one hundred dollar compound interest notes . . . of [which] twenty-five thousand dollars' worth were sent to England, and we received exchange for them. The rest were disposed of to the banks."[88] She then circulates "as many bogus United States notes and bonds as we could, especially as we would serve the double purpose of aiding the Confederate and injuring the Federal government, and as, moreover, we would be assisted by prominent Federal officials."[89] At another moment, she reveals that she carried with her "ninety-three thousand dollars . . . and had in deposit in several banks over fifty thousand dollars," all of which she used for the Southern cause.[90]

Velazquez also engages in a bigger scheme, which includes "not only dealing in genuine—borrowed for the purpose from the treasury—and bogus Federal securities, but Confederate bogus bonds also. These bonds were to be, as far as practicable, put upon the English market, at the best rates that could be gotten for them, and our—that is, the Confederate—share of the proceeds was to go into a general fund, to be used for advancing the inter-ests of the cause."[91] These numerous illegal schemes are significant in help-ing her express affiliation to the Confederate cause, as well as in furthering the cause of Confederate autonomy and statehood. Indeed, these expres-sions of autonomy and affiliation, Velazquez stresses, are intertwined with the very creation of the Confederate person in ways that include, but also extend beyond, citizenship.

The American State and Citizenship at the End of the War

While Velazquez's narrative is critical to understanding Confederate state-hood and membership within it, Ripley's *From Flag to Flag* illustrates the importance of unlawful transnational trade in defining the limits of U.S. territory at the end of the Civil War. My analysis of Ripley thus highlights the importance of the transnational illegal marketplace in the production of new national spaces. The crisis of war allows Ripley to fashion herself as a manager capable of controlling difficult labor populations, a utilitarian homemaker skilled in carving out a domestic space regardless of wealth and location, and an erudite voyager, tracing trade and travel routes among the U.S. South, the U.S. Southwest, Mexico, and Cuba. Ultimately, Ripley's sub-ject position in this transnational economic circuit signals her emergence as a liberal person in the United States and abroad. After all, though she might have been limited to the domestic sphere before the onset of the Civil War, the war forces her to become more enterprising. Ripley's entrance into a liberal economic sphere links departure from the home to national exile and to the expression of full personhood in the absence of the properties of recognition and citizenship.[92] Although she repeatedly stresses her reli-ance on antebellum conceptions of Southern femininity, Ripley's initiation into the shadow economy is matched by her exit from the domestic space: her departure from the space of the home, as well as her exile from the nation-state signals her increased mobility and visibility as an economic or commercial subject, even as this mobility is catalyzed by her dispossession.

In participating in the shadows of legal trade, Ripley expresses a trans-national economic subjectivity that supplements that of which she has been dispossessed (citizenship and property) and demonstrates the adverse ef-fects of being deprived of recognition in all forms.[93] However, mobility and visibility, antithetically, do not produce recognition. Rather, because this increased mobility is a symptom of the lack of recognition experienced by Southerners, Ripley's narrative seems to suggest that it is the deprivation of recognition that forces women out of the shadows of the domestic sphere. For this reason, Ripley's visibility as a vaguely enterprising woman is matched by her discretion about the extent of her participation in the shadows of the federal government. Unlike Velazquez, therefore, Ripley frames this economic visibility not as an alternative to national recognition but, rather, as the only recourse for Confederate women who would otherwise prefer to remain within the bounds of the domestic sphere. It is, moreover, an undesirable outcome for Southern women.

Therefore, Ripley does not directly mention her role in this trade even when she describes in vivid detail the various actors participating in and transactions related to blockade running. She writes,

> The Confederate Government made stupendous efforts to procure army supplies through Mexico; but the great distance, scarcity of transportation, lack of harmony between the several branches of the service, and the unscrupulousness of speculators, interfered with well-laid plans, diminished anticipated results, and subjected the officers of the department to severe criticism for their failure to furnish the army with everything needed, and vituperation from every contractor who did not get the pound of flesh demanded. Traders shipped hither merchandise of every description, with the expectation of selling to the Confederate authorities at such fabulous profit as would warrant taking proportionate hazard in regard to securing payment, all tending to wild speculation, reckless business methods, and amazing complications.[94]

In this passage, the reader cannot help but wonder how Ripley is privy to this information without being embedded in the business of blockade running. In being acutely aware of blockade running taking place in Matamoros while also representing the varied cast of speculators and businesspeople trading in Mexico, a group to which Ripley belongs, she asserts her participation in the trade as both exceptional and banal. Indeed, the Mexican government's increased scrutiny of the family's participation in commercial life in Matamoros proves Mexico to be an economically inhospitable nation for the Ripley family. Given the relationship to property that Ripley is eager to establish throughout the narrative, it is no surprise that she leaves Matamoros precisely six weeks before the fall of the Confederacy.

More importantly, in framing her departure from Matamoros and egress from blockade running as preempting the fall of the Confederacy, Ripley reinforces the central role of blockade running (and blockade runners, by extension) in the creation and maintenance of the Confederate state. This moment also demonstrates Ripley's ingeniousness as a writer. Lest she face criticism for witnessing the defeat of the South in such close proximity to the Confederacy, she frames her departure from Matamoros in ways that replicate the language describing her departure from the South at the onset of the war: her property is threatened. Hence, in drawing a parallel between the grim position of property in the antebellum South and in Matamoros, Ripley avoids being mischaracterized as a traitor by faulting dispossession for her emigration once again.

Moreover, by depicting Matamoros as dispossessing its residents of property and thus being unable to sustain a vibrant economic life, Ripley warns against replicating Mexico's weak relation to property at a historical moment when the U.S. nation is once again grappling with the material properties of the citizen. Although the decline of Matamoros's economy into "sleepy insignificance" is framed as a direct result of the end of the shadow economy, the fall of Matamoros is concurrent with the emergence of a newly united U.S. nation.[95] She writes, "We prayed for only that little strip, that Dixie-land, and the Lord gave us the whole country from the lakes to the Gulf, from ocean to ocean—all dissensions settled, all dividing lines wiped out—a united country forever and ever!"[96] Although this moment anticipates Ripley's desire to return to the United States as a member of the newly integrated national body, it also reveals the intersections of unlawful exchange and a state in flux. Ripley's departure from the corrupt and economically debased Matamoros, paired with what seems to be a discomfort in fully admitting to her participation in blockade running (and thereby admitting to her treasonous behavior), demonstrates her desire to be economically and politically represented rather than remain in the shadows and on the margins of the U.S. state at the end of the Civil War.

And yet, before returning to the United States, Ripley and her family first move to Cuba, where Ripley's property faces a similar fate as in the antebellum United States. Cuba is initially presented as a fertile area because of its natural productive capacity, but it, too, is an economically unproductive place for the Ripley family. Commercial life in Havana is as ineffective and lawless as that in Mexico. For example, though by moving to Cuba she means to replicate her lost Southern plantation life, what she encounters instead is a difficult ecological and economic terrain. This is clearly seen in the difficulties encountered by Ripley when both she and her husband are attempting to purchase a sugar plantation on the island. She writes that, after numerous failed attempts at buying plantations with imperfect titles and minor liens, "at last a plantation was found, so hopelessly in debt, so wretchedly managed, in such bad repute from lack of energy and care, that the owners (three brothers) offered to sell it, or rather consented to allow it to be sold under the heavy mortgage."[97] Even then, however, Ripley complains that "in Cuba the laws are so complex, the officials so full of dishonest trickery, that oftentimes the laws seem framed to obstruct rather than to facilitate justice."[98] Ripley's representation of Cuba is therefore replete with descriptions of it as a lawless space that sounds familiar, given her depiction of Mexico and its disregard for personal property. Moreover, her portrayal of the Cuban state as always threatening the sanctity of private property echoes her representations of the Union at the onset of the war. Cuban attitudes toward property, Ripley suggests, are dangerous and limit one's full expression of belonging and personhood.

To emphasize this point, Ripley narrates her experience of a second loss of property on the island, with the "innumerable taxes, forced loans and impressments of horses and cattle from the planters in every district" a result of the threat of insurrection on the island.[99] She adds, "There were war-taxes, church-taxes, taxes to repair bridges we had never heard of, and to make roads we could never travel."[100] Because taxation is an expression of state power, the excessive taxation is ideologically similar to the "appropriation of property" described by Ripley while she is still in the South. In this instance, she sees excessive taxation to be akin to dispossession, which results in the depletion of the economic vitality of the island. Indeed, this moment also brings to mind the famous American slogan, "No Taxation Without Representation," as an expression of self-rule and a critique of exploitation. Thus, Ripley complains that the "superb province, whose natural resources are almost inexhaustible, has been bled to death by the leeches and parasites to whom her welfare and government were intrusted."[101] The lack of integrity of property paired with excessive taxation on the island produces what Ripley calls a set of "impoverished owners."[102] Said differently, by using the paradoxical term, "impoverished owners," Ripley underscores that property without a promise of its protection by the state is worthless.

Thus, it is no surprise that to underscore how property loses its value without state protection, while also emphasizing that without state protection the person is not under obligation to follow its laws, Ripley focuses on the long history of piracy in Cuba. Even the *independistas* (Cuban independent fighters) are described as freebooters in the text. In describing Carlos Garcia, a general in the Cuban War of Independence, she writes that he was a "renowned freebooter, . . . always accompanied with a band of from ten to twenty men, he rode where he please, overawed the planter on his large estate, curse the poor peasant in his hut, took the fine horses and carefully hoarded doubloons of the humble farmer."[103] As Ripley understands it, free-booting and piracy are part of the origins of Cuban national history, and in Ripley's estimation, Cuban independistas' disregard for the property of others is an extension of the Cuban character. Ripley notes, "There were bands of freebooters—not a result of government oppression—who made robbery their only pursuit. They swept over the island with the fleetness of the wind; here to-day and there to-morrow, possessing such a thorough knowledge of all the wild country around that a place of concealment or an avenue of escape was always open to them. They did not go in detached parties, but in well-organized bands, and were a law unto themselves, bid-ding all government defiance, long before the insurrection was in existence. Indeed, marauding bands of like nature have flourished since the earliest days of *civilization* in Cuba."[104] Cuban national character, as Ripley repre-sents it, is piratic because it is structured on disregard for property. Funda-mentally, Cuba, like Mexico, is shown to be a site of lawlessness and propertied recklessness. Rule of law, while largely absent, is overbearing and incapable of protecting private property even when it is present.

In her view, the absent protections of property result in Cuba lagging in its progress toward liberalism. In Ripley's view, the right to and respect for property are the primary qualities of liberal modernity, and her descrip-tions of the Cuban economy are therefore full of images of its idleness and lack of industriousness. "Nobody seemed to be working," she writes, "every living thing had a lazy, idle air, and poor Don Pedro who belonged to a race that could not economize time, labor, or anything else, was harassed because he could not get his cane cut, for lack of help. When plans involving econ-omy of time and curtailment of domestic service were suggested, to help him out of his financial difficulties, his doleful answer was ever '*No se pu-ede!*' ('Impossible!')."[105] This representation of Cuba helps to frame it as an-tithetical to the development of the liberal person precisely because neither the Spanish colonial regime nor the independistas respect and encourage the acquisition and protection of property. In other words, although the re-bellious spirit of the independistas, in resisting a repressive colonial regime, might have otherwise resonated with the exiled Ripley, the independistas' lack of respect for private property makes this revolutionary movement an imperfect solution to the frustration of living in a colonial regime. In sum, her experience with being dispossessed once again in Cuba makes locations outside the U.S. nation-state undesirable sites for settlement. The relative fragility of property in both Mexico and Cuba reveals the formative importance of property in Ripley's feeling of belonging. Moreover, because Cuba was seen as a site for American expansion and the extension of slavery, Ripley's depiction of Cuba seems to suggest that the U.S. nation-state, having just fought a war of property, would endure a similar fate if it lacked adequate protection of property.

However, this crisis of property is perhaps expressed most clearly in Ripley's observation of the changing labor relations on the island, the introduction of Chinese coolie labor in particular. More specifically, her observations of emerging wage labor on the island helps to indicate her own position in the shifting political economy of the island as someone who witnesses her own dispossession while simultaneously observing other people being endowed with the property of personhood. In part this is because the presence of the contract especially serves as a physical marker of personhood under the law. Ripley writes, "Each man, before embarking from China, subscribed to a printed contract, one page in Spanish and the other in Chinese characters, setting forth that Ah Sin (Christian name José), province of Macao, is contracted with his own *free-will* and consent to—'La Alianza y Co.'—to do field-labor."[106] Ripley notes that every coolie "carried his contract on his person, and never hesitated to assert his rights, but sometimes had to be reminded that the planter also had rights."[107] Ripley's use of "rights" is resonant precisely because it is her "right" to property that is most compromised throughout the memoir.

Thus, while the contract stands in for the fiction of the "voluntary" nature of immigrant labor and indentured servitude in the global South, it is also a surrogate for the liberal fiction of autonomy and freedom in the marketplace.[108] After all, the contract is intended to safeguard the property of the free person and the properties in the free person. Indeed, the contract creates the contractual subject as a unique or singular person endowed with limited, albeit important, rights. Said differently, the property of the contract creates the very liberal subject that it protects. Moreover, it helps to distinguish the Chinese laborer from "the negroes, direct descendants of imported Africans," who "were more or less stupid and stolid, like 'dumb-driven cattle.'"[109] The Chinese laborer, as Ripley understands him or her, troubles the boundary between the liberal, wage laborer (racialized as white) and the abject, enslaved body (racialized as black). Moreover, in Ripley's view, the contracted, indentured Chinese laborer troubles the distinction between the black enslaved subject, who lacks all forms of personhood, and the white Confederate woman, who lacks formal rights and citizenship. That the indentured laborer is endowed with the property of the contract (and of personhood by extension), while Ripley faces dispossession repeatedly across the Americas, is especially offensive to Ripley given the racial differences between her and the Chinese laborer. Said differently, that the contract legitimizes the (albeit limited) personhood of the Chinese laborer, and that it creates a propertied person only underscores Ripley's own repeated dispossession, thereby requiring that she return to the United States at the end of the Civil War to claim the property of citizenship.

Although these moments seem to demonstrate Ripley's awareness of economic and social life on the island, which in turn clarifies her own position vis-à-vis conversations about rights and property in the creation and legitimation of full personhood (which Ripley sees as consisting of a free, represented, and protected population), they also show her dissatisfaction with Cuba and Mexico as sites of resettlement. Thus, while Ripley critiques the failed economic life on the island, at the same time, living there allows her to further refine her understanding of the particularities of property in the Americas. Given the increasing tensions on the island between Spaniards and insurgents, Ripley's departure from the island is the only possible response to being confronted with the systematic loss of property and overtaxation. The travelogue, therefore, must necessarily end with Ripley's return and reincorporation into the U.S. national body as its subject. Indeed, this expression of a desire for membership in the postbellum nation-state comes at the end of the travelogue: Ripley uses her U.S. citizenship in order to avoid paying war taxes in Cuba. Ripley conveys to the tax collectors that "our ideas of proper allegiance would not permit citizens of the United States to pay the war-taxes of a foreign government; that we had been cautioned to maintain strict neutrality with Spain and her colony."[110] In this fantastic moment of reversal, it is war that catalyzes Ripley's reunion with the newly integrated U.S. nation-state. By refusing to participate in the project of Cuban state building, Ripley asserts her belonging and adherence to the U.S. national project. Thus, during the postwar period, which is marked by the increased codification of U.S. citizenship, as well as its attendant rights and privileges, Ripley returns to the United States.

Ripley's persistent expression of her refusal of any other national affiliation reflects an ambition entirely different from Velazquez's. Velazquez's narrative is a cautionary tale that expresses the danger of being deprived of the properties of citizenship in times of crisis. Thus, while Ripley returns to the United States, Velazquez is driven into exile at the end of the war: "I longed to quit the scene of so much misery, and fully sympathized with those who preferred to fly from the country of their birth, and to seek homes in other lands, rather than to remain and be victimized, as they were being, by the wretches who had usurped all control of the affairs of the late rebel states."[111] These emigrants are looking to "find homes for themselves and their children in some land where they could live in peace and quietness, and enjoy the fruits of their labor without fear of being plundered."[112] For this reason, she travels through Latin America to different Confederate colonies, to "find out all I could about the natural resources of Venezuela, for the purpose of advising my friends in New Orleans."[113] The last chapters of the narrative are dedicated to observations of different South American countries, and she spends considerable time writing a manual for achieving wealth in these different locations, though, by Velazquez's own admission, "the schemings of ambitious politicians," as well as the revolutions taking place in these areas, once again make property very vulnerable.[114] Thus, like Ripley, Velazquez must tour Latin America to seek new sites of colonization but must inevitably fail: the only desirable solution is for the United States to uphold and preserve the properties of Americans.

Conclusion

Ripley's and Velazquez's narratives are about property on several different registers, the loss of property both national and material at the onset of the Civil War, and the interrelationship between the autonomy of property and of the recognized subject. Given the precarious position of these properties, Ripley's and Velazquez's participation in blockade running serves as a dramatization of the debates taking place over Confederate diplomatic recognition, as well as a critique of the deprivation of personal recognition instigated by Lincoln's blockade. Their narratives, while belonging to a longer tradition of Civil War–era blockade running adventure novels, are unique in exposing the political stakes of participating in blockade running and illegal forms of property ownership more generally. These stakes surpass any private gain or benefit. Rather, Ripley's and Velazquez's autobiographies demonstrate how participation in blockade running functions as an expression of resistance to national and diplomatic erasure. Moreover, these texts dramatize the ways in which Confederate populations navigated the dispossession of property and rights at the onset of the war, both politically and economically. For this population, participation in illegal forms of property ownership, as seen in blockade running, also demonstrates the importance of property in the creation of the rights-bearing subject capable of being protected by the state. By being dispossessed of property and of rights, these populations are forced to seek the protections attached to property elsewhere. However, Ripley's travelogue in particular demonstrates the futility of these exercises and posits that return to the United States as a recognized person is the best option.

Not only is the Confederate subject a type of pirate at the onset of the Civil War, but I want to stress how these texts further representations of the antebellum South as a piratic region, characterized by law breaking and, because of its disavowal of and resistance to federal law, assertions of independence in the face of unjust restrictions. However, rather than seeing the South as a piratic force, this chapter views it as engaging in forms of exchange that help to shape national policies regarding the properties of rights and the rights of property. In this context, the wartime trade that figures so prominently in Southern travelogues and adventure novels is less an act of resistance than an assertion of property ownership that stands in for citizenship when it is absent. In this context, the South is not a rogue region that, through its participation in smuggling and blockade running, is defying restrictive national laws. Rather, through its defiance, the South is participating in the active creation of the new nation.

Afterword
Pirates, Terrorists, Narcotraffickers

On Friday, June 30, 1704, six pirates were executed along the Charles River in Boston, and their dying speeches were recorded, including the speech of one Captain John Quelch. Quelch states, "Gentlemen, 'tis but little I have to speak: what I have to say is this, I desire to be informed for what I am here, I am condemned only upon circumstances. I forgive all the world: so the lord be merciful to my soul."[1] As with the pirates examined in this book, Quelch can be understood to be a historical figure who attributes his turn to the shadowy trade to a corrupt social and political climate.

However, before dying, Quelch also warns the spectators. He cautions that "they should also take care how they brought money into New-England, to be hanged for it!"[2] Quelch's warning does not clarify the subject of his admonition. Indeed, his utterance suggests that the character of exchange, or the means by which money is brought to New England, can be recast as unlawful regardless of the person's intent. Said differently, the character of a person's property and act of exchange can shift from being lawful to unlawful depending on the legal conventions of the period. After all, Quelch began his career aboard a privateering vessel, a licensed vessel of war also oftentimes used for mercantile ventures. Regardless of how Quelch began his career, he is hanged as a pirate, even inspiring a sermon by Cotton Mather. However, I begin with this anecdote not only because of how Quelch captivated the colonial imaginary but also because Quelch was the first person to be tried for the crime of piracy under maritime law outside England. That is to say, Quelch was tried for the crime of piracy without a jury. In many ways, Quelch's case exemplifies the exceptional crime of piracy, and the exceptional punishments used to discipline pirates.

More than two hundred years later, the crimes of piracy and armed robbery continue to be incontrollable, as evidenced not just by their persistence but also by the uptick in piracy in the 2000s. The seizure of MV *Faina* in September 2008 and the MV *Maersk Alabama* in April 2009 in particular captured the American imagination. After all, the seizure of the *Maersk Alabama* came to be dramatized in the film *Captain Phillips*, mentioned in the introduction. These years also coincided with increased anxiety about a number of different piracies, including heightened intellectual piracy with the popularity of sites like the Pirate Bay and WikiLeaks.[3] The increase in intellectual and nautical piracy also corresponded with heightened panic about narcotrafficking in the American hemisphere, as well as increased securitization against terrorism worldwide.

The problem of piracy, I want to underscore, has dovetailed with other extralegal crimes that threatened U.S. property and sovereignty. Indeed, narcotraffickers, like pirates, have recently come to be understood as terrorists, promoting and inflicting a type of harm so injurious that it can only be framed an "inexplicable villainy," to borrow Shannon Lee Dawdy's term in reference to piracy.[4] In 2011, for example, following a rash of particularly violent and gruesome events on the U.S. side of the U.S.-Mexico border, Texas congressman Michael McCaul took aim at the Arellano Félix organization, Los Zetas, La Familia Michoacana, and the Beltrán, Sinaloa, Juárez, and Gulf cartels in order to try to curb the violence resulting from narcotrafficking.[5] Under McCaul's proposed bill, the government would have been permitted to freeze any funds found to be tied to these organizations and would have enhanced the criminal penalties for those found aiding the cartels under the U.S. Patriot Act. The proposed bill would have used the act to reclassify narcotrafficking as a terroristic act. Indeed, this would have been a departure from American domestic and international policy justified by the War on Drugs.[6]

McCaul's bill would have criminalized engagement in narcotrafficking not as a crime in the American criminal justice system but rather as a behavior that threatens the very integrity of the American state. McCaul uses the definition of terrorism under federal law, "to intimidate a civilian population or a government by assassination or kidnappings," to propose that the cartels "fall squarely into that definition," in order to establish the threat posed by the narcotrafficker.[7] As I want to underscore, in using the Patriot Act to argue for the extrajudicial use of force against the narcotrafficker, McCaul links the narcotrafficker not just to the modern-day terrorist but also to a long line of historical "terrorists" including the pirate. Indeed, this echoes John C. Yoo's position, mentioned in the introduction, when he publicly states that terrorism requires an extrajudicial response, just as piracy did in antiquity. Terrorists, narcotraffickers, and pirates all test the limits of American jurisprudence: in addition to making possible possessory behaviors outside the law that function as surrogates for rights in a dispossessive state, these figures have, at different times, helped to expand and consolidate the powers of the state. As this afterword's opening anecdote suggests, we have been wrestling with the question of extralegal forms of exchange and violence since before the invention of America.

However, in these final pages, I want to consider the importance of acts of piracy, terrorism, and narcotrafficking in helping to consolidate and expand the reach of U.S. state power. The U.S. state has grown and been strengthened by framing certain behaviors as requiring extralegal measures to suppress acts of "inexplicable villainy." Indeed, perhaps this is why piracy continues to matter. The U.S. state has grown strong using the language of piracy to justify extrajudicial forms of punishment. The debates around the existence of Guantanamo Bay and drone strikes point to the capaciousness of the language of terrorism, which has been borrowed from the language of piracy in legitimizing extrajudicial expressions of state power. Indeed, the existence of extrajudicial spaces and expressions of state power, which run counter to the protections guaranteed by the state, have made apparent the need to sustain and perpetuate the language of piracy.[8] The language legitimating drone strikes, for example, has demonstrated the imperfect and incomplete extension of the protections attached to U.S. citizenship. And so, while this book has explored issues of piracy to answer questions around property and citizenship in American antebellum life arising from the unequal extensions of and precariousness of both citizenship and property rights in this period, piracy's significance has not diminished in the years since the Civil War's conclusion. Instead, it would seem that the persistence of shadow and illegal markets in the United States suggests that citizenship does not alleviate the problems to which piracy seems like an adequate response—namely, economic disenfranchisement and marginalization.

Said differently, the language of piracy persists for reasons other than piracy's interrelation with property. Piracy matters to the state because, in utilizing the language of piracy, the state can justify a number of different actions. The language of piracy can instantiate a number of corollary effects that go beyond those explored in these pages. To take up the question of extrajudicial force against U.S. citizens abroad, for example, means that the figure of the pirate and his position under the law continue to matter greatly to what we have come to attach to the rights of citizenship. In a document known as "The Holder Letter," which discloses the use of drone strikes on Americans abroad, Attorney General Eric H. Holder implies that citizenship alone is insufficient in protecting persons from U.S. state violence. Holder writes, "Based on generations-old legal principles and

Supreme Court decisions handed down during World War II, as well as during the current conflict, it is clear and logical that United States citizenship alone does not make such individuals immune from being targeted. Rather, it means that the government must take special care and take into account all relevant constitutional considerations, the laws of war, and other law with respect to U.S. citizens—even those who are leading efforts to kill their fellow, innocent Americans."[9] Said differently, even when the rights and protections attached to citizenship have been codified, these rights can be stripped when the citizen commits an act of exceptional violence. These acts include terrorism and narcotrafficking, as noted in McCaul's statement, but in the past have also included acts of piracy.

Indeed, the state employs a number of mechanisms to dispossess persons of certain rights and protections. As demonstrated in the language used in the Holder letter, the dispossession of certain American citizens of the rights to due process through indefinite detention or drone strikes can be justified using the language of exceptional criminality and terrorism. The Department of Justice's rationale for authorizing force against U.S. citizens abroad goes as far as to evoke the language of war. Holder states, "The Supreme Court has long 'made clear that a state of war is not a blank check for the President when it comes to the rights of the Nation's citizens.' But the Court's case law and longstanding practice and principle also make clear that the Constitution does not prohibit the Government it establishes from taking action to protect the American people from the threats posed by terrorists who hide in faraway countries and continually plan and launch plots against the U.S. homeland."[10] This letter gestures to the long history of using violence against persons who pose a "threat" to the integrity of the U.S. nation-state. However, given the terrorist's inimical position to the state, the language passed down from the Supreme Court, which becomes the basis for the justification used by the Department of Justice to legitimize these strikes, points to a contradiction in the adjudication of the crime of terrorism. The charge of terrorism, like the charge of piracy at different moments in American jurisprudence, transforms the citizen into the alternative: the enemy. After all, the phrase "to protect the American people from the threats posed by terrorists who hide in faraway countries" suggests that terrorists belong to a class of foreign enemies hostile and injurious to the well-being of the U.S. nation-state, as well as its lawful members or citizens. And so, the memo suggests, to be a terrorist is antithetical to being an "American person." Therefore, to dispossess the American person of his nationality and his rights of citizenship requires that the American person be recast as a terrorist with whom one can exist in a state of war. Indeed, Holder's position uses the language of war to justify drone attacks on U.S. citizens abroad.

However, Holder's justification, I want to underscore, goes one step further by echoing the language used by President Abraham Lincoln during the imposition of the blockade cited in chapter 5.[11] In both cases, the American citizen comes to be recast as an inimical figure to the U.S. nation-state, against whom there exists a state of war. As the case of the blockade at the onset of the U.S. Civil War demonstrates, to classify an American person as an enemy means that the American person belongs to a class of recognized belligerents. And yet, as with members of the Confederacy, U.S. citizens belonging to terroristic organizations pose a problem to the clear designations of and separation between the citizen and the enemy. This paradox, between the public enemy, a label that signals that the person belongs to a separate sovereign state against whom one can wage war, and another class of stateless enemies, raises the question of recognition once again.[12] As with the pirates of antiquity, the modern-day terrorist or narcotrafficker is a figure whose presence troubles the ambiguous and fungible legal designations for persons who threaten the state. As *hostis humani generis*, the pirate and terrorist are exiled from the private protections of the state and the public protections abstractly promised under the law of nations. The terrorist and the narcotrafficker, like the pirate, are neither citizens nor lawful enemies. Indeed, their indeterminate position vis-à-vis a number of legal traditions leaves this population vulnerable to a range of different forms of violence.

Thus, the rights and privileges attached to U.S. citizenship continue to be precarious and contingent even with the crystallization of national citizenship after the conclusion of the Civil War. As in the case of the terrorist in U.S. law in the wake of the war on terror, the rights attached to citizenship can be annulled and revoked, and the citizen can be recast as a figure antithetical to citizenship altogether. While *Fugitives, Smugglers, and Thieves* has taken up the question of extralegal forms of property ownership understood through the framework of piracy, as I have also shown in the preceding chapters, piracy matters greatly to understanding U.S. citizenship. Piracy has always impacted and been affected by questions of membership and belonging in a national community. Indeed, it matters deeply that extralegal acts of violence, the formative language used to describe the crime of piracy, continue to shape the language of citizenship. Moreover, the citizen can be impacted by language adjudicating the crime of piracy, as well as other exceptional crimes, including treason and terrorism, that take place on the fringes of American territory and on the periphery of any individual state's power. In other words, piracy and other exceptional crimes are critical to understanding the state's capacity to restrict recognition and exile persons from the category of the citizen.

The narcotrafficker and the terrorist, like the pirate of antiquity, are figures that continue to test the authority of and the limits of the state. More importantly, these figures bring to the surface the ways in which the language of citizenship can be undone by the language of exceptional criminality, which has its origins in the language used to describe the pirate and the crime of piracy. As I have shown, piracy is not simply about property. Rather, the pirate brings to the surface the complicated relationship between the individual and the state. Notwithstanding the continued significance and persistence of shadow economies, piracy and the pirate continue to matter because of what they make perceptible for the study of the state and the protections it offers to its members. The pirate, the narcotrafficker, and the terrorist are figures that trouble the state and that make apparent the legal contortions the state must undergo in order to retitle citizens as *hostis humani generis*, or enemies of mankind. Piracy matters now, just as it always has, because piracy is critical to the study of property, to the study of the person, and to the study of the state.

Notes

Introduction

1. Commonly thought to be a pseudonym for Daniel Defoe, though this has been contested.

2. Though the subject of the "attack" or "aggressive" action is left unclear, the term was taken up by the Greek historian Polybius to mean the "naval marauders" of classical antiquity (Alfred P. Rubin and Boczek, "Private and Public History," 38).

3. This book builds on contemporary scholarship in hemispheric American studies, as well as critical debates in comparative regional and global Southern studies that have drawn attention to the complex networks of material and intellectual exchange across regional and national borders. For work in hemispheric American studies, see Handley, *Postslavery Literatures in the Americas*; Gruesz, *Ambassadors of Culture*; Levander and Levine, *Hemispheric American Studies*; Luis-Brown, *Waves of Decolonization*; and Murphy, *Hemispheric Imaginings*. For works in comparative Southern studies, see Smith and Cohn, *Look Away!*, and Cohn, *History and Memory*.

4. There is a vast archive of historical and empirical work on the study of the pirate, from which parts of this project have emerged. These works include Bromley, *Corsairs and Navies, 1660–1760*; Rediker, *Between the Devil*; and Rediker, *Villains of All Nations*. It is also indebted to work on smuggling in the American context. See Andreas, *Smuggler Nation*; Andrew W. Cohen, *Contraband*; Dawdy, *Building the Devil's Empire*; and Luskey and Woloson, *Capitalism by Gaslight*.

5. Grahn, *Political Economy of Smuggling*, xv.

6. See Hartman, *Scenes of Subjection*; McKittrick, *Demonic Grounds*; and Sharpe, *Ghosts of Slavery*.

7. United States v. Palmer, 16 U.S. 610, 610 (1818).

8. Heller-Roazen, *Enemy of All*; Fenn, "Justinian." For discussions of common law and piracy, see Coke, *Institutes of the Lawes of England*.

9. Hall, *Treatise on International Law*, 268.

10. Ibid., 310–11.

11. Indeed, this is a common interpretation of piracy, as also seen in Heller-Roazen, *Enemy of All*.

12. Blackstone, *Commentaries*, 71.

13. Dawdy, "Why Pirates Are Back," 373–74.

14. Ibid.

15. Indeed, Jody Greene's antecedent for the extrajuridical use of force against terrorists is the use of force against the pirate (Greene, "Hostis Humani Generis").

16. See Burgess, *Politics of Piracy*; Hanna, *Pirate Nests*; Latimer, *Buccaneers of the Caribbean*; Mylonas, *Politics of Nation-Building*; Thomson, *Mercenaries, Pirates, and Sovereigns*; and Ruff, *Violence in Early Modern Europe*.

17. Thomson, *Mercenaries, Pirates, and Sovereigns.*

18. Ibid., 140.

19. This rich scholarship begins with Samuel Eliot Morison's seminal work on Atlantic maritime life (*Maritime History of Massachusetts Bay*) and ends with recent works such as Burg, *Sodomy and the Pirate Tradition*; Leeson, *Invisible Hook*; Linebaugh and Rediker, *Many-Headed Hydra*; Pennell, *Bandits at Sea*; Rediker, *Between the Devil*; Rediker, *Villains of All Nations*; and Turley, *Rum, Sodomy, and the Lash.*

20. Leeson, *Invisible Hook*; Rediker, *Villains of All Nations.*

21. See Heyman and Smart, *States and Illegal Practices*; Neuwirth, *Shadow Cities*; Neuwirth, *Stealth of Nations*; Perlman, *Myth of Marginality*; Roy and AlSayyad, *Urban Informality*; Smart, "Unruly Places"; Venkatesh, *Off the Books*; and Wacquant, *Urban Outcasts.*

22. Lewis, "Economic Development."

23. Hobsbawm, *Primitive Rebels.*

24. Dawdy, *Building the Devil's Empire*, 243.

25. Peñalver and Katyal, "Property Outlaws."

26. Rediker, *Between the Devil*, 251.

27. Dawdy and Bonni, "Towards a General Theory of Piracy," 679.

28. Rediker, *Villains of All Nations*, 26.

29. Linebaugh and Rediker, *Many-Headed Hydra*, 163.

30. See Karraker, *Piracy Was a Business*; Leeson, *Invisible Hook*; Starkey, *British Privateering Enterprise*; and Starkey, "Pirates and Markets."

31. See Rediker, *Between the Devil.*

32. Knighton, "Wreck of the *Corsair*," 91.

33. Though not referring to piracy explicitly, the editors of the recent edited volume *Capitalism by Gaslight* note that it is imperative that scholars "examine the many people, goods, transactions, strategies, and economic practices that have been obscured by nineteenth-century debates about the meanings of economic activity and more recent arguments about what constituted capitalism" (Luskey and Woloson, introduction to *Capitalism by Gaslight*, 2). These editors make visible the properties and exchanges in the shadows of—but directly adjacent to—the above-board economic activities that helped to shape the American political economy of the eighteenth and nineteenth centuries. These activities, the editors propose, give us a glimpse of the numerous but less well-known moments of self-creation in the narratives of American capitalist expansion, transformation, and revolution.

34. Turley, *Rum, Sodomy, and the Lash*, 36.

35. The transgressive characteristics of the pirate extend even to expressions of sexuality and desire that might be impermissible on land. For example, in his seminal study of sexuality at sea, Turley notes, "The pirate lived outside the boundaries of conventional European society," thus making it possible for him to transgress sexually, as well as economically and politically (ibid., 2). This subject is also taken up in Burg, *Sodomy and the Pirate Tradition.*

36. Certainly, there are other traditions in the study of citizenship that I could also draw on, such as the concepts of civil, political, and social citizenship outlined by T. H. Marshall in *Citizenship and Social Class*. While some forms of citizenship ensure the enjoyment of the rights purportedly guaranteed by the state (social citizen-

ship), others, such as political citizenship, refer to the right to exercise political power through voting, for example. Social citizenship in particular ensures the right to "maintain cultures and languages differing from the dominant ones without losing civil or political rights or membership in the national community" (Glenn, *Unequal Freedom*, 80). Social citizenship has expanded to include cultural citizenship (see Ong, "Cultural Citizenship as Subject-Making"), sexual citizenship (Berlant and Warner, "Sex in Public"), and economic citizenship (seen in New Deal policies), for example. And yet, even Marshall acknowledges that civil citizenship, or the rights necessary to experience freedom, includes "liberty of the person, freedom of speech, thought and faith," but also the "right to own property and to conclude valid contracts" (Marshall, *Citizenship and Social Class*, 10).

37. Locke, *Second Treatise of Government*, 19.

38. Hartog, "Constitution of Aspiration," 1021.

39. Locke, *Second Treatise of Government*, 90.

40. Alexander, *Commodity and Propriety*, 1.

41. Locke, *Second Treatise of Government*, 46.

42. Incidentally, the Fourth Amendment also delimits the right to privacy through the right to the protection of property, ensuring "the right of the people to be secure in their persons, houses, papers, and effects, against unreasonable searches and seizures." The right to privacy, in other words, is parsed out through the state's guarantee to not interfere with the subject's property.

43. Blackstone, *Commentaries*, 374.

44. See Horwitz, *Transformation of American Law*, and Alexander, *Commodity and Propriety*.

45. Hohfled, "Fundamental Legal Conceptions"; Banner, *American Property*.

46. Best, *Fugitive's Properties*, 131.

47. For literature on the significance of property ownership as a cornerstone of liberal thought in the United States and American political economy, see Banner, *American Property*; Henry C. Carey, *Past*; Gore, *Property, Its Duties and Rights*; Hacker, *Triumph of American Capitalism*; Hartz, *Liberal Tradition in America*; Macpherson, *Political Theory of Possessive Individualism*; Macpherson, "Introduction"; Pocock, *Politics, Language, and Time*; Pocock, *Virtue, Commerce, and History*; Purdy, *Meaning of Property*; Schlatter, *Private Property*; Skidmore, *Right of Man to Property!*; and Wood, *Radicalism of the American Revolution*.

48. Purdy, *Meaning of Property*, 32.

49. Ibid., 17.

50. Ibid., 2.

51. Tocqueville, *Democracy in America*, 11.

52. Ibid., 13.

53. Hamilton, "Federalist Paper No. 71," 430.

54. See Katherine Adams, *Owning Up*; Castronovo and Nelson, *Materializing Democracy*; Coviello, *Intimacy in America*; Dillon, *Gender of Freedom*; Dillon, *New World Drama*; and Nelson, *National Manhood*.

55. For some examples of work on the state and its dispossession of citizenship, personhood, and property for certain populations in scholarship as diverse as literary

studies, history, and legal studies, see Best, *Fugitive's Properties*; Hartman, *Scenes of Subjection*; Ngai, *Impossible Subjects*; Harris, "Whiteness as Property"; and Penningroth, *Claims of Kinfolk*.

56. Tirres, "Ownership without Citizenship," 45.

57. Kunal Parker develops this idea of black foreigners by tracing the development of some sense of national citizenship rooted in fundamental and movable national rights in the early nineteenth century. These rights, Parker argues, included the privilege of passing through or residing in any state of one's choosing "for the purposes of trade, agriculture, professional pursuits, or otherwise," and these rights come to be framed as rights to travel through national (as well as state) territories (Kunal Parker, "Citizenship and Immigration Law," 177). As Parker argues, laws limiting black movement, settlement, ownership, and belonging identified them as perpetually foreign.

58. Ibid., 174.

59. Ibid., 183.

60. Best's *Fugitive's Properties* examines the homology between legal and commodity forms, arguing that the "expressive similarities and structural connections between fugitive persons and fugitive personhood" shape the development of intellectual property law (17). Meanwhile, Jeffory A. Clymer's *Family Money* examines the social forms of property and family through the structures of racial difference in the nineteenth century. This work examines how literary authors reimagine the conditions of wealth when the law is contradictory and contingent and especially when law forecloses personal property rights for enslaved populations. Finally, Joan Dayan's "Legal Slaves and Civil Bodies" examines the social and civil death of the enslaved person through the lens of property. Indeed, this work borrows from Hartman's *Scenes of Subjection*, which examines the civic death of dispossessed slaves as property. For historical treatments, see Penningroth, *Claims of Kinfolk*, and Schweninger, *Black Property Owners*.

61. See Harris, "Whiteness as Property," and Hartman, *Scenes of Subjection*.

62. Harris, "Whiteness as Property." More recently, Alexander Weheliye's *Habeas Viscus*, for example, expands on Hortense Spiller's work by looking to the place of race in the creation of the category of the human.

63. Coviello, *Intimacy in America*.

64. Peñalver and Katyal, "Property Outlaws."

65. See Keynes, *Undeclared War*; London, *Victory in Tripoli*; Oren, *Power, Faith, and Fantasy*; Smethurst, *Tripoli*; Toll, *Six Frigates*; and Tucker, *Stephen Decatur*. Indeed, Edward Keynes considers the first Barbary War to be one of several "undeclared wars," which include the Civil and Vietnam Wars (91). These wars stand in contradistinction to publicly declared wars such as the Mexican-American War, the Spanish-American War, and the two world wars.

66. Allison, *Stephen Decatur*, 217. Also see Cooper, *History of the Navy*; Louras, *James Fenimore Cooper*; and Tucker, *Stephen Decatur*.

67. Blum, "Pirated Tars, Piratical Texts," 137.

68. See Armstrong, "Captivity and Cultural Capital"; Armstrong and Tennenhouse, "American Origins"; Armstrong and Tennenhouse, *Imaginary Puritan*; Baepler, "Re-

writing the Barbary Captivity Narrative"; Baepler, *White Slaves, African Masters*; Blum, "Pirated Tars, Piratical Texts"; and Blum, *View from the Masthead*.

69. Baepler, "The Barbary Captivity Narrative in American Culture," 220.

70. Ibid., 224.

71. A few works examine American maritime life and the creation of American national identity, for example, Gilje, *To Swear Like a Sailor*. This work looks to the American maritime world to argue that sailors helped to create a distinct American national identity as the "common man." Paul A. Gilje's earlier work, *Liberty on the Waterfront*, examines the importance of early American sailors in resisting Great Britain during the Revolutionary War. Only one work in history explicitly treats citizenship's interrelationship with maritime labor, and even this work overlooks piracy. This work, Perl-Rosenthal, *Citizen Sailors*, however, is extremely valuable in its discussion of how postrevolutionary sailors helped to create the first model of U.S. citizenship.

72. Such as those proposed by Hartman in *Scenes of Subjection*.

73. This is, in part, Hartman's argument in her seminal work, *Scenes of Subjection*, and Lisa Lowe's argument in *The Intimacies of Four Continents*, both of which examine the place of the dehumanized property of the slave at the heart of European liberalism. More recently, Dillon has looked to performance and the theater in the eighteenth century as spaces of world making, or new publics that are responding to the problematics of colonialism, which "subtends and structures new dispensations of political freedom insofar as they depend on a shadow economy of dispossession" (Dillon, *New World Drama*, 8).

74. Roberts, "Dispossession and Cosmopolitan Community," 254.

75. Ibid.

76. Those undertaken in Gerassi-Navarro, *Pirate Novels*; Moore, *Pirates and Mutineers*; and Turley, *Rum, Sodomy, and the Lash*, for example. Moreover, I depart from a related canon of criticism on sea literature due to my focus on figures other than sailors and maritime laborers. Indeed, the criticism on maritime life and oceanic narratives is vast, with notable titles including Blum, *View from the Masthead*; Margaret Cohen, *Novel and the Sea*; and Philbrick, *James Fenimore Cooper*. Margaret Cohen, for example, furthers an "adventure poetics," which, as Cohen sees it, is a "traveling genre" popularized by Daniel Defoe (Margaret Cohen, *Novel and the Sea*, 8).

77. Woertendyke, *Hemispheric Regionalism*, 4.

78. Ibid., 8.

79. Yoo, quoted in Mayer, "Outsourcing Torture."

80. Cicero, *De Officiis* (On duties), cited in Heller-Roazen, *Enemy of All*, 101.

81. Greene, "Hostis Humani Generis."

Chapter One

1. After all, piracy is in part a behavior that has existed in response to monopolistic state authority, as Kenneth Kinkor argues (Kinkor, "Black Men under the Black Flag," 197).

2. See Hartman, *Scenes of Subjection*, and Lisa Lowe, *Intimacies of Four Continents*.

3. Wayne Franklin, *James Fenimore Cooper*, xi.

4. Indeed, it is no surprise that Simms would use piracy to allegorize this dispossession, given that the Confederacy viewed their dispossession as a form of colonial domination.

5. For works on American literature and maritime life, see Bender, *Sea-Brothers*; Blum, *View from the Masthead*; Peck, "Repossession of America"; and Springer, *America and the Sea*.

6. In *Building the Devil's Empire*, Shannon Lee Dawdy examines the importance of piracy and smuggling in the development of New Orleans's political economy in the eighteenth century, for example. In his work on smuggling, Peter Andreas writes that "smuggling—and attempts to police it—have made and remade America, from the illicit molasses in colonial times to drug trafficking today. . . . Smuggling, it turns out, has been as much about building up the American state as about subverting it" (Andreas, *Smuggler Nation*, x–xi). For works looking to piracy specifically, see Katherine Anderson, "Female Pirates and Nationalism," and Gerassi-Navarro, *Pirate Novels*.

7. "No es el nombre de mis padres el que voy a buscar en ese tiempo, puesto que cuando mis padres me lo negaron, es que no me creyeron digno de llevarle. Voy a buscar, señora, el nombre que satisface más al justo orgullo del hombre. Voy a buscar el nombre que se forma por los propios méritos, no el que se toma prestado de los ajenos" (Ancona, *El filibustero*, 30). Unless otherwise noted, translations are my own.

8. Gerassi-Navarro, *Pirate Novels*, 96.

9. Ibid.

10. The Jacinto Canek rebellion of 1761, for example, resulted in the death of a number of Spanish officials. Indeed, it was a difficult region to control because of its geographic location. This rebelliousness persisted even after Mexican independence. Yucatán declared itself an autonomous region in 1823 and 1841. The state even appealed to the United States for annexation during the Mexican-American War. Moreover, the Caste War (1847–1901) also demonstrated the revolutionary spirit pervasive in this region.

11. Gallant, "Brigandage, Piracy, Capitalism, and State-Formation," 37.

12. Adam Smith, *Wealth of Nations*, 3:378.

13. Ibid.

14. Ancona, *El filibustero*, v.

15. Gerassi-Navarro, *Pirate Novels*, 100.

16. Ibid., 101.

17. Peck, "Repossession of America," 597.

18. Cooper, *Water-Witch*, 2.

19. Ibid., 108.

20. Ibid., 288–89.

21. Ibid., 118.

22. Ibid., 94.

23. Ibid., 99.

24. Ibid., 295.

25. Ibid., 140.

26. Ibid., 83.

27. Ibid., 84.

28. Ibid., 181.

29. What Andy Doolen calls the promises and perils of the interracial and international exchange taking place in eighteenth-century New York (Doolen, *Fugitive Empire*, 15).

30. Cooper, *Water-Witch*, 28–29.

31. Cooper, *Sea Tales*, 436.

32. Ibid., 778.

33. Ibid., 519.

34. Ibid., 614.

35. Ibid., 685.

36. Ibid., 865.

37. Peck, "Repossession of America," 598.

38. Cooper, *Sea Tales*, 868 (italics mine).

39. Ibid., 514.

40. Ibid., 565.

41. Ibid., 725–26 (italics mine).

42. Ibid., 725.

43. Cooper, *American Democrat*, 77–78, 135.

44. Cooper, *Water-Witch*, 12.

45. "Following Scott, when reviewers before 1860 laid out a history of prose fiction, they generally used the term *romance* to refer to the form throughout the ages and the term *novel* to imply a modem type distinguished by its concentration on the ordinary and the contemporary. Then they slid into using the term *romance* to mean pre-modern types of novels, those produced in the past century which depended on supernatural and marvelous events to resolve their plots and to achieve their effects" (Baym, "Concepts of the Romance," 437).

46. Berger, "Killing Tom Coffin."

47. Simms, *Yemassee*, 1:121.

48. Mayfield, " 'The Soul of a Man!,' " 479.

49. Collins, "Experiments in Realism," 9.

50. See Collins, "Experiments in Realism"; Fox-Genovese, "Fettered Mind"; Guilds, *William Gilmore Simms*; Hoefer, " 'The Slaves That They Are' "; King, "Foolish Talk 'about Freedom' "; Mayfield, " 'The Soul of a Man!' "; Charles S. Watson, *From Nationalism to Secessionism*; and Wimsatt, *Major Fiction of William Gilmore Simms*.

51. Simms, *Yemassee*, 1:100.

52. Ibid., 1:96.

53. Ibid., 1:122.

54. Fox-Genovese, "Fettered Mind," 633.

55. Simms, *Yemassee*, 2:27–28.

56. *"Ramon,"* 35–36.

57. Ibid., 37.

58. Ibid., 54.

59. Ibid., 98–99.

60. Philbrick, *James Fenimore Cooper*, 94.

61. *"Ramon,"* 98–99.

62. Philbrick, *James Fenimore Cooper*, 88.

Chapter Two

1. Indeed, it would seem that this is, in part, the reason why destroying currency is considered to be a federal crime: "Whoever mutilates, cuts, defaces, disfigures, or perforates, or unites or cements together, or does any other thing to any bank bill, draft, note, or other evidence of debt issued by any national banking association, or Federal Reserve bank, or the Federal Reserve System, with intent to render such bank bill, draft, note, or other evidence of debt unfit to be reissued, shall be fined under this title or imprisoned not more than six months, or both" (Coins and Currency, 18 U.S.C. § 333 [1948]).

2. U.S. Const. art. III, § 3.

3. The yellow fever epidemic of Philadelphia in the summer of 1793, as Andy Doolen has written, delivered a devastating blow to the young nation's capital. As he writes, the epidemic killed five thousand of the city's residents and drove more than three times as many residents to the countryside (Doolen, *Fugitive Empire*, 77). The epidemic was seen as a product of the ills of American commercial society, as well as a foreign contagion, the contagion of blackness and black revolution in particular (Gould, "Race, Commerce"). After all, Haitian uprisings had begun two years prior and news of this conflict had begun washing up on American shores in ways that produced extreme anxiety.

4. Charles Brockden Brown, *Arthur Mervyn*, 17.

5. Ibid., 16.

6. Ibid., 17.

7. Mihm, *Nation of Counterfeiters*, 31. The value of currency, however, "was not something inert, something inherent in the note itself, the way that gold in a coin was thought to have intrinsic value. Far from it: value was something that materialized and became tangible when the note was exchanged, when one person put confidence in the note of another" (ibid., 10).

8. For works in history looking to counterfeiting, see Benner, *Fraudulent Finance*; Mihm, *Nation of Counterfeiters*; Kenneth Scott, *Counterfeiting in Colonial America*; and Tremmel, *Counterfeit Currency*. Other works, such as Fliegelman's *Prodigals and Pilgrims*, look to the place of antiauthoritarian activity in the early republic. For works looking specifically to representations of counterfeiting in American literature, see Anthony, *Paper Money Men*; Baker, *Securing the Commonwealth*; Balkun, *American Counterfeit*; Germana, *Standards of Value*; Henkin, *City Reading*; and Mihm, "Alchemy of the Self." These works are diverse in their assessment of counterfeiting. Some of them have looked broadly to value and form, while others look more closely at the place of the counterfeiter in nineteenth-century American life. As some critics note, circulating counterfeit currency also requires that the subject imitate a proper economic subject, to become a confidence man or woman, what Peter Jaros calls "a public specter," and execute a performance that, as Stephen Mihm and Jaros argue, relies on "theatricality" (Jaros, "Personating Stephen Burroughs"; Mihm, *Nation of Counter-*

feiters, 37). In part, this is aligned with a more recent strain of criticism such as William Huntting Howell's *Against Self-reliance*, which argues against dominant modes of reading American autonomous exceptionalism.

9. Mihm, *Nation of Counterfeiters*, 79. Indeed, this is, in part, Howell's argument in *Against Self-reliance*, where he argues that imitation is critical to the project of American independence, though Howell does not examine the place of counterfeiting in these debates.

10. Batchelder, "Counterfeiting of Colonial Paper Money."

11. Quoted in Wood, *Revolutionary Characters*, 135.

12. Hamilton, "Federalist, No. 30," 188.

13. See the bundle-of-rights theory furthered in Hohfled, "Fundamental Legal Conceptions," and Honoré, "Ownership."

14. Breck, *Historical Sketch*, 6.

15. Although language expressly stating the counterfeiter's inimical position to the state might not be present in the Constitution, the Constitution mentions only three federal criminal offenses punishable by death: treason, piracy, and counterfeiting. Article I, Section 8, of the U.S. Constitution enumerates the powers of Congress, which include the power "to provide for the punishment of counterfeiting the Securities and current coin of the United States" (U.S. Const. art. I, § 8).

16. State v. Tutt, 18 S.C.L. 44, 45 (1831). This is also the language used in Title 18 of the U.S. Federal Criminal Code mentioned in n. 1.

17. Ibid.

18. Batchelder, "Counterfeiting of Colonial Paper Money," 30.

19. State v. Tutt, 18 S.C.L. 44, 45 (1831).

20. Fox v. State of Ohio, 46 U.S. 410, 411 (1847).

21. Mihm, *Nation of Counterfeiters*, 108.

22. In an age of rampant counterfeiting, the "well-worn" bank note, authentic or counterfeit, was most valuable and reliable because its worn appearance demonstrated the note had passed through many trusting hands.

23. Ibid., 25, 15.

24. Ibid., 14.

25. Citing a quote by John Quincy Adams from 1837, Mihm notes that, for Adams, "the only difference between a bank director and a counterfeiter . . . was that the counterfeiter gave 'evidence of superior skill and superior modesty'" (Mihm, *Nation of Counterfeiters*, 9). Mihm continues, "Wildcat banks, unincorporated banks, and fraudulent, nonexistent banks established by frontier financiers all blurred the boundaries between legitimate banking and outright fraud. . . . Indeed, the wildcat banker came to be seen as a more disturbing figure than a conventional counterfeiter" (ibid., 160).

26. Mihm, *Nation of Counterfeiters*, 315.

27. Ibid., 307.

28. In his seminal work, *A Nation of Counterfeiters*, Mihm has called confidence men like Burroughs the embodiment of the democratic self-fashioning subject that defines this period. He argues that "new possibilities emerged for middling white men like Burroughs; they could now become architects of their own destiny, instead of remaining mired in inherited roles and obligations. It followed that social roles,

like theatrical parts, could be assumed and abandoned at will" (ibid., 37). This work has looked to Burroughs's memoir to argue that Burroughs represents a new form of American individualism, self-interest, and enterprise (Williams, "Rogues, Rascals and Scoundrels," 13). Yet, as some critics have argued, Burroughs's memoir represents an anarchic view of individualism, and the imitability of currency and character had, in his view, "dissolved the organic bonds of traditional society" (Kaplan, "Theft and Counter-theft," 520).

29. Burroughs's career, according to Mihm, "mirrored the final dissolution of the colonial architecture of authority, and its replacement by a more raucous and individualistic expression of political and economic power.... In his attacks (rhetorical and otherwise) on this older order, Burroughs enjoyed a certain kinship with a new breed of self-made political and economic entrepreneurs with whom he shared a scorn of prerogative and inherited rights," a view supported by many critics of Burroughs's work (Mihm, *Nation of Counterfeiters*, 56). For a similar argument, also see Daniel A. Cohen, *Pillars of Salt*. He is the self-made subject that Franklin imagines to be at the heart of the American economic person (Downes, *Democracy, Revolution, and Monarchism*).

30. Burroughs, *Memoirs*, 7.

31. Ibid., 270.

32. Indeed, this is especially true given the property restrictions on both free and enslaved black persons of the antebellum period. Therefore, the pleasures gained from property are neither uniformly granted nor uniformly accessed. The property of whiteness, understood through specific ethnic qualifications, in other words, is intertwined with the pleasures of property. Moreover, given the ties between property and personhood, the types of possession made possible by possessing whiteness are critical in the creation of person. As I show in the following chapter, for example, by being denied the rights to the primary possession of the body, in addition to a range of other properties, enslaved black persons were denied the property of personhood. Conversely, black persons were denied the property of citizenship, a deprivation underwritten and bolstered by the laws denying enslaved persons a range of different properties. In fact, the denial of personhood, or exclusion from the category of person or human, is tied to both whiteness and property. Said differently, self-possession is attached to whiteness, and whiteness provides a framework for normative personhood. However, despite these complicated and confusing dynamics, what remains true is that property provides the framework for understanding the qualities of both person and citizen.

33. Burroughs, *Memoirs*, 267.

34. Ibid., 95.

35. Ibid.

36. Ibid.

37. As Daniel E. Williams notes, Burroughs echoes the Declaration of Independence by writing, "Happiness is the pursuit of all" (Williams, "In Defense of Self," 110).

38. Burroughs, *Memoirs*, 98.

39. Ibid., 100.

40. Ibid., 101–2.

41. Ibid., 102.

42. Ibid., 38.

43. As Christopher Jones argues, Burroughs's use of the picaresque, an episodic narrative that recounts the adventures of a youth, functions to critique extant social, religious, and political authority (Christopher Jones, "Praying upon Truth").

44. Burroughs, *Memoirs*, 182–83.

45. Ibid., 183 (italics mine).

46. Ibid., 119.

47. Ibid., 141.

48. Ibid., 209.

49. Ibid., 119.

50. For example, scholars have examined the novel's depiction of the yellow fever outbreak in Philadelphia, arguing that yellow fever was associated with blackness and the threat of the spread of black revolution across the hemisphere in the wake of Haitian independence (Gould, "Race, Commerce"). Doolen's work on the novel explores the relationship between the development of the American political economy, its dependence on slave labor, and the terror this generated in the national imaginary (Doolen, *Fugitive Empire*). He frames the threat of black revolution through yellow fever contagion and the discourse of health. Robert Levine argues that the many unforeseen "revolutions" in the novel (the plot twists, the deaths, the impersonations) are representative of a period in postrevolutionary America in which the Revolution was seen as "a blow to the imagination, an unexpected disorienting shock, an unforeseen upheaval that makes a mockery of stabilizing controls and simple cause-effect schematizations" (Levine, "Arthur Mervyn's Revolutions," 145). In *The Culture and Commerce of the Early American Novel*, Stephen Shapiro argues the shifts in perspective in *Arthur Mervyn* reflect the changing economic climate during the period. Finally, some others have examined this gothic novel as offering a "model of community" that reflects the changing ethnic demography in the postrevolutionary nation-state (Roberts, "Gothic Enlightenment," 308). One critic writes "Arthur Mervyn's story illustrates the destruction of Philadelphia and seeks to construct a global consciousness about an individual's resilience during a localized outbreak" (Tarr, "Infectious Fiction," 152). These works also acknowledge the importance of secrets and secrecy in these novels in facilitating American national growth both domestically and abroad, since secrecy is associated as much with American revolution and radicalism as with mercenary plots against the fledgling nation (Downes, "Constitutional Secrets").

51. Mathew Carey, *Short Account*, 11–12.

52. Ibid., 55.

53. Charles Brockden Brown, *Arthur Mervyn*, 36.

54. Ibid., 32.

55. Ibid., 64.

56. Ibid., 242.

57. Ibid., 29, 32; Philip Barnard and Stephen Shapiro, introduction to ibid., xliii.

58. Charles Brockden Brown, *Arthur Mervyn*, 320.

59. Ibid., 230.

60. Ibid., 215.

61. Ibid., 216.

62. Ibid., 74.

63. Ibid.

64. Ibid.

65. Ibid.

66. Madison, *Papers*, 266.

67. Charles Brockden Brown, *Arthur Mervyn*, 148. Indeed, even the envelope structure of the text, which includes a number of first-person authorial voices, is a formal rehearsal of Brown's understanding of the lack of any singular American person. Moreover, this narrative structure closely parallels the various chambers and antechambers of Welbeck's gothic Philadelphia home, where Welbeck hides his secrets and schemes.

68. Hsuan Hsu has studied Brown's other works of fiction to examine the role of ventriloquism and vocal displacements as emblematic of the ethos of democratic expansionism that characterized the early nineteenth century, in that it exposes "the horrific violence and brutal displacements that [expansion] both requires and disavows" (Hsu, *Geography*, 26).

69. This has been informed by work on Brown's skepticism of speculation and rampant economic liberalism in the postrevolutionary state. See Ostrowski, " 'Fated to Perish by Consumption,' " and Weyler, *Intricate Relations*.

70. Charles Brockden Brown, *Arthur Mervyn*, 69.

71. Ibid., 70.

72. Trilling, *Sincerity and Authenticity*.

73. Charles Brockden Brown, *Arthur Mervyn*, 40.

74. Ibid., 63.

75. Ibid., 79.

76. Ibid., 305.

77. Burroughs, *Memoirs*, 82.

78. Charles Brockden Brown, *Arthur Mervyn*, 172.

79. Ibid., 175.

80. Ibid., 92.

81. Ibid., 124.

82. Ibid., 125.

83. Ibid., 46.

84. Ibid.

85. Ibid., 153.

86. As Cathy Davidson writes, Mervyn's "best con, perhaps (the issue is not conclusively resolved in the novel), is his resolute insistence that he had never conned anyone" (Davidson, *Revolution and the Word*, 345).

87. Ziff, *Writing in the New Nation*, 77.

88. Barosky, "Legal and Illegal Moneymaking," 536.

89. For this observation, I thank Molly Brady.

90. Eric P. Newman, "Franklin Making Money More Plentiful," 348; Benjamin Franklin, "Account of the Devices."

91. Benjamin Franklin, *Autobiography*, 64.

92. As Mihm writes, "Long before the outlaws of the late nineteenth century seized the popular imagination, tales of individual counterfeiters became the scrim through which people experiencing the market revolution could perceive and project their hopes, fears, anxieties, envy, and admiration" (Mihm, *Nation of Counterfeiters*, 16).

93. Lukasik, *Discerning Characters*, 2.

94. Ibid., 5.

95. Watts, *Writing and Postcolonialism*, 109.

96. Mihm, *Nation of Counterfeiters*, 226.

Chapter Three

1. The lack of an ending is particularly interesting given that this type of revolution never took place historically on the island. Several incidents, including the Conspiración de La Escalera in 1843 and the Ten Years' War, did mobilize Afro-Cubans against slavery. However, Cuban independence was not achieved until 1898, and even then it was not the slave-led democracy envisioned by Delany.

2. U.S. Senate, Alabama, *Digest of the Laws*, 392.

3. This is perhaps most clearly echoed in the use of the term "contraband" during the Civil War to refer to escaped slaves or to slaves who joined the Union army. The term itself *not only* suggests that slave escape is a crime committed by a slave but also reasserts the place of the enslaved body as an object of contraband in the event of slave escape. The usage of this term congeals the close relation between slave body and illegal good that I will argue Delany encourages as a test of the conceits and limits of the liberal state.

4. See Shelby, "Two Conceptions of Black Nationalism"; Stein, "'Christian Nation Calls'"; Whitlow, "Revolutionary Black Novels"; and Zeugner, "Note on Martin Delany's *Blake*."

5. See Chiles, "Within and without Raced Nations"; Clymer, "Martin Delany's *Blake*"; Crane, "Lexicon of Rights"; Ernest, *Resistance and Reformation*; Gilroy, *Black Atlantic*; Levine, *Martin Delany*; and John Lowe, "'Calypso Magnolia.'" These studies argue that the presence of the transnational and transatlantic in the text works against nation-based conceptions of blackness. They suggest that black political life requires a pan-African sensibility that is irreducible to culture but rather international in nature.

6. See Chiles, "Within and without Raced Nations"; Doolen, "'Be Cautious'"; and Sundquist, *To Wake the Nations*. Eric Sundquist argues that the rebirth of African American resistance and revolution is crucial to the American Renaissance. Andy Doolen's examination also includes a discussion of this novel as a historiographic text in which Delany reinserts the black subject into U.S. historical narratives, events, and locations. His analysis of *Blake*, however, is especially significant given his examination of it as a text that unmoors rights from American revolutionary rhetoric and ideology. Katy Chiles's is a discussion of intratextuality and the importance of *Blake*'s serialization to the consolidation of the U.S. nation-state.

7. See Nwankwo, "Promises and Perils," and Rowe, "United States Literary Culture."

8. See Crane, "Lexicon of Rights"; Hartman, *Scenes of Subjection*; and Stanley, *From Bondage to Contract*. These works have exposed the fault lines of the liberal promise of rights, focusing specifically on modes of critiquing universal humanism's inability to account for the enslaved subject. Rather than examine the ideology of slavery, this scholarship has instead focused on material relations of power (laws around the contract and property ownership, for example).

9. For example, Lisa Lowe has argued in "Intimacies of Four Continents" that these ideas of individual liberty relied on a guarantee of freedom that was dialectically situated against the "unfreedoms" of the New World that emerged from slave, indigenous, and coolie labor in the Americas. In essence, she argues that universal humanism has never been universal, nor have liberal principles been afforded equally to all. Lowe suggests that liberal humanism paradoxically relies on exclusion and the subjugation of certain populations. When discussing Hegel, Lowe notes that Hegel defines the freedoms guaranteed in liberal humanism "as a condition achieved through a developmental process in which the individual first possessed him- or herself, his or her own interiority, then put his will in an object through labor, and then made a contract to exchange the thing" (Lisa Lowe, "Intimacies of Four Continents," 201).

10. Much more radically, Delany also advocated for a slave insurrection in the United States and discussed the possibility of fomenting such a revolution with the radical abolitionist John Brown. The period in which Delany advocated for insurrection was conterminous with the period (roughly from the early 1840s to the early 1860s) in which he advocated for emigration. He, along with Brown, was interested in developing a sovereign territory for African Americans modeled after the Cherokee nation and other Indian tribes. By the early 1860s, Delany had a renewed interest in integrationism.

11. Floyd J. Miller, introduction to *Blake*, by Delany, xiii.

12. Ibid., xiv. Although not discussing Delany's *Blake* specifically, Rachel Adams's *Continental Divides* illustrates the significance of thinking about "geographies of freedom" for enslaved bodies in contemporary American (U.S., Canadian, and Mexican) literature. Her study thus illustrates the importance of thinking about these routes of freedom transnationally in order to unearth the modes through which they reconfigure American space.

13. Delany, "Condition, Elevation, Emigration and Destiny," 213.

14. Delany, "Political Destiny," 247. In his writings after the end of the Civil War, Delany amends his earlier distrust of voting by repeatedly urging Andrew Johnson to support the enfranchisement of African Americans.

15. Delany, "Condition, Elevation, Emigration and Destiny," 214.

16. Delany, "Political Destiny," 247. Unsurprisingly, Delany's formulation of rights, both political and civil, is informed by discourses on natural rights, particularly those that informed the French Revolution.

17. Delany, "Homes for the Freedmen," 425.

18. Washington, *Up from Slavery*, 315.

19. Washington, *American Negro*, 243.

20. Ibid., 18.

21. Adam Smith, *Wealth of Nations*, 2:88.

22. Ibid., 2:90–91.

23. Washington, *American Negro*, 240–41.

24. The politics of respectability is seen as a "deliberate concession to mainstream societal values," and a "strict adherence to what is socially deemed 'respectable'" at the cost of replicating discourses that are "culturally defensive, patriarchal, and heterosexist" in nature (Gross, "Examining the Politics of Respectability in African American Studies"). For more on works that critically examine the politics of respectability, see Berry, *Politics of Parenthood*; Griffin, "Black Feminists and DuBois"; Gross, *Colored Amazons*; Schechter, *Ida B. Wells-Barnett*; White, *Dark Continent of Our Bodies*; and Wolcott, *Remaking Respectability*. These works have examined the politics of respectability in the context of black womanhood. However, few have analyzed law breaking and the politics of respectability. For a treatment of this, see Elijah Anderson, *Code of the Street*, and Austin, "'Black Community.'"

25. For literary treatments, see Best, *Fugitive's Properties*, and Clymer, *Family Money*. For historical treatments, see Penningroth, *Claims of Kinfolk*, and Schweninger, *Black Property Owners*.

26. Keckley, *Behind the Scenes*. As Dorothy Porter notes in her introduction to the 1968 edition of the novel, "Mrs. Keckley hoped to obtain funds from the sale of the book to assist Mrs. Lincoln with her financial problems" (Porter, introduction to *Behind the Scenes*, by Keckley, n.p.).

27. Perhaps this is Keckley's reproduction of Harriet E. Wilson's *Our Nig*. Wilson's narrative, too, reflects a self-awareness of its own circulation, and the narrative ends with an appeal to the reader so that the author may realize her economic independence. Though not an autobiography, the novel's slippage between first and third person implicates the reader in an economy of readership that will presumably help uplift the author. Like Keckley, Wilson is dramatically self-aware of the purpose of writing, and in a radically mimetic moment, we see how her economic subjectivity is intertwined with the reader's act of reading (and purchasing) the text.

28. Henson, *Life*, 23–24.

29. Henson, *Life*.

30. Bibb, *Narrative*.

31. Ibid., 17.

32. Douglass, *My Bondage and My Freedom*, title page.

33. Douglass, "Nature of Slavery," 431.

34. Purdy, *Meaning of Property*, 91.

35. Quoted in James McCune Smith, introduction to *My Bondage and My Freedom*, by Douglass, xx–xxi.

36. In *Behind the Scenes*, Keckley creates a Contraband Relief Fund, which I see as an expression of her participation in the shadows of lawful enterprise even when her self-fashioning as an economic subject relies on the visibility and the circulation of her body, as well as the body of her text. Moreover, as I will discuss in chapter 4, Keckley's circulation helps to assert her position as an increasingly autonomous economic subject at the onset of the Civil War, a condition that she shares with white Confederate women. In fact, it is her participation in the Contraband Relief Fund

that doubly allows her to become the public face of a charitable organization, even when this organization is indirectly aiding escaped slaves when slave escape is explicitly outlawed and punished as though it were the theft of property.

37. Delany, "Political Destiny," 272.

38. This reflects classical liberalism's account of the development of man from an individual in the state of nature to the man who is citizen-subject. After the subject has possession of the inalienable self and other alienable property, John Locke suggests, the subject can then exchange the freedoms he experienced in the state of nature for the rights, safety, and protections attached to belonging to a civil or political society. The state of nature, according to Locke, drives toward the fulfillment of desire and the acquisition of property. He writes,

> Man being born, as has been proved, with a title to perfect freedom, and an uncontrouled enjoyment of all the rights and privileges of the law of nature, equally with any other man, or number of men in the world, hath by nature a power, not only to preserve his property, that is, his life, liberty and estate, against the injuries and attempts of other men; but to judge of, and punish the breaches of that law in others, as he is persuaded the offence deserves, even with death itself, in crimes where the heinousness of the fact, in his opinion, requires it. But because no *political society* can be, nor subsist, without having in itself the power to preserve the property, and in order thereunto, punish the offences of all those of that society; there, and there only is *political society*, where every one of the members hath quitted this natural power, resigned it up into the hands of the community in all cases that exclude him not from appealing for protection to the law established by it. (Locke, *Second Treatise of Government*, 46)

39. Though there has been a great deal of work on the psychic, affective, and symbolic freedoms that slaves experienced, they exist on a different register from what we are able to see in *Blake*. See Boritt and Hancock, *Slavery, Resistance, Freedom*; Camp, *Closer to Freedom*; Hammond and Mason, *Contesting Slavery*; Norrece T. Jones Jr., *Born a Child of Freedom*; and Oaks, *Slavery and Freedom*.

40. This is also echoed in W. E. B. Du Bois's work. He writes that "the piratical voyages" of slave traders take place with impunity under the American flag, "for there was seldom a United States cruiser to be met with, and there were, on the other hand, diplomats at Washington so jealous of the honor of the flag that they would prostitute it to crime rather than allow an English or a French cruiser in any way to interfere" (Du Bois, *Suppression*, 144).

41. Douglass, *My Bondage and My Freedom*, 161.

42. Ibid., 375.

43. Ibid.

44. Douglass, "Internal Slave Trade," 446.

45. Bibb, *Narrative*, 60–61.

46. Douglass, *My Bondage and My Freedom*, 159; Bibb, *Narrative*, 61.

47. Douglass, *My Bondage and My Freedom*, 310.

48. Ibid., 63, 64, 65.

49. Ibid., 36, 37.

50. Ibid., 346.

51. Brisbane, "Narrative of Albert and Mary."

52. Ibid., 113.

53. Ibid.

54. Ibid., 104.

55. Ibid., 105

56. Delany, *Blake*, 3. This moment also underscores the critique articulated in *Ramon, the Rover of Cuba*, that is, that piracy is taking place with impunity on American shores.

57. The 1827 Supreme Court decision in the case of *U.S. v. Gooding* found that owners of vessels being fitted for the slave trade could be indicted for participation in that trade, even when the defendant is not participating in the trade itself. In a case very similar to the one described at the beginning of *Blake*, John Gooding, owner of a vessel called the *General Winder* located in the port of Baltimore, had the intent of using said vessel to transport slaves from Africa to sell in Cuba. The courts admitted as evidence the testimony of Peter Coit, a man living in Saint Thomas who was approached by the captain of the *General Winder* to engage in the slave trade. After asking Captain Hill who was paying for said slaving expedition, Coit testified that Hill informed him that it was Gooding. Using the Slave Trade Act of 1789, 1808, and 1818, the courts upheld the decision to find Gooding guilty of breaking the law.

58. Delany, *Blake*, 295.

59. Delany, "Annexation of Cuba," 162.

60. An Act to Continue in Force "An Act to Protect the Commerce of the United States and Punish the Crime of Piracy," and Also to Make Further Provisions for Punishing the Crime of Piracy of 1820, 601 U.S.C. § 4 (1820).

61. Fugitive Slave Law of 1850, 462 U.S.C. § 7 (1850).

62. In *Runaway Slaves*, John Hope Franklin and Loren Schweninger acknowledge that despite the lack of exact figures having to do with the financial loss of runaways to planters and slave owners, "the financial expenditures for advertisements, rewards, slave hunters, jail fees, travel, and other expenses" (289), added to the loss of labor, turmoil caused by runaways on the plantation, and the loss of property, result in a significant loss for the slave owners.

63. Best, *Fugitive's Properties*, 17.

64. Delany, *Blake*, 287.

65. Douglass, "Nature of Slavery," 429–30.

66. Douglass, *My Bondage and My Freedom*, 190.

67. Ibid., 188–89.

68. Ibid.

69. Ibid., 190–91.

70. Ibid., 191.

71. Ibid., 190.

72. Delany, *Blake*, 32.

73. Ibid., 31.

74. Ibid., 84.

75. Delany is responding to the history of the passport as a marker of citizenship and also as an artifact that the U.S. national government began issuing exclusively in 1856. See Torpey, *Invention of the Passport*.

76. Delany, *Blake*, 135.

77. In *Neither Fugitive Nor Free*, Edlie L. Wong discusses the importance passports as "political documentation of citizenship," writing that its denial to "free black Americans" reconfirmed this population's "statelessness" (242).

78. The decade in which *Blake* is set was witness to three U.S. attempts to purchase Cuba from Spain, as well as numerous U.S. filibustering expeditions to the island. However, as we come to see in Delany's representation of Cuba, despite U.S. ambitions for the island, Cuba's treatment of its black population differs greatly from the United States' treatment in ways that resonate as more progressive. In *Blake*, the island offers free Afro-Cubans the rights so central to the foundation of personhood, and these rights to liberty, equality, and justice in turn directly threaten the institution of slavery.

79. See Guterl, "American Mediterranean," and Levander, "Confederate Cuba."

80. Delany, "Annexation of Cuba," 165.

81. Ibid.

82. Delany, *Blake*, 183.

83. Though the act of purchasing the self does emerge in U.S. slave narratives, this type of activity is seen as an exception rather than the rule of law as it was in Cuba, though some figures estimate that 42 percent of freedmen living in Ohio in 1839 had bought themselves out of slavery. For examples, see Douglass, *Narrative of the Life*, in *Autobiographies*; Douglass, *My Bondage and My Freedom*; Douglass, *Life and Times*, in *Autobiographies*; Equiano, *Interesting Narrative*; Keckley, *Behind the Scenes*; Venture Smith, *Narrative of the Life*; and Troy, *Hair-Breadth Escapes*. However, several of these narratives center on being cheated during or after the sale, thus demonstrating the precariousness and unreliability of purchasing one's freedom.

84. Delany, *Blake*, 184.

85. It is not enough to say that piracy is an anarchic act. Rather, piracy challenges the state while also allowing for a more thorough transnational economic history to emerge in its wake. Piracy, after all, is also part of the social, political, and economic order that it is always contesting. Therefore, piracy reorganizes the social, economic, and legal institutions since piracy exists alongside and in opposition to a varied set of interlocking state institutions that attempt to restrict it. Piracy grates against a system that relies on the rights of some at the expense of the rights of others, and it creates new models of social organization.

86. Jeffory A. Clymer has suggested that Blake's act of piracy resignifies the "legal understanding of slave traders as pirates. By (almost) making Blake into this figure of a pirate, even as the ship's white crew would also have legally been considered pirates, Delany multiplies the scene's levels of bitter irony concerning property ownership" (Clymer, "Martin Delany's *Blake*," 724).

87. In the many texts on piracy, Marcus Rediker and others have illustrated the significance of maritime life in the development of egalitarianism, suggesting that the pirate ship in international waters functions as the great equalizer. Pirates pose a

threat to individual nation-states and serve to destabilize the very order of the state, but they are also a varied cast of characters from different racial, ethnic, national, and economic groups. Peter Linebaugh and Rediker write that "the pirate ship was egalitarian in a hierarchical age, as pirates divided their plunder equally, leveling the elaborate structure of pay ranks common to all other maritime employments. . . . Pirates were class-conscious and justice-seeking. . . . Indeed, the 'Distribution of Justice' was a specific practice among pirates" (Linebaugh and Rediker, *Many-Headed Hydra*, 163).

88. Delany, *Blake*, 207.

89. Ibid., 209.

90. Clymer, "Martin Delany's *Blake*," 724.

91. Delany, *Blake*, 238.

92. Ibid., 273.

93. Quoted in Hartog, "Constitution of Aspiration," 1018.

94. Hartog, "Constitution of Aspiration," 1017.

95. Pole, *Pursuit of Equality*, 358.

Chapter Four

1. A note on the terminology used to describe the borderlands populations I examine over the course of this chapter: I will move back and forth between "Californio" and "Mexican" for the remainder of this work. While Ruiz de Burton insists on using "Spano American" to designate her position as a white Mexican, or Californio, I insist on using the term "Mexican" so as to designate the ways in which borderlands persons were racialized by the conclusion of the Mexican-American War. After all, Ruiz de Burton insists on racializing Californios as white precisely because, by the date of the romance's publication in 1885, there was no distinction between white and indigenous Mexicans: an "inaccuracy" or imprecision Ruiz de Burton was eager to counter with this historical novel. I also use the term "hidalgo" to signal the particular landed and classed position of the Alamar family, and other dispossessed wealthy Mexican persons living in the borderlands. Thus, while the term "hidalgo," too, is racialized, I use this term to specifically designate a community of propertied Spaniards (and later, Mexicans) who were given title to land by the Spanish Crown.

2. Ruiz de Burton, *Squatter and the Don*, 85.

3. Ibid.

4. Adelman and Aron, "From Borderlands to Borders," 816.

5. Previous work on identity formation in this time period has focused on shifting racial and ethnic relations in the borderlands. This work on identity has focused on the split between Californio or Tejano self-identification and Anglo interpellation. Rosaura Sánchez has argued, for example, that "despite critical changes in property relations and political power, all of which admittedly play a significant role in the construction of identity, several other discourses (those of language, loyalty, religion, culture, family, national origin, and, last but not least, a shared history, a memory of an imagined territorial community and a shared oppression) continue to interpellate them as Californios or Tejanos while at the same time combining disjunctively

with hegemonic discourses to produce a new inchoate identity, one no longer based on territorial nationalism but rather grounded on a strong sense of ethnic identity" (Sánchez, *Telling Identities*, 4). For work on race, whiteness, and the construction of racial and ethnic identity in the borderlands as refracted through this novel, see Aranda, "Contradictory Impulses," and Luis-Brown, "'White Slaves.'"

6. For notable examples, see Chavez-Garcia, *Negotiating Conquest*; De León, *They Called Them Greasers*; Deena González, *Refusing the Favor*; Johannsen, *To the Halls*; Lima, *Latino Body*; Monroy, *Thrown among Strangers*; Montejano, *Anglos and Mexicans*; Paredes, *With His Pistol*; Peréz, *Decolonial Imaginary*; Pitt, *Decline of the Californios*; Rodríguez, *Literatures*; Roybal, *Archives of Dispossession*; Saldívar *Border Matters*; and Sánchez, *Telling Identities*.

7. Ruiz de Burton, *Squatter and the Don*, 297.

8. For some examples of work in this field, see Banner, *How the Indians*; Grande, *Red Pedagogy*; Saunt, *New Order of Things*; and Robertson, *Conquest by Law*.

9. I do not attend to the particularities of Native American relations to property in part because to do so responsibly would require expertise in a large and well-established field of study. I am especially sensitive and attentive to the encroachment on this field of study by non-Native scholars.

10. In *How the Indians Lost Their Land*, Stuart Banner writes that *Johnson v. M'Intosh* is the cornerstone of the legal study of property.

11. Ruiz de Burton, *Squatter and the Don*, 215.

12. Lima, *Latino Body*, 4.

13. As David Kazanjian has argued, "The U.S.-Mexico War was not simply a trial run for the Civil War . . . not fought primarily over slavery . . . and did not only affect black and white racial formations," but rather it also "transformed U.S. imperialism from white settler colonialism to neocolonialism, and it produced white, Indian, Mexican, and, eventually, Chicano racial formations that blended the assimilative mode of civilization policy with the eradicative mode of removal policy" (Kazanjian, *Colonizing Trick*, 176). He notes that "the U.S.-Mexico War can no longer be considered just a 'border war,' either in the geographic sense of the territories wrested from Mexico and annexed by the United States, or in the metaphorical sense of the subsequent, racially and nationally hybrid identity formations produced in annexed California, Texas, New Mexico, and Arizona" (ibid., 176).

14. Ruiz de Burton, *Squatter and the Don*, 215.

15. Ibid., 135.

16. Ibid., 160.

17. Ibid., 163.

18. Pita and Sánchez, introduction to *Squatter and the Don*, by Ruiz de Burton, 19.

19. The secularization law of 1833, passed in California, also changed the shape of ownership in these borderland territories, as land was wrested from missions and grants were given to the members of the Abila, Bernal, Carrillo, Castro, de la Guerra, Higuero, Pacheco, Peralta, Pico, Sanchez, and Vallejo families (Gates, "California Land Act of 1851," 396). In a paired effort to settle the frontier, the Mexican government also offered land grants to citizens of up to forty-eight thousand acres of land, and by some estimations the Mexican government had awarded approximately 750

land grants by 1846. Though there was an eleven-league (approximately fifty thousand acres) limitation on colonizable lands, this quota was unlawfully surpassed by many land grant recipients in the years leading up to the Mexican-American War. As a result Mexican claims "averaged between 17,000 and 19,000 acres, but several Mexican families held estates in excess of 300,000 acres" (Pisani, "Squatter Law in California," 287).

20. See De León, *They Called Them Greasers*, and Johannsen, *To the Halls*. This kind of hostility toward Mexicans is reflected in the imaginative literature, as well as in historical documents. For example, in *The Literatures of the U.S.-Mexican War*, Jaime Javier Rodríguez notes that George Lippard's 1847 *Legends of Mexico*, which combines "surreal recreations of the war's early battles" with a "dismissive use of historical facts," echoes the belief in Mexico and Mexicans as threatening to the "mythology of 'America'" through "the charge that Mexicans are antidemocratic" (Rodríguez, *Literatures*, 3, 4).

21. Caughfield, *True Women and Westward Expansion*, 43.

22. Ibid., 44.

23. Indeed, the seeming feudal nature of Mexican land ownership was framed as the product of the usufruct structure of the *ejido* system of the pre-Columbian era in Mexico, as well as the *latifundio* system of the post-Independence era. See Florescano, "Colonial Latifundio." As Enrique Florescano writes, "In the indigenous mentality, there was no concept of individual property. The land belonged to the community; the individual only had the right of usufruct, and only so long as he complied with the duties and obligations that the communities imposed" (ibid., 131).

24. De León, *They Called Them Greasers*, 27.

25. Ibid., 31.

26. Pisani, "Squatter Law in California," 290.

27. Caughfield, *True Women and Westward Expansion*, 53.

28. Ibid., 286.

29. Montejano, *Anglos and Mexicans*; Rodríguez, *Literatures*, 215.

30. Kaup, "Unsustainable Hacienda," 578; Montejano, *Anglos and Mexicans*, 76–77.

31. Ruiz de Burton, *Squatter and the Don*, 83.

32. Ibid., 116.

33. Ibid., 102.

34. Zimmerman, *Panic!*, 6.

35. Paredes, *With His Pistol*, 10.

36. As De León writes about Anglo and Texan-Mexican relations in the aftermath of the Mexican-American War, when "Anglos insisted that Tejanos were culturally dissimilar from themselves and were thus unassimilable; that because of Mexican culture, the difficulties Tejanos faced were of their own making; and that Mexican Americans complacently accepted their fate of social inequality," they were ignoring a long history of protest and demands for social reform in Mexico (De León, *They Called Them Greasers*, 105).

37. Sánchez, *Telling Identities*, 105.

38. See Coronado, "Historicizing." In this chapter Raúl Coronado discusses an alternative genealogy of liberalism in the Spano-American world that originates in the late eighteenth century in Philadelphia.

39. See Rodríguez O., *Independence of Spanish America*, and Esdaile, *Spain in the Liberal Age.*

40. Sánchez, *Telling Identities*, 96–97.

41. Ibid., 96.

42. Ibid., 99.

43. Ibid., 128.

44. Ibid.

45. Ibid., 129. For example, the first federal constitution of 1857 abolished colonial monopolies and promised reformed laws that would facilitate free trade. Silvestre Villegas Revueltas notes, "These reformist efforts, to create a more efficient tax-free trade, to make the government more efficient, and to increase circulation of real estate and with it the idea of extending the number of property owners, show another facet of these moderate liberals that goes beyond the resolution of political conflicts [in Mexico]" ("Este intento de reforma, en cuanto a crear un comercio más expedito, libre de impuestos, la promesa de adelgazar y hacer eficiente la marcha del gobierno y subrepticiamente anunciar la circulación de la propiedad raíz y con ello la idea de extender la cantidad de propietarios, muestran la otra faceta de estos liberales moderados que va más allá de la solución de los conflictos políticos") (Villegas Revueltas, *El liberalismo moderado en Mexico*, 107; translation mine).

46. Sánchez, *Telling Identities*, 102.

47. Ibid., 103.

48. Ibid., 102.

49. Ibid., 132.

50. Ibid., 131, 96.

51. See John González, "Romancing Hegemony"; Pita and Sánchez, introduction to *Squatter and the Don*, by Ruiz de Burton.

52. Numerous critics have taken up the topic of whiteness in this novel. Jesse Alemán has written convincingly about the contingency of whiteness in *The Squatter and the Don* and *Who Would Have Thought It?* (1872) (Alemán, "Citizenship Rights and Colonial Whites," 7). John González's essay on *The Squatter and the Don* argues that resistance to U.S. colonialism takes the form of mixed marriages and the struggle to make Californios visible as white, which in turn helps us rethink the fictions of U.S. citizenship and national affiliation (John González, "Romancing Hegemony"). José F. Aranda Jr. has argued that Ruiz de Burton's novels insist "on the need to formulate histories and analyses that place some people of Mexican descent at the center of discourses more typically associated with Anglo America" (Aranda, "Contradictory Impulses," 554). By putting pressure on the way race works in the novel, David Luis-Brown reveals the models through which the borderlands *criollo*, or hidalgo, is represented and treated as white, in part because the indigenous and mestizos are treated as nonwhite (Luis-Brown, "'White Slaves'").

53. Rodríguez, *Literatures*, 20–21.

54. Ibid., 63.

55. As Juan Poblete discusses in "Citizenship and Illegality," though in reference to a related archive of Gold Rush literature, the presence of "American, Chilean, Peruvian, Mexican, Californio, Chinese, [and] Australian" miners in California, all

"making private claims in what were legally federal lands," is a generative site for understanding the complicated negotiations of race, property, and citizenship in the United States (179). As he writes, "To be Chilean came to mean being a racialized, second- or third-class inhabitant whose only right or, even more, whose natural destiny was to work servicing American citizens. To be called 'Chilean' in this context—not unlike being called 'Mexican' in the United States today—became an index of a longstanding racialized dialectic between (white) Americans and their Latino others" (ibid., 283). Though he is discussing a different ethnic population at a later historical moment, Poblete's contribution is to our understanding of comparative racialization in this region in the second half of the nineteenth century and of the way race, property, and citizenship intersect in this period.

56. Horsman, *Race and Manifest Destiny*.

57. Robinson, *Land in California*, 111.

58. Ibid.

59. Bogue, "Social Theory and the Pioneer," 22.

60. Clay and Troesken, "Squatting," 207.

61. Quoted in Krall, *Proving Up*, 41.

62. Pisani, "Squatter Law in California," 282.

63. Ibid.

64. Bogue, "Social Theory and the Pioneer," 22.

65. Ruiz de Burton, *Squatter and the Don*, 173.

66. Ibid.

67. Ibid., 161.

68. Ibid., 187.

69. This is perhaps best exemplified in James Fenimore Cooper's 1848 novel, *Jack Tier: or, The Florida Reef*, set during the Mexican-American War, and whose villain, Stephen Spike, is a pirate smuggling gunpowder to Mexico. It is not so much that *Jack Tier* represents squatting as a form of piracy, but rather that the war surfaces crises of property that are in part expressed through the figure of the American pirate, a mercenary with no national allegiance even in times of war and also with no allegiance to the integrity of property.

70. Ruiz de Burton, *Squatter and the Don*, 92.

71. Ibid., 286.

72. Grodin, Massey, and Cunningham, *California State Constitution*, 11.

73. Dawdy and Bonni, "Towards a General Theory of Piracy," 686.

74. Krall, *Proving Up*, 44.

75. Lance Newman, "Free Soil," 140.

76. Ibid.

77. Quoted in Clay and Troesken, "Squatting," 216.

78. Reddy, *Freedom with Violence*, 64.

79. Ruiz de Burton, *Squatter and the Don*, 62.

80. Ibid., 173.

81. Ibid., 97.

82. Ibid., 56.

83. Hurtado, *Intimate Frontiers*, 24.

84. Ibid.

85. Sánchez, *Telling Identities*, 216.

86. Deena González, *Refusing the Favor*, 110.

87. Peréz, *Decolonial Imaginary*, 81.

88. Dekker, *American Historical Romance*, 41.

89. See Dawson, "Ruiz de Burton's Emotional Landscape." Melanie V. Dawson discusses the loss of property through the lens of affect theory.

90. Chavez-Garcia, *Negotiating Conquest*, 54.

91. Hurtado, *Intimate Frontiers*, xxiii. A point reinforced by Laura Woodworth-Ney, who writes, "Under Spanish and Mexican law, women could own land and could receive land grants. Between 1796 and 1846, 7 percent of the land grants in California were awarded to women. By 1844, 13 percent of Los Angeles households were headed by women" (Woodworth-Ney, *Women in the American West*, 83).

92. Lecompte, "Independent Women," 18–19. Also see Weber, *Mexican Frontier*, and Schuele, "Community Property Law."

93. Deere and León, "Liberalism," 650–51.

94. Ibid., 655–56.

95. Grodin, Massey, and Cunningham, *California State Constitution*, 4.

96. California Const. (1850), art. I, § 1, http://leginfo.ca.gov/const-toc.html.

97. Grodin, Massey, and Cunningham, *California State Constitution*, 6.

98. Sánchez, *Telling Identities*, 198.

99. Ibid., 200.

100. Ibid.

101. Ruiz de Burton, *Squatter and the Don*, 44.

102. Pita and Sánchez, introduction to *Squatter and the Don*, by Ruiz de Burton, 15.

103. Crawford, "María Amparo Ruiz Burton," 207.

104. Alemán, "Novelizing National Discourses," 44.

105. Ruiz de Burton, *Squatter and the Don*, 338.

106. Lye, *America's Asia*.

Chapter Five

1. Edward McPherson, *Political History*, 149.

2. Ibid.

3. Ibid. The language of the blockade, which quickly moves from privateering (by invoking the letter of marque) to piracy, and which also juxtaposes these activities to the proper and lawful activities of the citizen, draws on a long and complicated legal and political history of defining piracy in both municipal and public international law. I am also invoking a long tradition in international legal theory of reading the pirate.

4. Berwanger, *British Foreign Service*, 57.

5. Ripley, *From Flag to Flag*; Velazquez, *Woman in Battle*.

6. The very question of black personhood, as discussed in chapter 3, hinges on the qualities of person as juxtaposed to the qualities of property: the difference between property in person and property of person.

7. Reidy, "African American Struggle," 214.

8. Wahl, *Bondsman's Burden*.

9. Velazquez, *Woman in Battle*, 606.

10. As Caroline Levander writes in "Confederate Cuba," Cuba figures prominently in the literature of the antebellum period as a site of possible Confederate expansion. Thus, it is not surprising that, when dispossessed, the Velazquez family moves to the island in order to access territorial possession. These are the same reasons that eventually catalyze Ripley's move to Cuba two decades later. In other words, I want to stress that both Ripley's and Velazquez's narratives center on overlapping forms of territorial dispossession for which Cuba is a stopgap. The problem is that, as both Velazquez and Ripley are clear to express in their memoirs, belonging in Cuba does not approximate U.S. citizenship. As a result, their relationship to both Cuba and the United States is fraught with uncertainty and insecurity.

11. Velazquez, *Woman in Battle*, 248.

12. As reflected in Alemán, "Crossing the Mason-Dixon Line"; Clinton, "'Public Women' and Sexual Politics"; and Young, *Disarming the Nation*.

13. Velazquez, *Woman in Battle*, 45.

14. In *Swindler, Spy, Rebel*, Kathleen De Grave argues that confidence women are distinct from everyday pretenders in that they "involved intricate disguises, a careful manipulation of people's expectations, and a joy in the tricks one pulled" (112). De Grave argues that Velazquez cross-dresses "as much for sport as for patriotism, impelling [her] to exaggerate her male impersonation and test its limits," and thus Velazquez qualifies as a confidence woman (ibid.).

15. Robin Sager's "Multiple Metaphoric Civil Wars" analyzes the varied ethnic performances in the memoir, from her performance as a Confederate soldier and its implied racial affiliation, to her later performance as Cuban in light of the failing Southern cause, in order to highlight the inconsistencies in Velazquez's ethnic and class identification.

16. Young, *Disarming the Nation*, 165.

17. Elizabeth Young identifies gender counterfeit working in tandem with historical inauthenticity in the creation of a compelling memoir. Young looks to the fictive elements in the narrative, which she suggests Velazquez borrows from the picaresque and the adventure novel, to argue that Velazquez's mobility between different genres is reflected in the mobility she gains from cross-dressing (Young, *Disarming the Nation*).

18. Ibid., 165.

19. While Young has argued that *The Woman in Battle* is "a metaphorical point of exchange for intersections between individual bodies and the national body politic," and calls the many boundary crossings in the novel both a "fantasy and nightmare," she misses the opportunity to examine these boundary crossings as unlawful economic transactions and expressions (Young, *Disarming the Nation*, 156).

20. Young, *Disarming the Nation*.

21. While some recent critics have read Velazquez's narrative within the counterfactual, with the promise of French and British involvement on behalf of the Confederacy (occasioned by a need for Southern cotton in the world market, especially in the face of the blockade), even these moments do not prompt critics to explore

the significance of the blockade in literature of the period (Hutchison, "On the Move Again," 425).

22. Isenberg, *Sex and Citizenship*, 7–8.

23. Drew Gilpin Faust has written of this "homespun revolution" that though it overemphasized the impact of the production of domestic textiles, it does reflect white Southern women's undertaking of "unaccustomed sorts of economic production" (Gilpin Faust, *Mothers of Invention*, 51). It also framed "economically independent southern households as essential to the political independence of the nation" (ibid., 45).

24. Ibid., 218. In *The Southern Lady*, Anne Firor Scott also discusses the importance of the Civil War in the progression toward suffrage in the United States.

25. Gardiner, "Foreign Travelers' Accounts of Mexico"; Friend, "Texan of 1860"; Sutherland, "Looking for a Home."

26. Tyler, "Cotton on the Border." For works examining the persistence of the importance of cotton in both Southern and world markets even after the onset of war, see Susan Lee, *Westward Movement*; William Parker, *Structure of the Cotton Economy*; Bruchey, *Cotton*; and Wright, *Political Economy*. The limited work on the economics of the Civil War includes Thornton and Ekelund, *Tariffs, Blockades, and Inflation*.

27. Guterl, "After Slavery.

28. Edlie L. Wong, *Racial Reconstruction*, 17.

29. Susanna Michele Lee, *Claiming the Union*; Reidy, "African American Struggle."

30. Bergman and Bernardi, *Our Sister's Keepers*; Burgett, *Sentimental Bodies*; Carlin, "'What Methods Have Brought Blessing'"; Ginzberg, *Women and the Work*; Perry and Weaks-Baxter, *History of Southern Women's Literature*; and Moss, *Domestic Novelists*.

31. Andreas, *Smuggler Nation*, 157–58. Lebergott, "Through the Blockade," for example, makes the case that cotton running has been overestimated. Owsley, *King Cotton Diplomacy*, continues to be the standard source on the importance of cotton during the Civil War. Also see James McPherson, *Battle Cry of Freedom*, and Wise, *Lifeline of the Confederacy*.

32. Andreas, *Smuggler Nation*, 158.

33. Durham, *High Seas and Yankee Gunboats*; Taylor, *Running the Blockade*; William Watson, *Adventures of a Blockade Runner*.

34. Taylor, *Running the Blockade*.

35. Ibid., viii–ix.

36. Ibid.

37. Ibid., 3.

38. Ibid., viii–ix.

39. Watson, *Adventures of a Blockade Runner*. Watson's narrative begins by stressing the isolation experienced by the Southern states at the outset of the war given that they "almost entirely depended upon the export of their stable products" (ibid., 2). The only recourse Southerners have, Watson suggests, is to participate in law-breaking forms of trade. Blockade running becomes a means of creating and sustaining economic life in a devastated climate where, as Watson describes, "factories were closed from want of raw material and thousands of operatives thrown out of employment" and "the seas, which three years previously had been thickly studded with the white sails of shipping, were now deserted, and nearly as solitary as

when discovered by Columbus" (ibid., 2–3). Watson's narrative presents blockade running as a reprieve from the "misery and privation" endured by Southerners (ibid., 3). Finally, participation in blockade running and other illegal enterprises becomes a part of Confederate identity and is generative of a range of other economic activities in the shadows of law: from the restaurants operating "under tarpaulins spread over poles" to the "rough wooden sheds hastily knocked together . . . used as grocery stores and rum mills," the narrative highlights how marginalized populations in peripheral locations (both ideologically and spatially) are able to create rituals of survival (ibid., 26).

40. Ibid., 315–16.

41. Ibid., 34 (emphasis in original).

42. Ibid., 1–2.

43. Prize Cases, 67 U.S. 635 (1863).

44. Prize Cases, 67 U.S. 635, 636 (1863).

45. Ibid.

46. Ibid., 672.

47. Ibid.

48. Ibid.

49. Ibid.

50. Ibid., 671.

51. Ibid., 666.

52. Ibid., 699.

53. Ibid., 673.

54. Ibid., 674.

55. Ibid., 687.

56. Ibid.

57. Susanna Michele Lee, *Claiming the Union*, 1.

58. Ibid. As Lee underscores, this process was particularly resonant for formerly enslaved persons who could at once gain national recognition and citizenship, as well as property by proving their fealty to the Union.

59. Ibid.

60. Ripley, *From Flag to Flag*, 51, 52.

61. Ibid., 53.

62. Ibid., 49–50.

63. Ibid., 162–63.

64. Velazquez, *Woman in Battle*, 269–70.

65. Ibid., 236.

66. Ibid., 536.

67. "Bounty jumping" describes the act of taking a bounty or a reward for enlistment into the federal army and then stealing this money.

68. Velazquez, *Woman in Battle*, 488.

69. Ibid., 489.

70. Ibid., 490–91.

71. Ibid., 491.

72. Ibid.

73. Ibid.

74. Ibid.

75. Ibid., 387.

76. Ibid.

77. Ibid.

78. Ibid., 389.

79. Ibid., 7.

80. [C. J. Worthington], introduction to *Woman in Battle*, by Velazquez, [8].

81. Ibid., 8.

82. Velazquez, *Woman in Battle*, 458.

83. Ibid., 455.

84. Ibid.

85. Ibid., 299.

86. Ibid., 299–300.

87. Ibid., 248.

88. Ibid., 484.

89. Ibid., 469.

90. Ibid., 504.

91. Ibid., 474.

92. In *The Gender of Freedom*, Elizabeth Maddock Dillon argues that women continuously negotiate a liberal meaning of value.

93. For a discussion of how selfhood has come to be articulated in relation to the nation and to empire, see Wai-chee Dimock's *Empire for Liberty*. This seminal work examines forms of individuation that emerge through articulations of self as nation and nation as self. For Dimock the logics of freedom and empire overlap, and this necessitates an examination of American literature as always already engaging with the overlaps of liberal individuation and empire-building processes.

94. Ripley, *From Flag to Flag*, 121–22.

95. Ibid., 124.

96. Ibid.

97. Ibid., 149.

98. Ibid., 150.

99. Ibid., 205.

100. Ibid.

101. Ibid., 294.

102. Ibid., 293.

103. Ibid., 218.

104. Ibid., 217.

105. Ibid., 233.

106. Ibid., 176 (emphasis added).

107. Ibid., 177.

108. Yun, *Coolie Speaks*, xx. Lisa Yun argues that the "contract" was used to produce a "mobile slave" rather than produce a free liberal subject due to the restrictive legal structures already in place on the island (ibid., xx–xxi).

109. Ripley, *From Flag to Flag*, 180.

110. Ibid., 206.

111. Velazquez, *Woman in Battle*, 536.

112. Ibid.

113. Ibid., 545.

114. Ibid., 551–52.

Afterword

1. *Account of the Behaviour*, 3.

2. Ibid.

3. Dawdy, "Why Pirates Are Back."

4. Ibid., 373–374.

5. Aguilar, "Bill Seeks to Designate."

6. In discussing the interesting position of the narcotrafficker within a political and criminal category, I am deliberately excluding the U.S. War on Drugs, which, as scholars have argued, was not a war between states but rather an ideological tool of neoliberal expansion in Latin America implemented by Richard Nixon in 1970 (see De La Barra and Buono, *Latin America*; Blakely, *State Terrorism and Neoliberalism*; Corva, "Neoliberal Globalization"; and Petras and Veltmeyer, *Beyond Neoliberalism*).

7. Aguilar, "Bill Seeks to Designate."

8. Greene, "Hostis Humani Generis."

9. Holder, "Holder Letter," 2.

10. Hamdi v. Rumsfeld 542 U.S. 507, 536 (2004) and Youngstown Sheet & Tube Co. v. Sawyer 343 U.S. 578, 587 (1952), cited in Holder, "Holder Letter," 4.

11. See Holder, *Lawfulness of a Lethal Operation*, and Holder, "Holder Letter."

12. This is a paradox articulated by Jody Greene in "Hostis Humani Generis," which looks to the catachrestic quality of terms such as "pirate" and "terrorist."

Bibliography

An Account of the Behaviour and Last Dying Speeches of the Six Pirates. Boston: N. Boone, 1704.

Adams, John Quincy. *Argument of John Quincy Adams before the Supreme Court of the United States, in the Case of the United States, Appellants, vs. Cinque, and Others, Africans.* New York: Negro University Press, 1969.

Adams, Katherine. *Owning Up: Privacy, Property, and Belonging in U.S. Women's Life Writing.* Oxford: Oxford University Press, 2009.

Adams, Rachel. *Continental Divides: Remapping the Cultures of North America.* Chicago: University of Chicago Press, 2009.

Adelman, Jeremy, and Stephen Aron. "From Borderlands to Borders: Empires, Nation-States, and the Peoples in between in North American History." *American Historical Review* 104 (1999): 814–41.

Aguilar, Julián. "Bill Seeks to Designate Drug Cartels as Terrorists." *Texas Tribune*, April 21, 2012.

Alemán, Jesse. "Citizenship Rights and Colonial Whites: The Cultural Work of María Amparo Ruiz de Burton's Novels." In *Complicating Constructions: Race, Ethnicity, and Hybridity in American Texts*, edited by David S. Goldstein and Audrey B. Thacker, 3–30. Seattle: University of Washington Press, 2007.

———. "Crossing the Mason-Dixon Line in Drag: The Narrative of Loreta Janeta Velazquez, Cuban Woman and Confederate Soldier." In *Look Away! The U.S. South in New World Studies*, edited by Jon Smith and Deborah Cohn, 110–29. Durham, NC: Duke University Press, 2004.

———. "Novelizing National Discourses: History, Romance, and Law in *The Squatter and the Don.*" In *Recovering the U.S. Hispanic Literary Heritage*, vol. 3, edited by Ramón A. Gutiérrez, Genaro M. Padilla, and María Herrera-Sobek, 38–49. Houston: Arte Público, 2000.

Alexander, Gregory S. *Commodity and Propriety: Competing Visions of Property in American Legal Thought, 1776–1970.* Chicago: University of Chicago Press, 2008.

Allison, Robert J. *Stephen Decatur: American Naval Hero, 1779–1820.* Amherst: University of Massachusetts Press, 2005.

Ancona, Eligio. *El filibustero: Novela historica.* Mérida, Mexico: Editorial Yucatense "Club del Libro," 1950.

Anderson, Elijah. *Code of the Street: Decency, Violence, and the Moral Life of the Inner City.* New York: W. W. Norton, 1999.

Anderson, Katherine. "Female Pirates and Nationalism in Nineteenth-Century American Popular Fiction." In *Pirates and Mutineers of the Nineteenth Century: Swashbucklers and Swindlers*, edited by Grace Moore, 95–116. Burlington, VT: Ashgate, 2011.

Andreas, Peter. *Smuggler Nation: How Illicit Trade Made America*. New York: Oxford University Press, 2013.

Anthony, David. *Paper Money Men: Commerce, Manhood, and the Sensational Public Sphere in Antebellum America*. Columbus: University of Ohio Press, 2009.

Aranda, José F., Jr. "Contradictory Impulses: María Amparo Ruiz de Burton, Resistance Theory, and the Politics of Chicano/a Studies." In "No More Separate Spheres!," special issue, *American Literature* 70 (1998): 551–79.

Armstrong, Nancy. "Captivity and Cultural Capital in the English Novel." *Novel* 31, no. 3 (1998): 373–98.

Armstrong, Nancy, and Leonard Tennenhouse. "The American Origins of the English Novel." *American Literary History* 4, no. 3 (1992): 386–410.

———. *The Imaginary Puritan: Literature, Intellectual Labor, and the Origins of Personal Life*. Berkeley: University of California Press, 1992.

Austin, Regina. " 'The Black Community,' Its Lawbreakers, and a Politics of Identification." In *Critical Race Theory: The Cutting Edge*, edited by Richard Delgado and Jean Stefancic, 290–301. Philadelphia: Temple University Press, 2000.

Baepler, Paul. "The Barbary Captivity Narrative in American Culture." *Early American Literature* 39, no. 2 (2004): 217–46.

———. "Rewriting the Barbary Captivity Narrative: The Perdicaris Affair and the Last Barbary Pirate." *Prospects* 24 (1999): 177–212.

———. *White Slaves, African Masters: An Anthology of the American Barbary Captivity Narratives*. Chicago: University of Chicago Press, 1999.

Baker, Jennifer J. *Securing the Commonwealth: Debt, Speculation, and Writing in the Making of Early America*. Baltimore: Johns Hopkins University Press, 2005.

Balkun, Mary McAleer. *The American Counterfeit: Authenticity and Identity in American Literature and Culture*. Tuscaloosa: University of Alabama Press, 2006.

Banner, Stuart. *American Property: A History of How, Why, and What We Own*. Cambridge, MA: Harvard University Press, 2011.

———. *How the Indians Lost Their Land: Law and Power on the Frontier*. Cambridge, MA: Harvard University Press, 2005.

Barosky, Todd. "Legal and Illegal Moneymaking: Colonial American Counterfeiters and the Novelization of Eighteenth-Century Crime Literature." *Early American Literature* 47, no. 3 (2012): 531–60.

Batchelder, Robert F. "The Counterfeiting of Colonial Paper Money: As Seen through the Letter of Signer of the Declaration of Independence, Josiah Bartlett." *Old York Road Historical Society Bulletin* 37 (1977): 28–32.

Baym, Nina. "Concepts of the Romance in Hawthorne's America." *Nineteenth-Century Fiction* 38, no. 4 (March 1984): 426–43.

Bender, Bert. *Sea-Brothers: The Tradition of American Sea Fiction*. Philadelphia: University of Pennsylvania Press, 1988.

Benner, Judith Ann. *Fraudulent Finance: Counterfeiting and the Confederate States, 1861–1865*. Hillsboro, TX: Hill Junior College Press, 1970.

Berger, Jason. "Killing Tom Coffin: Rethinking the Nationalist Narrative in James Fenimore Cooper's *The Pilot*." *Early American Literature* 43, no. 3 (2008): 664–65.

Bergman, Jill, and Debra Bernardi, eds. *Our Sister's Keepers: Nineteenth-Century Benevolence Literature by American Women*. Tuscaloosa: University of Alabama Press, 2005.

Berlant, Lauren, and Michael Warner. "Sex in Public." *Critical Inquiry* 24, no. 2 (1998): 547–66.

Berry, Mary Frances. *The Politics of Parenthood: Child Care, Women's Rights, and the Myth of the Good Mother*. New York: Penguin, 1994.

Berwanger, Eugene H. *The British Foreign Service and the American Civil War*. Lexington: University Press of Kentucky, 1994.

Best, Stephen. *The Fugitive's Properties: Law and the Poetics of Possession*. Berkeley: University of California Press, 2004.

Bibb, Henry. *Narrative of the Life and Adventures of Henry Bibb, an American Slave, Written by Himself with an Introd. by Lucius C. Matlack*. New York, 1850.

Blackstone, William. *Commentaries on the Laws of England, Book the Fourth*. London: A. Stahan, 1825.

Blakely, Ruth. *State Terrorism and Neoliberalism: The North in the South*. New York: Routledge, 2009.

Blum, Hester. "Pirated Tars, Piratical Texts: Barbary Captivity and American Sea Narratives." *Early American Studies* 1, no. 2 (Fall 2003): 133–59.

———. *The View from the Masthead: Maritime Imagination and Antebellum American Sea Narratives*. Chapel Hill: University of North Carolina Press, 2008.

Bogue, Allan G. "Social Theory and the Pioneer." *Agricultural History* 34, no. 1 (January 1960): 21–34.

Boritt, Gabor S., and Scott Hancock, eds. *Slavery, Resistance, Freedom*. Oxford: Oxford University Press, 2007.

Breck, Samuel. *Historical Sketch of Continental Paper Money*. Philadelphia: John C. Clark, 1843.

Brisbane, W. H. "Narrative of Albert and Mary." In *Autographs for Freedom*, edited by Julia Griffiths, 77–127. Auburn, UK: Alden, Beardsley, 1850.

Bromley, J. S. *Corsairs and Navies, 1660–1760*. London: Hambledon, 1987.

Brown, Charles Brockden. *Arthur Mervyn; or, Memoirs of the Year 1793*. Edited by Philip Barnard and Stephen Shapiro. Indianapolis: Hackett, 2008.

Brown, Gillian. *Domestic Individualism: Imagining Self in Nineteenth-Century America*. Berkeley: University of California Press, 1992.

Bruchey, Stuart, ed. *Cotton and the Growth of the American Economy, 1790–1860*. New York: Harcourt, Brace and World, 1967.

Burg, B. R. *Sodomy and the Pirate Tradition: English Sea Rovers in the Seventeenth-Century Caribbean*. New York: New York University Press, 1983.

Burgess, Douglas R., Jr. *The Politics of Piracy: Crime and Civil Disobedience in Colonial America*. Lebanon, NH: University Press of New England, 2014.

Burgett, Bruce. *Sentimental Bodies: Sex, Gender, and Citizenship in the Early Republic*. Princeton, NJ: Princeton University Press, 1998.

Burroughs, Stephen. *Memoirs of the Notorious Stephen Burroughs*. Boston: Charles Gaylord, 1835.

Camp, Stephanie M. H. *Closer to Freedom: Enslaved Women and Everyday Resistance in the Plantation South*. Chapel Hill: University of North Carolina Press, 2004.

Cantú, Roberto. "Hybrid Resolutions: Liberal Democracy and Ethnic Identity in Montserrat Fontes's *Dreams of the Centaur*." *Arizona Journal of Hispanic Cultural Studies* 4 (2000): 141–58.

Carey, Henry C. *The Past, the Present, and the Future*. New York: Augustus M. Kelley, 1967.

Carey, Mathew. *A Short Account of the Malignant Fever*. Philadelphia: printed by author, 1794.

Carlin, Deborah. "'What Methods Have Brought Blessing': Discourses of Reform in Philanthropic Literature." In *The (Other) American Traditions: Nineteenth-Century Women Writers*, edited by Joyce W. Warren, 203–25. New Brunswick, NJ: Rutgers University Press, 1993.

Castronovo, Russ, and Dana D. Nelson. *Materializing Democracy: Toward a Revitalized Cultural Politics*. Durham, NC: Duke University Press, 2001.

Caughfield, Adrienne. *True Women and Westward Expansion*. College Station: Texas A&M University Press, 2005.

Chavez-Garcia, Miroslava. *Negotiating Conquest: Gender and Power in California, 1770s to 1880s*. Tucson: University of Arizona Press, 2006.

Chiles, Katy. "Within and without Raced Nations: Intratextuality, Martin Delany, and *Blake; Or the Huts of America*." *American Literature* 80, no. 2 (2008): 323–52.

Clay, Karen, and Werner Troesken. "Squatting and the Settlement of the United States: New Evidence from Post-Gold Rush California." *Advances in Agricultural Historical Economics* 1 (2000): 207–33.

Clinton, Catherine. "'Public Women' and Sexual Politics during the American Civil War." In *Battle Scars: Gender and Sexuality in the American Civil War*, edited by Catherine Clinton and Nina Sibler, 61–77. New York: Oxford University Press, 2006.

Clymer, Jeffory A. *Family Money: Property, Race, and Literature in the Nineteenth Century*. Oxford: Oxford University Press, 2013.

———. "Martin Delany's *Blake* and the Transnational Politics of Property." *American Literary History* 15, no. 4 (2003): 709–31.

Cohen, Andrew W. *Contraband: Smuggling and the Birth of the American Century*. New York: W. W. Norton, 2015.

Cohen, Daniel A. *Pillars of Salt, Monuments of Grace: New England Crime Literature and the Origins of American Popular Culture, 1674–1860*. Amherst: University of Massachusetts Press, 1993.

Cohen, Margaret. *The Novel and the Sea*. Princeton, NJ: Princeton University Press, 2010.

Cohn, Deborah. *History and Memory in the Two Souths: Recent Southern and Spanish American Fiction*. Nashville: Vanderbilt University Press, 1999.

Coke, Edward. *The Third Part of the Institutes of the Laws of England: Concerning High Treason, and other Pleas of the Crown and Criminal Causes*. London: W. Clarke and Sons, 1817.

Collins, Kevin. "Experiments in Realism: Doubling in Simms's 'The Cassique of Kiawah.'" *Southern Literary Journal* 34, no. 2 (Spring 2002): 1–13.

Cooper, James Fenimore. *The American Democrat, or Hints on the Social and Civic Relations of the United States of America.* Cooperstown, NY: H. and E. Phinney, 1838.

———. *History of the Navy of the United States of America.* New York: G. P. Putnam, 1856.

———. *Sea Tales: "The Pilot" and "The Red Rover."* New York: Library of America, 1991.

———. *The Water-Witch, or, the Skimmer of the Seas.* New York: Houghton, Mifflin and Company 1884.

Coronado, Raúl. "Historicizing Nineteenth-Century Latina/o Textuality." In *The Latino Nineteenth Century: Archival Encounters in American Literary History*, edited by Rodrigo Lazo and Jesse Alemán, 49–70. New York: New York University Press, 2016.

Corva, Dominic. "Neoliberal Globalization and the War on Drugs: Transnationalizing Illiberal Governance in the Americas." *Political Geography* 27, no. 2 (2008): 176–93.

Coviello, Peter. *Intimacy in America: Dreams of Affiliation in Antebellum Literature.* Minneapolis: University of Minnesota Press, 2005.

Crane, Gregg D. "The Lexicon of Rights, Power, and Community in *Blake*: Martin R. Delany's Dissent from Dred Scott." *American Literature* 68, no. 3 (1996): 527–53.

Crawford, Kathleen. "María Amparo Ruiz Burton: The General's Lady." *The Journal of San Diego History* 30, no. 3 (September 1984): 198–211.

Davidson, Cathy. *Revolution and the Word: The Rise of the Novel in America.* Oxford: Oxford University Press, 1988.

Dawdy, Shannon Lee. *Building the Devil's Empire: French Colonial New Orleans.* Chicago: University of Chicago Press, 2008.

———. "Why Pirates Are Back." *Annual Review of Law and Social Science* 7 (December 2011): 361–85.

Dawdy, Shannon Lee, and Joe Bonni. "Towards a General Theory of Piracy." *Anthropological Quarterly* 85, no. 3 (2012): 673–99.

Dawson, Melanie V. "Ruiz de Burton's Emotional Landscape: Property and Feeling in *The Squatter and the Don.*" *Nineteenth-Century Literature* 63, no. 1 (2008): 41–72.

Dayan, Joan. "Legal Slaves and Civil Bodies." *Nepantla: Views from South* 2, no. 1 (2001): 3–39.

Deere, Carmen, and Magdalena León. "Liberalism and Married Women's Property Rights in Nineteenth-Century Latin America." *Hispanic American Historical Review* 85, no. 4 (2005): 627–78.

De Grave, Kathleen. *Swindler, Spy, Rebel: The Confidence Woman in Nineteenth-Century America.* Columbia: University of Missouri Press, 1995.

Dekker, George. *The American Historical Romance.* Cambridge: Cambridge University Press, 1993.

De La Barra, Ximena, and Richard Alan Dello Buono. *Latin America after the Neoliberal Debacle: Another Region Is Possible*. Lanham, MD: Rowman and Littlefield, 2009.

Delany, Martin. "Annexation of Cuba." In *Martin Delany: A Documentary Reader*, edited by Robert Levine, 160–66. Chapel Hill: University of North Carolina Press, 2003.

———. *Blake; or, The Huts of America*. Boston: Beacon, 1970.

———. "The Condition, Elevation, Emigration, and Destiny of the Colored People of the United States." In *Martin Delany: A Documentary Reader*, edited by Robert Levine, 189–216. Chapel Hill: University of North Carolina Press, 2003.

———. "Homes for the Freedmen." In *Martin Delany: A Documentary Reader*, edited by Robert Levine, 425–30. Chapel Hill: University of North Carolina Press, 2003.

———. "Political Destiny of the Colored Race on the American Continent." In *Martin Delany: A Documentary*, edited by Robert Levine, 245–79. Chapel Hill: University of North Carolina Press, 2003.

De León, Arnoldo. *They Called Them Greasers: Anglo Attitudes toward Mexicans in Texas, 1821–1900*. Austin: University of Texas Press, 1983.

Dillon, Elizabeth Maddock. *The Gender of Freedom: Fictions of Liberalism and the Literary Public Sphere*. Stanford, CA: Stanford University Press, 2004.

———. *New World Drama: The Performative Commons in the Atlantic World, 1649–1849*. Durham, NC: Duke University Press, 2014.

Dimock, Wai-chee. *Empire for Liberty: Melville and the Poetics of Individualism*. Princeton, NJ: Princeton University Press, 1989.

Doolen, Andy. "'Be Cautious of the Word "Rebel"': Race, Revolution, and Transnational History in *Martin Delany's Blake; or, The Huts of America*." *American Literature* 81, no. 1 (2009): 153–79.

———. *Fugitive Empire: Locating Early American Imperialism*. Minneapolis: University of Minnesota Press, 2005.

Douglass, Frederick. *Autobiographies: "Narrative of the Life of Frederick Douglass, an American Slave"; "My Bondage and My Freedom"; "Life and Times of Frederick Douglass."* New York: Library of America, 1994.

———. "The Internal Slave Trade: Extract from an Oration, at Rochester, July 5, 1852." In *My Bondage and My Freedom*, 446–50. New York: Miller, Orton and Mulligan, 1855.

———. *My Bondage and My Freedom*. New York: Miller, Orton and Mulligan, 1855.

———. "The Nature of Slavery: Extract from a Lecture on Slavery, at Rochester, December 1, 1850." In *My Bondage and My Freedom*, 429–34. New York: Miller, Orton and Mulligan, 1855.

Downes, Paul. "Constitutional Secrets: 'Memoirs of Carwin' and the Politics of Concealment." *Criticism* 39, no. 1 (Winter 1997): 89–117.

———. *Democracy, Revolution, and Monarchism in Early American Literature*. Cambridge: Cambridge University Press, 2002.

Du Bois, W. E. B. *The Suppression of the African Slave-Trade to the United States of America 1638–1870*. New York: Dover, 1970.

Durham, Roger S. *High Seas and Yankee Gunboats: A Blockade-Running Adventure from the Diary of James Dickson.* Columbia: University of South Carolina Press, 2005.

Equiano, Olaudah. *The Interesting Narrative of the Life of Olaudah Equiano; or, Gustavus Vassa, the African.* New York: Simon and Brown, 2013.

Ernest, John. *Resistance and Reformation in Nineteenth-Century African-American Literature: Brown, Wilson, Jacobs, Delany, Douglass, and Harper.* Jackson: University Press of Mississippi, 1995.

Esdaile, Charles J. *Spain in the Liberal Age.* Oxford: Blackwell, 2000.

Fenn, Percy Thomas, Jr. "Justinian and the Freedom of the Sea." *American Journal of International Law* 19, no. 4 (October 1925): 716–27.

Fliegelman, Jay. *Prodigals and Pilgrims: The American Revolution against Patriarchal Authority, 1750–1800.* Cambridge: Cambridge University Press, 1982.

Florescano, Enrique. "The Colonial Latifundio." In *The Mexico Reader: History, Culture, Politics*, edited by Gilbert M. Joseph and Timothy J. Henderson, 131–40. Durham, NC: Duke University Press, 2002.

Fox-Genovese, Elizabeth. "The Fettered Mind: Time, Place, and the Literary Imagination of the Old South." *Georgia Historical Quarterly* 74, no. 4 (1990): 622–50.

Franklin, Benjamin. "Account of the Devices on the Continental Bills of Credit." In *Writings*, 734–38. New York: Library of America, 1987.

———. *The Autobiography of Benjamin Franklin.* London: George Bell and Sons, 1884.

Franklin, John Hope, and Loren Schweninger. *Runaway Slaves: Rebels on the Plantation.* Oxford: Oxford University Press, 2000.

Franklin, Wayne. *James Fenimore Cooper: The Early Years.* New Haven, CT: Yale University Press, 2007.

Friend, Llerena B. "The Texan of 1860." *Southwestern Historical Quarterly* 62, no. 1 (July 1958): 1–17.

Gallant, Thomas. "Brigandage, Piracy, Capitalism, and State-Formation: Transnational Crime from a Historical World-Systems Perspective." In *States and Illegal Practices*, edited by Josiah McConnell Heyman, 25–61. Oxford: Berg, 1999.

Gardiner, C. Harvey. "Foreign Travelers' Accounts of Mexico, 1810–1910." *The Americas* 8, no. 3 (January 1952): 321–51.

Gates, Paul. "The California Land Act of 1851." *California Historical Quarterly* 50, no. 4 (December 1971): 395–430.

Gerassi-Navarro, Nina. *Pirate Novels: Fictions of Nation Building in Spanish America.* Durham, NC: Duke University Press, 1999.

Germana, Michael. *Standards of Value: Money, Race, and Literature in America.* Iowa City: University of Iowa Press, 2009.

Gilje, Paul A. *Liberty on the Waterfront: American Maritime Culture in the Age of Revolution.* Philadelphia: University of Pennsylvania Press, 2012.

———. *To Swear Like a Sailor: Language, Meaning, and Culture in the American Maritime World, 1750–1850.* Cambridge: Cambridge University Press, 2016.

Gilpin Faust, Drew. *Mothers of Invention: Women of the Slaveholding South in the American Civil War.* Chapel Hill: University of North Carolina Press, 2004.

Gilroy, Paul. *The Black Atlantic: Modernity and Double Consciousness.* London: Verso, 1993.

Ginzberg, Lori D. *Women and the Work of Benevolence: Morality, Politics, and Class in the Nineteenth-Century United States.* New Haven, CT: Yale University Press, 1990.

Glenn, Evelyn Nakano. *Unequal Freedom: How Race and Gender Shaped American Citizenship and Labor.* Cambridge, MA: Harvard University Press, 2002.

González, Deena. *Refusing the Favor: The Spanish-Mexican Women of Santa Fe, 1820–1880.* New York: Oxford University Press, 1999.

González, John. "Romancing Hegemony: Constructing Racialized Citizenship in María Amparo Ruiz de Burton's *The Squatter and the Don.*" In *Recovering the U.S. Hispanic Literary Heritage,* vol. 2, edited by Erlinda Gonzales-Berry and Chuck Tatum, 23–39. Houston: Arte Público, 1996.

González Stephan, Beatriz. *La historiografía literaria del liberalismo hispanoamericano del siglo XIX.* Havana: Casa de las Américas, 1987.

Gore, Charles, ed. *Property, Its Duties and Rights: Historically, Philosophically, and Religiously Regarded.* London: Macmillan, 1915.

Gould, Philip. "Race, Commerce, and the Literature of Yellow Fever in the Early National Philadelphia." *Early American Literature* 35, no. 2 (2000): 157–86.

Grahn, Lance. *The Political Economy of Smuggling: Regional Informal Economies in Early Bourbon New Granada.* Boulder, CO: Westview, 1997.

Grande, Sandy. *Red Pedagogy: Native American Social and Political Thought.* Lanham, MD: Rowman and Littlefield, 2004.

Greene, Jody. "Hostis Humani Generis." *Critical Inquiry* 34, no. 4 (Summer 2008): 683–705.

Griffin, Farah Jasmine. "Black Feminists and DuBois: Respectability, Protection, and Beyond." *Annals of the American Academy of Political and Social Science* 568 (March 2000): 28–40.

Grodin, Joseph R., Calvin R. Massey, and Richard B. Cunningham. *The California State Constitution: A Reference Guide.* Westport, CT: Greenwood, 1993.

Gross, Kali N. *Colored Amazons: Crime, Violence, and Black Women in the City of Brotherly Love, 1880–1910.* Durham, NC: Duke University Press, 2006.

———. "Examining the Politics of Respectability in African American Studies." *Almanac: Journal of Record, Opinion, and News* 43, no. 28 (April 1997), http://www.upenn.edu/almanac/v43/n28/benchmrk.html.

Gruesz, Kristen Silva. *Ambassadors of Culture: The Transamerican Origins of Latino Writing.* Princeton, NJ: Princeton University Press, 2002.

Guilds, John Caldwell. *William Gilmore Simms and the American Frontier.* Athens: University of Georgia Press, 1997.

Guterl, Matthew Pratt. "After Slavery: Asian Labor, the American South, and the Age of Emancipation." *Journal of World History* 14, no. 2 (June 2003): 209–41.

———. "An American Mediterranean: Haiti, Cuba, and the American South." In *Hemispheric American Studies,* edited by Caroline Levander and Robert Levine, 96–115. New Brunswick, NJ: Rutgers University Press, 2008.

Hacker, Louis. *The Triumph of American Capitalism: The Development of Forces in American History to the End of the Nineteenth Century*. New York: Simon and Schuster, 1940.

Hall, William Edward. *A Treatise on International Law*. Oxford: Clarendon, 1895.

Hamilton, Alexander. "Federalist, No. 30." In *The Federalist*, edited by Jacob E. Cooke, 188–90. Middletown, CT: Wesleyan University Press, 1961.

———. "Federalist Paper No. 71." In *The Federalist Papers*, edited by Clinton Rossiter, 429–34. New York: Signet, 2003.

Hammond, John Craig, and Matthew Mason, eds. *Contesting Slavery: The Politics of Bondage and Freedom in the New American Nation*. Charlottesville: University of Virginia Press, 2011.

Handley, George. *Postslavery Literatures in the Americas: Family Portraits in Black and White*. Charlottesville: University of Virginia Press, 2000.

Hanna, Mark G. *Pirate Nests and the Rise of the British Empire, 1570–1740*. Chapel Hill: University of North Carolina Press, 2015.

Harper, Judith E. *Women during the Civil War: An Encyclopedia*. New York: Routledge, 2003.

Harris, Cheryl I. "Whiteness as Property." *Harvard Law Review* 106, no. 8 (June 1993): 1707–91.

Hartman, Saidiya V. *Scenes of Subjection: Terror, Slavery, and Self-making in Nineteenth-Century America*. Oxford: Oxford University Press, 1997.

Hartog, Hendrik. "The Constitution of Aspiration and 'The Rights That Belong to Us All.'" *Journal of American History* 74, no. 3 (1987): 1013–34.

Hartz, Louis. *The Liberal Tradition in America: An Interpretation of American Political Thought since the Revolution*. New York: Harcourt, Harvest, 1955.

Heller-Roazen, Daniel. *The Enemy of All: Piracy and the Law of Nations*. New York: Zone Books, 2009.

Henkin, David M. *City Reading: Written Words and Public Spaces in Antebellum New York*. New York: Columbia University Press, 1998.

Henson, Josiah. *The Life of Josiah Henson, Formerly a Slave, Now an Inhabitant of Canada, as Narrated by Himself*. Boston: A. D. Phelps, 1849.

Heyman, Josiah McConnell, and Alan Smart. *States and Illegal Practices*. Oxford: Berg, 1999.

Hobsbawm, Eric J. *Primitive Rebels: Studies in Archaic Forms of Social Movement in the 19th and 20th Centuries*. New York: W. W. Norton, 1959.

Hoefer, Anthony Dyer. "'The Slaves That They Are' and the Slaves That They Might Become: Bondage and Liberty in William Gilmore Simms's *The Yemassee*." In "Racial Desire(s)," special issue, *MELUS* 34, no. 3 (Fall 2009): 115–32.

Hohfled, Wesley. "Fundamental Legal Conceptions as Applied in Judicial Reasoning." *Yale Law Journal* 26 (1917): 710–70.

Holder, Eric H., Jr. "The Holder Letter." To Patrick J. Leahy. *Washington Post*, May 22, 2013.

———. *Lawfulness of a Lethal Operation Directed against a U.S. Citizen Who Is a Senior Operational Leader of Al-Qa'ida or an Associated Force*. Washington, DC: United States Department of Justice, 2013.

Honoré, A. M. "Ownership." In *Oxford Essays in Jurisprudence*, edited by A. G. Guest, 107–47. Oxford: Oxford University Press, 1961.

Horsman, Reginald. *Race and Manifest Destiny: The Origins of American Racial Anglo-Saxonism*. Cambridge, MA: Harvard University Press, 1981.

Horwitz, Morton J. *The Transformation of American Law, 1780–1860*. Cambridge, MA: Harvard University Press, 1977.

Howell, William Huntting. *Against Self-reliance: The Arts of Dependence in the Early United States*. Philadelphia: University of Pennsylvania Press, 2015.

Hsu, Hsuan. *Geography and the Production of Space in Nineteenth-Century American Literature*. Cambridge: Cambridge University Press, 2010.

Hurtado, Albert. *Intimate Frontiers: Sex, Gender, and Culture in Old California*. Albuquerque: University of New Mexico Press, 1999.

Hutchison, Coleman. "On the Move Again: Tracking the 'Exploits, Adventures, and Travels of Madame Loreta Janeta Velazquez.'" *Comparative American Studies* 5, no. 4 (2007): 423–40.

Isenberg, Nancy. *Sex and Citizenship in Antebellum America*. Chapel Hill: University of North Carolina Press, 1998.

Jaros, Peter. "Personating Stephen Burroughs: The Apparitions of a Public Specter." *Early American Literature* 44, no. 3 (2009): 569–603.

Johannsen, Robert W. *To the Halls of the Montezumas: The Mexican War in the American Imagination*. Oxford: Oxford University Press, 1985.

Jones, Christopher. "Praying upon Truth: *The Memoirs of Stephen Burroughs* and the Picaresque." *Early American Literature* 30 (1995): 32–50.

Jones, Norrece T., Jr. *Born a Child of Freedom, yet a Slave: Mechanisms of Control and Strategies of Resistance in Antebellum South Carolina*. Hanover, NH: Wesleyan University Press, 1990.

Kaplan, Catherine. "Theft and Counter-theft: Joseph Plumb Martin's Revolutionary War." *Early American Literature* 41, no. 3 (2006): 515–34.

Karraker, Cyrus. *Piracy Was a Business*. Rindge, NH: Richard R. Smith, 1953.

Kaup, Monika. "The Unsustainable Hacienda: The Rhetoric of Progress in Jovita González and Eve Raleigh's *Caballero*." *MFS: Modern Fiction Studies* 51, no. 3 (Fall 2005): 561–91.

Kazanjian, David. *The Colonizing Trick: National Culture and Imperial Citizenship in Early America*. Minneapolis: University of Minnesota Press, 2003.

Keckley, Elizabeth. *Behind the Scenes; or, Thirty Years a Slave and Four Years in the White House*. New York: Arno, 1968.

Keynes, Edward. *Undeclared War: Twilight Zone of Constitutional Power*. University Park: Pennsylvania State University Press, 2004.

King, Vincent. "Foolish Talk 'about Freedom': Simms's Vision of America in *The Yemassee*." *Studies in the Novel* 35, no. 2 (Summer 2003): 139–48.

Kinkor, Kenneth. "Black Men under the Black Flag." In *Bandits at Sea: A Pirates Reader*, edited by C. R. Pennell, 195–210. New York: New York University Press, 2001.

Knighton, Andrew Lyndon. "The Wreck of the *Corsair*: Piracy, Political Economy and American Publishing." In *Pirates and Mutineers of the Nineteenth Century:*

Swashbucklers and Swindlers, edited by Grace Moore, 79–94. Burlington, VT: Ashgate, 2011.

Krall, Lisi. *Proving Up: Domesticating Land in U.S. History*. Albany: State University of New York Press, 2010.

Latimer, Jon. *Buccaneers of the Caribbean: How Piracy Forged an Empire*. Cambridge, MA: Harvard University Press, 2009.

Lawson-Peebles, Robert. "Property, Marriage, Women, and Fenimore Cooper's First Fictions." In *James Fenimore Cooper: New Historical and Literary Contexts*, edited by W. M. Verhoeven, 47–70. Amsterdam: Rodopi, 1993.

Lazo, Rodrigo, and Jesse Alemán. *The Latino Nineteenth Century: Archival Encounters in American Literary History*. New York: New York University Press, 2016.

Lebergott, Stanley. "Through the Blockade: The Profitability and Extent of Cotton Smuggling, 1861–1865." *Journal of Economic History* 41, no. 4 (1981): 867–88.

Lecompte, Janet. "Independent Women of Hispanic New Mexico, 1821–1846." *Western Historical Quarterly* 12 (1981): 17–35.

Lee, Susan. *The Westward Movement of the Cotton Economy, 1840–1860: Perceived Interests and Economic Realities*. New York: Arno, 1977.

Lee, Susanna Michele. *Claiming the Union: Citizenship in the Post–Civil War South*. New York: Cambridge University Press, 2014.

Leeson, Peter T. *The Invisible Hook: The Hidden Economics of Pirates*. Princeton, NJ: Princeton University Press, 2009.

Levander, Caroline. "Confederate Cuba." *American Literature* 78, no. 4 (2008): 821–45.

Levander, Caroline, and Robert Levine, eds. *Hemispheric American Studies*. New Brunswick, NJ: Rutgers University Press, 2007.

Levine, Robert. "Arthur Mervyn's Revolutions." *Studies in American Fiction* 12, no. 2 (Autumn 1984): 145–60.

———. Introduction to *Martin Delany: A Documentary Reader*, edited by Robert Levine, 1–22. Chapel Hill: University of North Carolina Press, 2003.

———. *Martin Delany, Frederick Douglass, and the Politics of Representative Identity*. Chapel Hill: University of North Carolina Press, 1997.

Lewis, W. Arthur. "Economic Development with Unlimited Supplies of Labour." *Manchester School* 22, no. 2 (May 1954): 139–91.

Lima, Lázaro. *The Latino Body: Crisis Identities in American Literary and Cultural Memory*. New York: New York University Press, 2007.

Linebaugh, Peter, and Marcus Rediker. *The Many-Headed Hydra: Sailors, Slaves, Commoners, and the Hidden History of the Revolutionary Atlantic*. Boston: Beacon, 2000.

Locke, John. *Second Treatise of Government*. Edited by C. B. Macpherson. Indianapolis: Hackett, 1980.

London, Joshua. *Victory in Tripoli: How America's War with the Barbary Pirates Established the U.S. Navy and Shaped a Nation*. Hoboken, NJ: John Wiley and Sons, 2005.

Louras, Nick. *James Fenimore Cooper: A Life*. Alresford, UK: Chronos Books, 2016.

Lowe, John. "'Calypso Magnolia': The Caribbean Side of the South." *South Central Review* 22, no. 1 (2005): 54–80.

Lowe, Lisa. "Intimacies of Four Continents." In *Haunted by Empire: Geographies of Intimacy in North American History*, edited by Ann Laura Stoler, 191–212. Durham, NC: Duke University Press, 2006.

———. *The Intimacies of Four Continents*. Durham, NC: Duke University Press, 2015.

Luis-Brown, David. *Waves of Decolonization: Discourses of Race and Hemispheric Citizenship in Cuba, Mexico, and the United States*. Durham, NC: Duke University Press, 2008.

———. "'White Slaves' and the 'Arrogant Mestiza': Reconfiguring Whiteness in *The Squatter and the Don* and *Ramona*." *American Literature* 69 (1997): 813–39.

Lukasik, Christopher J. *Discerning Characters: The Culture of Appearance in Early America*. Philadelphia: University of Pennsylvania Press, 2011.

Luskey, Brian P., and Wendy A. Woloson, eds. *Capitalism by Gaslight: Illuminating the Economy of Nineteenth-Century America*. Philadelphia: University of Pennsylvania Press, 2015.

Lye, Colleen. *America's Asia: Racial Form and American Literature, 1893–1945*. Princeton, NJ: Princeton University Press, 2005.

Macpherson, C. B. "Introduction: The Meaning of Property." In *Property: Mainstream and Critical Positions*, edited by C. B. Macpherson, 1–13. Toronto: University of Toronto Press, 1978.

———. *The Political Theory of Possessive Individualism: Hobbes to Locke*. Oxford: Oxford University Press, 1962.

Madison, James. *The Papers of James Madison, vol. 1–17*. Edited by William T. Hutchinson, William M. E. Rachal, and Robert Allen Rutland. Chicago: University of Chicago Press, 1962.

Margulis, Jennifer. "Swarthy Pirates and White Slaves: Barbary Captivity in the American Literary Imagination." PhD diss., Emory University, 1999.

Marshall, T. H. *Citizenship and Social Class: And Other Essays*. Cambridge: Cambridge University Press, 1950.

Mayer, Jane. "Outsourcing Torture: The Secret History of America's 'Extraordinary Rendition' Program." *New Yorker*, February 8, 2005. http://www.commondreams.org/headlines05/0208-13.html.

Mayfield, John. "'The Soul of a Man!': William Gilmore Simms and the Myths of Southern Manhood." *Journal of the Early Republic* 15, no. 3 (Autumn 1995): 477–500.

McBride, Dwight. *Why I Hate Abercrombie & Fitch: Essays on Race and Sexuality*. New York: New York University Press, 2005.

McCullough, Kate. *Regions of Identity: The Construction of America in Women's Fiction, 1885–1914*. Stanford, CA: Stanford University Press, 1999.

McKittrick, Katherine. *Demonic Grounds: Black Women and the Cartographies of Struggle*. Minneapolis: University of Minnesota Press, 2006.

McPherson, Edward. *The Political History of the United States of America during the Great Rebellion*. Washington, DC: Philp and Solomons, 1865.

McPherson, James. *Battle Cry of Freedom: The Civil War Era*. New York: Oxford University Press, 1988.

Mihm, Stephen. "The Alchemy of the Self: Stephen Burroughs and the Counterfeit Economy of the Early Republic." *Early American Studies* 2, no. 1 (Spring 2004): 123–59.

———. *A Nation of Counterfeiters: Capitalists, Con Men, and the Making of the United States.* Cambridge, MA: Harvard University Press, 2007.

Monroy, Douglas. *Thrown among Strangers: The Making of Mexican Culture in Frontier California.* Berkeley: University of California Press, 1990.

Montejano, David. *Anglos and Mexicans in the Making of Texas, 1836–1986.* Austin: University of Texas Press, 1987.

Moore, Grace, ed. *Pirates and Mutineers of the Nineteenth Century: Swashbucklers and Swindlers.* Burlington, VT: Ashgate, 2011.

Morison, Samuel Eliot. *The Maritime History of Massachusetts Bay, 1783–1860.* Boston: Houghton Mifflin, 1978.

Moss, Elizabeth. *Domestic Novelists in the Old South: Defenders of Southern Culture.* Baton Rouge: Louisiana State University Press, 1992.

Murphy, Gretchen. *Hemispheric Imaginings: The Monroe Doctrine and Narratives of U.S. Empire.* Durham, NC: Duke University Press, 2005.

Mylonas, Harris. *The Politics of Nation-Building: Making Co-nationals, Refugees and Minorities.* Cambridge: Cambridge University Press, 2013.

Nelson, Dana. *National Manhood: Capitalist Citizenship and the Imagined Fraternity of White Men.* Durham, NC: Duke University Press, 1998.

Neuwirth, Robert. *Shadow Cities: A Billion Squatters, a New Urban World.* New York: Routledge, 2005.

———. *Stealth of Nations: The Global Rise of the Informal Economy.* New York: Random House, 2011.

Newman, Eric P. "Franklin Making Money More Plentiful." *Proceedings of the American Philosophic Society* 115 (October 1971): 341–49.

Newman, Lance. "Free Soil and the Abolitionist Forests of Frederick Douglass's 'The Heroic Slave.'" *American Literature* 81 (2009): 127–52.

Ngai, Mae. *Impossible Subjects: Illegal Aliens and the Making of Modern America.* Princeton, NJ: Princeton University Press, 2004.

Nwankwo, Ifeoma C. K. "The Promises and Perils of U.S. African American Hemispherism: Latin America in Martin Delany's *Blake* and Gayl Jones's *Mosquito.*" *American Literary History* 18, no. 3 (2006): 579–99.

Oaks, James. *Slavery and Freedom: An Interpretation of the Old South.* New York: W. W. Norton, 1990.

Ong, Aihwa. "Cultural Citizenship as Subject-Making." *Current Anthropology* 37, no. 5 (1996): 737–62.

Onuf, Peter. *Statehood and Union: A History of the Northwest Ordinance.* Bloomington: Indiana University Press, 1987.

Oren, Michael. *Power, Faith, and Fantasy: The United States in the Middle East, 1776 to the Present.* New York: W. W. Norton, 2007.

Ostrowski, Carl. "'Fated to Perish by Consumption': The Political Economy of *Arthur Mervyn.*" *Studies in American Fiction* 32, no. 1 (Spring 2004): 3–20.

Owsley, Frank Lawrence. *King Cotton Diplomacy: Foreign Relations of the Confederate States of America.* Tuscaloosa: University of Alabama Press, 2008.

Padilla, Genaro M. *My History, Not Yours: The Formation of Mexican American Autobiography.* Madison: University of Wisconsin Press, 1993.

Paredes, Américo. *With His Pistol in His Hand.* Austin: University of Texas Press, 1958.

Parker, Kunal. "Citizenship and Immigration Law, 1800–1924: Resolutions of Membership and Territory." In *The Cambridge History of Law in America*, vol. 2, *The Long Nineteenth Century*, edited by Michael Grossberg and Christopher Tomlins, 163–203. Cambridge: Cambridge University Press, 2008.

Parker, William, ed. *The Structure of the Cotton Economy of the Antebellum South.* Washington, DC: Agricultural History Society, 1970.

Paul, Heike, Alexandra Ganser, and Katharina Gerund, eds. *Pirates, Drifters, Fugitives: Figures of Mobility in the U.S. and Beyond.* Heidelberg: Universitätsverlag, 2012.

Peck, Daniel H. "A Repossession of America: The Revolution in Cooper's Trilogy of Nautical Romances." *Studies in Romanticism* 15, no. 4 (1976): 589–605.

Peñalver, Eduardo Moisés, and Sonia K. Katyal. "Property Outlaws." *University of Pennsylvania Law Review* 155 (2007): 1095–186.

Pennell, C. R., ed. *Bandits at Sea: A Pirates Reader.* New York: New York University Press, 2001.

Penningroth, Dylan. *The Claims of Kinfolk: African American Property and Community in the Nineteenth-Century South.* Chapel Hill: University of North Carolina Press, 2003.

Peréz, Emma. *The Decolonial Imaginary: Writing Chicanas into History.* Bloomington: Indiana University Press, 1999.

Perlman, Janice. *The Myth of Marginality: Urban Poverty and Politics in Rio de Janeiro.* Berkeley: University of California Press, 1976.

Perl-Rosenthal, Nathan. *Citizen Sailors: Becoming American in the Age of Revolution.* Cambridge, MA: Harvard University Press, 2015.

Perry, Carolyn, and Mary Weaks-Baxter, eds. *The History of Southern Women's Literature.* Baton Rouge: Louisiana State University Press, 2002.

Petras, James, and Henry Veltmeyer. *Beyond Neoliberalism: A World to Win.* Surrey, UK: Ashgate, 2011.

Philbrick, Thomas. *James Fenimore Cooper and the Development of American Sea Fiction.* Cambridge, MA: Harvard University Press, 1961.

Pisani, Donald J. "Squatter Law in California, 1850–1858." *Western Historical Quarterly* 25, no. 3 (Autumn 1994): 277–310.

Pitt, Leonard. *The Decline of the Californios: A Social History of the Spanish-Speaking Californians, 1846–1890.* Berkeley: University of California Press, 1966.

Poblete, Juan. "Citizenship and Illegality in the Global California Gold Rush." In *The Latino Nineteenth Century: Archival Encounters in American Literary History*, edited by Rodrigo Lazo and Jesse Alemán, 278–300. New York: New York University Press, 2016.

Pocock, J. G. A. *Politics, Language, and Time: Essays on Political Thought and History.* New York: Atheneum, 1973.

———. *Virtue, Commerce, and History: Essays on Political Thought and History, Chiefly in the Eighteenth Century.* New York: Cambridge University Press, 1985.

Pole, J. R. *The Pursuit of Equality in American History.* Berkeley: University of California Press, 1978.

Purdy, Jedediah. *The Meaning of Property: Freedom, Community, and the Legal Imagination.* New Haven, CT: Yale University Press, 2010.

"Ramon, the Rover of Cuba," and Other Tales. New York: Nafis and Cornish, 1843.

Reddy, Chandan. *Freedom with Violence: Race, Sexuality, and the US State.* Durham, NC: Duke University Press, 2011.

Rediker, Marcus. *Between the Devil and the Deep Blue Sea: Merchant Seamen, Pirates, and the Anglo-American Maritime World, 1700–1750.* Cambridge: Cambridge University Press, 1987.

———. *Villains of All Nations: Atlantic Pirates in the Golden Age.* Boston: Beacon, 2004.

Reidy, Joseph. "The African American Struggle for Citizenship Rights in the Northern United States during the Civil War." In *Civil War Citizens: Race, Ethnicity, and Identity in America's Bloodiest Conflict*, edited by Susannah J. Ural, 213–36. New York: New York University Press, 2010.

Reyes, Bárbara O. *Private Women, Public Lives: Gender and the Missions of the Californias.* Austin: University of Texas Press, 2009.

Ripley, Eliza McHatton. *From Flag to Flag: A Woman's Adventures and Experiences in the South during the War, in Mexico, and in Cuba.* New York: Appleton, 1889.

Roberts, Siân Silyn. "Dispossession and Cosmopolitan Community in Leonora Sansay's *Secret History*." In *The Haitian Revolution and the Early United States*, edited by Elizabeth Maddock Dillon and Michael Drexler, 250–65. Philadelphia: University of Pennsylvania Press, 2016.

———. "Gothic Enlightenment: Contagion and Community in Charles Brockden Brown's *Arthur Mervyn*." *Early American Literature* 44, no. 2 (2009): 307–32.

Robertson, Lindsay G. *Conquest by Law: How the Discovery of America Dispossessed Indigenous Peoples of Their Lands.* Oxford: Oxford University Press, 2005.

Robinson, W. W. *Land in California: The Story of Mission Lands, Ranchos, Squatters, Mining Claims, Railroad Grants, Land Scrip, Homesteads.* Berkeley: University of California Press, 1948.

Rodríguez, Jaime Javier. *The Literatures of the U.S.-Mexican War: Narrative, Time, and Identity.* Austin: University of Texas Press, 2010.

Rodríguez O., Jaime E. *The Independence of Spanish America.* Cambridge: Cambridge University Press, 1998.

Rowe, John Carlos. "Nineteenth-Century United States Literary Culture and Transnationality." *PMLA* 118, no. 1 (2003): 78–89.

Roy, Ananya, and Nezar AlSayyad. *Urban Informality: Transnational Perspectives from the Middle East, Latin America, and South Asia.* Oxford: Lexington, 2004.

Roybal, Karen. *Archives of Dispossession: Recovering the Testimonios of Mexican American Herederas, 1848–1960.* Chapel Hill: University of North Carolina Press, 2017.

Rubin, Alfred P., and B. A. Boczek. "Private and Public History; Private and Public Law." *Proceedings of the Annual Meeting (American Society of International Law)* 82 (April 20–23, 1988): 30–39.

Rubin, Louis D., Jr. *The Edge of the Swamp: A Study in the Literature and Society of the Old South*. Baton Rouge: Louisiana State University Press, 1989.

Ruff, Julius R. *Violence in Early Modern Europe, 1500–1800*. Cambridge: Cambridge University Press, 2001.

Ruiz de Burton, María Amparo. *The Squatter and the Don*. Edited by Beatrice Pita and Rosaura Sánchez. Houston: Arte Público, 1997.

Sager, Robin. "The Multiple Metaphoric Civil Wars of Loreta Janeta Velazquez's *The Woman in Battle*." *Southern Quarterly* 48, no. 1 (Fall 2010): 27–41.

Saldívar, José David. *Border Matters: Remapping American Cultural Studies*. Berkeley: University of California Press, 1997.

Sánchez, Rosaura. *Telling Identities: The Californio Testimonios*. Minneapolis: University of Minnesota Press, 1995.

Saunt, Claudio. *A New Order of Things: Property, Power, and the Transformation of the Creek Indians*. Cambridge: Cambridge University Press, 1999.

Schechter, Patricia. *Ida B. Wells-Barnett and American Reform, 1880–1930*. Chapel Hill: University of North Carolina Press, 2001.

Schlatter, Richard. *Private Property: The History of an Idea*. New Brunswick, NJ: Rutgers University Press, 1951.

Schuele, Donna. "Community Property Law and the Politics of Married Women's Rights in Nineteenth-Century California." *Western Legal History* 7 (1994): 248–52.

Schweninger, Loren. *Black Property Owners in the South, 1790–1915*. Urbana: University of Illinois Press, 1997.

Scott, Anne Firor. *The Southern Lady: From Pedestal to Politics, 1830–1930*. Charlottesville: University Press of Virginia, 1970.

Scott, Kenneth. *Counterfeiting in Colonial America*. Philadelphia: University of Pennsylvania Press, 1957.

Shapiro, Stephen. *The Culture and Commerce of the Early American Novel*. University Park: Pennsylvania State University Press, 2008.

Sharpe, Jenny. *Ghosts of Slavery: A Literary Archaeology of Black Women's Lives*. Minneapolis: University of Minnesota Press, 2003.

Shelby, Tommie. "Two Conceptions of Black Nationalism: Martin Delany on the Meaning of Black Political Solidarity." *Political Theory* 31, no. 5 (2003): 664–92.

Shell, Marc. *Money, Language, and Thought: Literary and Philosophic Economies from the Medieval to the Modern Era*. Baltimore: Johns Hopkins University Press, 1993.

Simms, William Gilmore. *The Yemassee: A Romance of Carolina, in Two Volumes*. New York: Harper and Brothers, 1844.

Skidmore, Thomas. *The Right of Man to Property!* New York: Burt Franklin, 1964.

Smart, Alan. "Unruly Places: Urban Governance and the Persistence of Illegality in Hong Kong's Urban Squatter Areas." *American Anthropologist* 103, no. 1 (2001): 30–44.

Smethurst, David. *Tripoli: The United States' First War on Terror*. New York: Presidio, 2006.

Smith, Adam. *An Inquiry into the Nature and Causes of the Wealth of Nations*. 4th ed. Goldsmiths'-Kress Library of Economic Literature, No. 13148. London: Printed for A. Strahan, and T. Cadell, 1786.

Smith, Jon, and Deborah Cohn. *Look Away! The U.S. South in New World Studies.* Durham, NC: Duke University Press, 2004.

Smith, Sidonie, and Julia Watson, eds. *Before They Could Vote: American Women's Autobiographical Writing, 1819–1919.* Madison: University of Wisconsin Press, 2006.

Smith, Venture. *A Narrative of the Life and Adventures of Venture, a Native of Africa: But Resident above Sixty Years in the United States of America, Related by Himself.* Middletown, CT: J. S. Stewart, 1897.

Springer, Haskell, ed. *America and the Sea: A Literary History.* Athens: University of Georgia Press, 1995.

Stanley, Amy Dru. *From Bondage to Contract: Wage Labor, Marriage, and the Market in the Age of Slave Emancipation.* Cambridge: Cambridge University Press, 1998.

Starkey, David J. *British Privateering Enterprise in the Eighteenth Century.* Exeter: University of Exeter Press, 1990.

———. "Pirates and Markets." In *Bandits at Sea: A Pirates Reader,* edited by C. R. Pennell, 107–24. New York: New York University Press, 2001.

Stein, Jordan Alexander. "'A Christian Nation Calls for Its Wandering Children': Life, Liberty, Liberia." *American Literary History* 19, no. 4 (2007): 849–73.

Sundquist, Eric. *To Wake the Nations: Race in the Making of American Literature.* Cambridge, MA: Harvard University Press, 1993.

Supreme Court of California, Points and Responses for Application of María Amparo Ruiz Burton for a Homestead, 1883.

Sutherland, Daniel E. "Looking for a Home: Louisiana Emigrants during the Civil War and Reconstruction." *Louisiana History: The Journal of the Louisiana Historical Association* 21, no. 4 (Autumn 1980): 341–59.

Tarr, Clayton Carlyle. "Infectious Fiction: Plague and the Novelist in *Arthur Mervyn* and *The Last Man.*" *Studies in the Novel* 47, no. 2 (Summer 2015): 141–57.

Taylor, Thomas E. *Running the Blockade: A Personal Narrative of Adventures, Risks, and Escapes during the American Civil War.* London: John Murray, 1896.

Thomson, Janice. *Mercenaries, Pirates, and Sovereigns: State-Building and Extraterritorial Violence in Early Modern Europe.* Princeton, NJ: Princeton University Press, 1994.

Thornton, Mark, and Robert B. Ekelund. *Tariffs, Blockades, and Inflation: The Economics of the Civil War.* Wilmington, DE: SR Books, 2004.

Tirres, Allison Brownell. "Ownership without Citizenship: The Creation of Noncitizen Property Rights." *Michigan Journal of Race and Law* 19, no. 1 (2013): 1–53.

Tocqueville, Alexis de. *Democracy in America and Two Essays on America.* London: Penguin Books, 2003.

Toll, Ian. *Six Frigates: The Epic History of the Founding of the U.S. Navy.* New York: W. W. Norton, 2006.

Torpey, John. *The Invention of the Passport: Surveillance, Citizenship and the State.* Cambridge: Cambridge University Press, 2000.

Tremmel, George B. *Counterfeit Currency of the Confederate States of America.* Jefferson, NC: McFarland, 2003.

Trilling, Lionel. *Sincerity and Authenticity*. Cambridge, MA: Harvard University Press, 1972.

Troy, William. *Hair-Breadth Escapes from Slavery to Freedom*. Manchester, UK: W. Bremner, 1861.

Tucker, Spencer. *Stephen Decatur: A Life Most Bold and Daring*. Annapolis, MD: Naval Institute Press, 2005.

Turley, Hans. *Rum, Sodomy, and the Lash: Piracy, Sexuality, and Masculine Identity*. New York: New York University Press, 1999.

Tyler, Ronnie C. "Cotton on the Border, 1861–1865." *Southwestern Historical Quarterly* 73, no. 4 (April 1970): 456–77.

U.S. Senate, Alabama. *A Digest of the Laws of the State of Alabama*. General Assembly, February 1843. Tuscaloosa: Marmaduke J. Slade, 1843.

Velazquez, Loreta Janeta. *The Woman in Battle: A Narrative of the Exploits, Adventures, and Travels of Madame Loreta Janeta Velazquez*. Richmond, VA: Dustin, Gilman, 1876.

Venkatesh, Sudhir Alladi. *Off the Books: The Underground Economy of the Urban Poor*. Cambridge, MA: Harvard University Press, 2009.

Villegas Revueltas, Silvestre. *El liberalismo moderado en Mexico, 1852–1864*. Mexico City: Universidad Nacional Autónoma de México, 1997.

Wacquant, Loïc. *Urban Outcasts: A Comparative Sociology of Advanced Marginality*. Cambridge, UK: Polity, 2008.

Wahl, Jenny Bourne. *The Bondsman's Burden: An Economic Analysis of the Common Law of Southern Slavery*. New York: Cambridge University Press, 1998.

Washington, Booker T. *The American Negro*. Boston: Small, Maynard, 1902.

———. *Up from Slavery*. New York: Doubleday, Page, 1907.

Watson, Charles S. *From Nationalism to Secessionism: The Changing Fiction of William Gilmore Simms*. Westport, CT: Greenwood, 1993.

Watson, William. *The Adventures of a Blockade Runner; or, Trade in Time of War*. London: T. Fisher, 1892.

Watts, Edward. *Writing and Postcolonialism in the Early Republic*. Charlottesville: University of Virginia Press, 1998.

Weber, David. *The Mexican Frontier, 1821–1846: The American Southwest under Mexico*. Albuquerque: University of New Mexico Press, 1982.

Weheliye, Alexander. *Habeas Viscus: Racializing Assemblages, Biopolitics, and Black Feminist Theories of the Human*. Durham, NC: Duke University Press, 2014.

Weyler, Karen. *Intricate Relations: Sexual and Economic Desire in American Fiction, 1789–1814*. Iowa City: University of Iowa Press, 2004.

White, E. Frances. *Dark Continent of Our Bodies: Black Feminism and the Politics of Respectability*. Philadelphia: Temple University Press, 2001.

Whitlow, Roger. "The Revolutionary Black Novels of Martin R. Delany and Sutton Griggs." *MELUS* 5, no. 3 (1978): 26–36.

Williams, Daniel E. "In Defense of Self: Author and Authority in the *Memoirs of Stephen Burroughs*." *Early American Literature* 25, no. 2 (1990): 96–122.

———. *Pillars of Salt: An Anthology of Early American Criminal Narrative*. Madison, WI: Madison House, 1993.

———. "Rogues, Rascals and Scoundrels: The Underworld Literature of Early America." *American Studies* 24, no. 2 (1983): 5–19.

Wimsatt, Mary Anne. *The Major Fiction of William Gilmore Simms*. Baton Rouge: Louisiana State University Press, 1989.

Winthrop, William. *Military Law and Precedents*. Washington, DC: Government Printing Office, 1920.

Wise, Stephen R. *Lifeline of the Confederacy: Blockade-Running during the Civil War*. Columbia: University of South Carolina Press, 1988.

Woertendyke, Gretchen. *Hemispheric Regionalism: Romance and the Geography of Genre*. Oxford: Oxford University Press, 2017.

Wolcott, Victoria W. *Remaking Respectability: African American Women in Interwar Detroit*. Chapel Hill: University of North Carolina Press, 2001.

Wong, Edlie L. *Neither Fugitive Nor Free: Atlantic Slavery, Freedom Suits, and the Legal Culture of Travel*. New York: New York University Press, 2009.

———. *Racial Reconstruction: Black Inclusion, Chinese Exclusion, and the Fictions of Citizenship*. New York: New York University Press, 2015.

Wood, Gordon. *The Radicalism of the American Revolution*. New York: Knopf, 1992.

———. *Revolutionary Characters: What Made the Founders Different*. New York: Penguin, 2006.

Woodworth-Ney, Laura. *Women in the American West*. Santa Barbara: ABC-CLIO, 2008.

Wright, Gavin. *The Political Economy of the Cotton South: Households, Markets, and Wealth in the Nineteenth Century*. New York: W. W. Norton, 1978.

Young, Elizabeth. *Disarming the Nation: Women's Writing and the American Civil War*. Chicago: University of Chicago Press, 1999.

Yun, Lisa. *The Coolie Speaks: Chinese Indentured Laborers and African Slaves of Cuba*. Philadelphia: Temple University Press, 2008.

Zeugner, John. "A Note on Martin Delany's *Blake*, and Black Militancy." *Phylon (1960-)* 32, no. 1 (1971): 98–105.

Ziff, Larzer. *Writing in the New Nation: Prose, Print, and Politics in the Early United States*. New Haven, CT: Yale University Press, 1991.

Zimmerman, David A. *Panic! Markets, Crisis, and Crowds in American Fiction*. Chapel Hill: University of North Carolina Press, 2006.

Index

Brown, Charles Brockden. See *Arthur Mervyn; or, Memoirs of the Year 1793* (Brown)

Burroughs, Stephen. See *Memoirs of the Notorious Stephen Burroughs* (Burroughs)

Bush, George W., 20

California Land Act of 1851, 109

Captain Phillips (film), 20, 168

Carey, Mathew, *A Short Account of the Malignant Fever*, 63

Caughfield, Adrienne, 116

Chase, Salmon P., 57

Cicero, 20

Citizenship and self-possession, 76–77, 81–82

Citizenship/property interdependence: and black exclusion, 11, 178n57; in Confederate women's travelogues, 150–51, 153–54; nature of, 9–12, 19; and nautical piracy narratives, 2, 3, 7, 13–14, 25–26, 27, 36–38, 39–40, 42–44; postbellum debates about, 150; and Preemption Act of 1841, 126–27; and Prize Acts (1863), 150; and Ruiz de Burton's inheritance claim, 132–33; and slave narratives, 81–82, 87–90; in *The Squatter and the Don* (Ruiz de Burton), 110, 113–14, 119, 121–22, 127–28, 130, 134–35. *See also* Person/property interdependence

Citizenship, Southern, dispossession by naval blockade terms, 138–39

Clymer, Jeffory A., 104

Coleridge, Samuel Taylor, 89

Colonial America: piracy in, 31–34; trade monopolies in, 31–32

Commentaries (William Blackstone), 5, 9

Commonwealth v. Turner (1827), 89

"The Condition, Elevation, Emigration and Destiny of the Colored People of the United States" (Martin Delany), 84–85

Confederacy: and counterfeiting/counterfeiters, 76; and Cuba, 100, 199n10; and Prize Cases (1863), 146–51; trade with defined as piracy, 136–37

Confederate diplomatic recognition: and blockade running, 137–39, 141, 143–46; debates dramatized in Confederate women's travelogues, 141, 143, 166; and Lincoln's naval blockade, 137–39, 141, 143–45

Confederate women's travelogues: assertion of citizenship through blockade running, 137, 140–41, 143, 166–67; blockade running as response to dispossession, 18–19, 137–39, 142, 151, 166; Confederate diplomatic recognition debates dramatized in, 141, 143, 166. *See also From Flag to Flag* (Ripley); *Woman in Battle* (Velazquez)

Confiscation Act (1862), 146

Continental Congress, 55, 183n15

Cooper, James Fennimore: and citizenship/property interdependence, 13, 26; conflicted approach to piracy, 38–39; *Letter to My Countrymen*, 38; and pirate figure, 15–16, 27, 38–39; on property, 38–39; *The American Democrat*, 38, 39; *The Pilot*, 39. *See also The Red Rover* (Cooper); *The Water Witch* (Cooper)

Counterfeiting/counterfeiters: and the Confederacy, 76, 158–59; Continental Congress on, 55, 183n15; democratization of property, 17, 52, 53, 57–59, 66; dispossession as justification for, 51–52; economic growth aided by, 56, 59–60; as federal vs. state crime, 50, 55–56, 183n15; as formative of nation-state, 52–54; and person/property interdependence, 51–54, 61–62, 66–73, 75; as piracy, 49–50; in print culture, 74–75; as subversive to nation-state, 55. *See also Arthur Mervyn; or, Memoirs of the*

151–53; and John Locke, 8–9, 126; and Mexican unsettlement, 110; and the self, 8, 76, 106–7, 184n32. *See also* Citizenship/property interdependence; Self-possession

Philadelphia: counterfeiting in, 51–52; yellow fever epidemic, 51, 63, 85n50, 182n3

The Pilot (James Fennimore Cooper), 39

Piracy: as act of restitution, 27, 30, 35; blockade running as, 18–19, 136–37, 138; in colonial America, 31–34; counterfeiting as, 16–17, 49–50; and Cuba, 162–63; etymology of, 2; as exceptional crime, 20–21, 168; as expanded category, 2–4, 13–14, 19, 20–21; extrajudicial force justified by, 5, 20–21, 169–70; fugitivity as, 17, 76–77, 81–82; and *hostis humani generis*, 5, 7, 20–21; justified by natural law, 31–32; legal definition of, 4–5; Lincoln's naval blockade as, 145; literature vs. historical records on, 3–4; persistence of, 168–69; as response to dispossession, 2, 138–39; as response to restrictive regimes, 6–7, 31–32; self-possession as, 76–77, 81–83, 90–91, 96–97; slavery as, 91–95; squatting as, 109, 122–26; state power expansion justified by, 5–6, 20–21, 45–47, 136–37, 169–72; as subversive to nation-state, 2, 15–16, 19; in support of nation-state, 138–39, 140–41, 143, 157–59, 180n6; terrorism linked with, 5, 20–21, 169–72; and U.S. citizenship rights, 172–73. *See also* Nautical piracy narratives; Pirate figure

Piracy, intellectual, 168–69

1820 Piracy Law, 95

Pirate figure: amplification of, 15–21; archetype of, 1–2, 28–30; blockade runner as, 18–19, 136–38; counterfeiter as, 16–17, 49–50; fugitive slave as, 17, 76–77, 81–82; issues represented by, 2–3; modernity exemplified

by, 7; in nautical piracy narratives, 15–16, 26–27, 27, 28, 30, 32–33, 36–39, 39, 39–41, 44–45; squatter as, 109, 122–26. *See also* Piracy

Pirate ships, features of, 6–7, 28–30, 33–34, 35–36, 103–4, 192–93n87

Pirates of the Caribbean (film), 20

Pisani, Donald J., 117, 123

Pole, J.R., 106

Preemption Act of 1841, 109, 113, 125, 126–27

Prize Cases (1863), 146–51; and legal status of Confederate property, 149–50; and legal status of Confederates, 146–49

Proclamation 81 "A Blockage of Ports in Rebellious States," 136

Property: alienability of, 43; black uplift through, 86–87; as contingent in "Narrative of Albert and Mary" (Brisbane), 94; as dangerous in *Arthur Mervyn* (Brown), 63–65; democratization through counterfeiting, 17, 53, 57–59; and natural rights, 8–10, 29–30; racial identity as, 12, 17, 26, 184n32; the self as, 8, 76, 106–7, 184n32.

Property/citizenship interdependence. *See* Citizenship/property interdependence

Property/person interdependence. *See* Person/property interdependence

Property rights: and corporations, 125–26; and Cuba, 161–64; expanded by piracy, 2–3; and Mexican civil law, 130–31; and Mexican liberal tradition, 119, 120–21; unlawful activity as assertion of, 159–61

Property rights of women: and Mexican-American War, 131; Mexican civil law vs. English common law, 130–31; upheld by California Constitutional Convention of 1849, 131

Purdy, Jeremiah, 10

Quelch, Captain John, 168

Racial identity: as property, 12, 17, 26, 184n32; in *The Squatter and the Don* (Ruiz de Burton), 121, 196n52
Railroad monopolies, compared to squatters, 125–26
Ramon, the Rover of Cuba (anonymous), 45–47
Rediker, Marcus, 6, 7
The Red Rover (James Fennimore Cooper): citizenship/property interdependence in, 36–38; egalitarianism in, 33; national identity creation, 35–36; piracy as act of restitution, 35; pirate figure in, 36–39. *See also* Cooper, James Fennimore
Reidy, Joseph, 138
Ripley, Eliza McHatton: *From Flag to Flag: A Woman's Adventures and Experiences in the South during the War, in Mexico, and in Cuba,* 18–19, 137, 141–43, 151–53, 159–67. *See also* Confederate women's travelogues
Roberts, Bartholomew "Black Bart," 1–2
Roberts, Silan, "Dispossession and Cosmopolitan Community in Leonora Sansay's *Secret History*," 14
Robinson, W.W., 122
Rodríguez, Jaime Javier, 121
Rousseau, Jean Jacques, *Discourse on Inequality*, 28
Ruff, Julius, 6
Ruiz de Burton, María Amparo: biographical information, 132–33; historical romances, 18; inheritance claim, 132–33. *See also The Squatter and the Don* (Ruiz de Burton)
Running the Blockade: A Personal Narrative of Adventures, Risks, and Escapes during the American Civil War (Thomas E. Taylor), 143–45

Sánchez, Rosaura, 119, 120, 128, 131
Santa Clara County v. Southern Pacific Railroad (1886), 125
Second Treatise of Civil Government (John Locke), 8–9
Self-creation: and counterfeiter, 51, 57, 183–84n28, 184n29; and the counterfeit person, 51–54, 66–73, 75; and the pirate, 28, 34
Self-possession: and citizenship, 76–77, 81–82; fugitivity as, 77, 81–82, 90–91, 96–97, 103; John Locke on, 8; Martin Delany on, 85–86; as piratical act, 76–77, 81–83, 90–91, 96–97; as property possession, 8, 76, 106–7, 184n32; and slavery, 76, 100–101. *See also* Person/property interdependence
Sharpe, Jenny, 4
A Short Account of the Malignant Fever (Mathew Carey), 63
Simms, William Gilmore: and dangers of property democratization, 26, 39–40; and pirate figure, 15–16. See also *The Yemassee* (Simms)
Slavery: dispossession likened to, 61–62; economic arguments against, 86–87, 92–93, 95; immigrant exploitation as, 154–55; as piracy, 91–95; and self-possession, 76, 100–101; in U.S. vs. Cuba, 100–101
Slave Trade Act of 1807, 95
Slave Trade Act of 1820, 95
Smith, Adam: economic argument against slavery, 86–87; on natural rights to property, 29–30; on property and power, 86
Smuggling: in 19th century Yucatan, 29–30; Adam Smith on, 29–30; as means of asserting Citizenship, 135. *See also* Blockade running
Southern Claims Commission, 150
Sovereignty, national. *See* Confederate diplomatic recognition
Sovereignty, personal. *See* Self-possession

Spanish Constitution of 1812, 119

The Squatter and the Don (María Amparo Ruiz de Burton): as allegory of Southern dispossession, 135; Anglo settlement compared to hidalgo colonization in, 114–15; citizenship/property interdependence in, 110, 113–14, 119, 121–22, 127–28, 130, 134–35; defense of Spanish land grant system, 114–15; as depiction of Mexican unsettlement, 109–10; Mexican liberal tradition highlighted, 118–19; Mexican women as creators of property in, 18, 129–30, 131–32; misuse of land as justification for dispossession, 115, 117, 121–22, 134–35; racial identity in, 121, 196n52; railroad appropriations critiqued in, 115, 125; squatter as propertied citizen in, 117–18; squatter as thief (or pirate) in, 113, 122–26; squatter/settler distinction erased in, 123–27. *See also* Ruiz de Burton, Maria Amparo

Squatter/settler: distinction erased, 123–27; as foundational American figure, 122, 127

Squatting: and dispossession, 18, 109, 113, 123, 125–27; legalization of, 109, 113, 125–27; as piracy, 109, 122–26

Stanton, Elizabeth Cady, 106–7

Star-Spangled Banner, parodied by *Vulture* anthem, 103–4

Statehood and Union (Peter Onuf), 122

State v. Antonio (1816), 55

State v. Tutt (1831), 55–56, 66

Supreme Court: and Confederate legal status, 146–51; and Native American dispossession, 111

Taylor, Thomas, *Running the Blockade: A Personal Narrative of Adventures, Risks, and Escapes during the American Civil War*, 143–45

Terrorism: as justification for extrajudicial force, 169–70; linked with piracy, 5, 20–21, 169–72

Tocqueville, Alexis de, 10

Treasure Island (Robert Louis Stevenson), 20

Treaty of Guadalupe Hidalgo (1848), 18, 109

Turley, Hans, 7

Turner, Fredrick Jackson, 122–23, 127

Up from Slavery (Booker T. Washington), 86

U.S. Patriot Act, 169

Velazquez, Loreta Janeta:
Woman in Battle: A Narrative of the Exploits, Adventures, and Travels of Madame Loreta Janeta Velazquez, 18–19, 137, 139–41, 153–59
See also Confederate women's travelogues

War on Drugs, 169

Washington, Booker T.: black uplift through education, 86; enfranchisement through property ownership, 87

Washington Crossing the Delaware (Emanuel Leutze), 2

The Water Witch; or, The Skimmer of the Seas (James Fennimore Cooper): egalitarianism in, 33–34; New Amsterdam as piratic society in, 33–34; piracy as response to restrictive regime in, 31–32; piracy justified by natural law, 31–32; pirate figure in, 28, 32–33. *See also* Cooper, James Fennimore

Watson, William, *The Adventures of a Blockade Runner: or, Trade in Time of War*, 145–46, 200n39

Watts, Edward, 75

Wealth of Nations (Adam Smith), 86

Whiteness, as property, 17, 26, 184n32

Wisconsin Convention of 1846, 11

Woertendyke, Gretchen, 16

Woman in Battle: A Narrative of the Exploits, Adventures, and Travels of Madame Loreta Janeta Velazquez (Loreta Janeta Velazquez): assertion of citizenship through blockade running, 140–41, 157–58; blockade running as act of war, 156–57; blockade running as response to dispossession, 18–19, 137; citizenship/property interdependence in, 153–54; counterfeiting in support of Confederate autonomy in, 158–59; cross-dressing as critical focus, 140, 199nn14, 15, 17; immigrant exploitation viewed as slavery, 154–55; national exile as solution, 165–66, 199n10; unlawful federal acts condemned, 154; war profiteering viewed as piracy, 155–56. *See also* Confederate women's travelogues

Wong, Edlie, 142–43

The Yemassee: A Romance of Carolina (William Gilmore Simms): and citizenship/property interdependence in, 27, 39–40, 42–44; historical context, 40–41; pirate figure in, 39–41, 42, 44–45; and Southern dispossession, 41–42. *See also* Simms, William Gilmore

Yemassee War (1715), 40

Yoo, John C.: on illegal combatants, 20–21; justification of extrajudicial force, 20–21, 169–70

Yucatan: 19th century piratic economy in, 29–30; rebelliousness of, 29, 180n10; as setting for *El filibustero* (Eligio Ancona), 27